25TH STREET CONFIDENTIAL

Pierce's
THE NEW
HEALY
HOTEL
CAFE
DRUGS
BECCO
FILMS
ARCADE HOTEL

25TH STREET CONFIDENTIAL

Drama, Decadence, and Dissipation along Ogden's Rowdiest Road

VAL HOLLEY

The University of Utah Press | SALT LAKE CITY

The Defiance House Man colophon is a registered trademark
of the University of Utah Press. It is based on a four-foot-tall
Ancient Puebloan pictograph (late PIII) near Glen Canyon, Utah.

17 16 15 14 3 4 5

LIBRARY OF CONGRESS CATALOGING-IN-PUBLICATION DATA

Holley, Val.
25th Street confidential : drama, decadence, and dissipation along
Ogden's rowdiest road / Val Holley.
pages cm
Includes bibliographical references and index.
ISBN 978-1-60781-268-5 (hardcover : alk. paper)
ISBN 978-1-60781-269-2 (paperback)
ISBN 978-1-60781-270-8 (ebook)
1. Twenty-fifth Street (Ogden, Utah)—History. 2. Ogden (Utah)—History.
3. Ogden (Utah)—Moral conditions—History. 4. Crime—Utah—Ogden—History.
5. Mormons—Utah—Ogden—History. I. Title.
F834.O3H65 2013
979.2'28—dc23
2013019417

Frontispiece courtesy of Special Collections Department, Stewart Library, Weber State University.
Photograph on facing page 140 courtesy of Special Collections Department, Stewart Library, Weber State University.

Printed and bound by Sheridan Books, Inc., Ann Arbor, Michigan

In memory of my uncle and great-uncle,
honorable public servants:

Dr. Merle Ekins Allen
mayor of Ogden, 1961–1965

Ernest R. Ekins
Ogden City Council, February–November 1961

And in memory of

Olin A. Kennedy
"grand old man of Ogden journalism"

O. A. Kennedy...had a genuine feeling for the past and he knew enough to do research.... We owe a good deal to men like him. Now that we are interested in western history we have such men to thank for the preservation of material, clues, leads, and records that would otherwise have disappeared entirely.

—Bernard DeVoto, 1943

CONTENTS

PREFACE

In 2008, when Robert Peery King first urged me to write a book about 25th Street, the thrill of the undertaking was immediate. You cannot grow up near Ogden without absorbing the street's legends of corruption, menace, and depravity. Larger-than-life personalities such as mayor Harman Peery or brothel chatelaine Rosetta Ducinnie Davie have become interwoven with its gaudy reputation.

Soon enough it was clear that a history of 25th Street would not be quite the romp I had anticipated. Historians who trod similar ground in other cities had already learned this. Richard Selcer, chronicler of the old Hell's Half Acre district in Fort Worth, Texas, observed, "What is 'known' today...is about two-thirds myth... The problem with getting to the historic roots is that the historical viewpoint languishes while the mythology is self-perpetuating."[1]

Selcer's words could have been written about Ogden's mistaken ideas of 25th Street's past. Few legends have been as persistent as the one about Kate Flint, madam of an opulent local establishment who asserted her high position in society by purchasing Brigham Young's carriage and parading up and down Ogden's streets in it. Then there is Fanny Dawson, perennially pegged as a cunning serial killer who masterminded the doping, robbery, and assassination of innocent saloon patrons. Neither account is true, but their perpetuity seems assured.[2] The conviction that Chicago bootlegger and crime boss Al Capone avoided the arm of the law by hiding out in Ogden during Prohibition is also mistakenly embedded in the local consciousness.[3]

Fortunately, the true history of 25th Street needs no embellishment to be salient and memorable. Its outsized role in Ogden annals, in fact, illuminates larger themes in Utah and U.S. history. Most significantly, 25th Street was a crucible of Mormon-Gentile conflict, especially after the Liberal Party deprived its rival, the People's Party, of control of Ogden's municipal government in 1889. In the twentieth century, the street was targeted in statewide Progressive-Era reform efforts, and, during Prohibition, came to epitomize the futility of liquor-abatement programs.

On a more mundane level, 25th Street was Ogden's proving ground in law enforcement and municipal governance. The city enriched its treasury and kept a lid on taxes thanks to fees and fines from the street's vicious establishments. It grappled continuously with the obligation to execute state liquor laws because the Utah Legislature declined to provide enforcement funds for them.

The ignominy attributed to 25th Street by the People's Party—the Mormons' political organization in Utah from 1870 to 1891—encouraged a perception that the street held no attraction for Mormons seeking business opportunities. However, as my research progressed, I found numerous examples of entrepreneurial Mormons who invested or participated in controversial 25th Street commercial ventures while remaining staunch and effective People's Party members.

Today, as 25th Street continues to recover from the deterioration and neglect of the mid-twentieth century, locals and guests are rediscovering its charm. Through strategically placed plaques and kiosks, the city encourages appreciation of and familiarity with the street's architectural and social history. Northern Utah demographics have changed dramatically since World War II, and Davis County's population now far outstrips Weber's, but between Ogden and Salt Lake City, there is no example of an historic metropolitan business district. As historians F. Ross Peterson and Robert Parson note, to preserve 25th Street is to "embrace a valuable legacy that can never be duplicated in any of the surrounding communities."[4]

ACKNOWLEDGMENTS

"Going the extra mile" doesn't adequately describe Sarah Langsdon, associate curator in Special Collections at Weber State University's Stewart Library, who took customer service to record levels and did everything in her power to support this project. The assistance of Sarah's coworkers—Melissa Johnson, Alixe Ogden, and Janessa Knotts—is gratefully appreciated.

Lee Witten, who volunteers his time as Union Station archivist, generously lent his assistance. Ogden is fortunate to have him.

The always-helpful staff of the Utah History Research Center—Doug Misner, Heidi Orchard, Heidi Stringham, Greg Walz, Alan Barnett, and Tony Castro—is the best I've encountered at any state historical society. Under the same roof, Cory Jensen and Christopher Hansen of the State Historic Preservation Office unearthed valuable documents and photographs.

Rebecca Ory Hernandez and Carla Price of Weber State University's Development Office opened doors, tracked down interviewees, and bent over backward to make my research expeditions to Ogden convenient and comfortable.

The *Standard-Examiner's* "Wasatch Rambler," Charles Trentelman, provides a clearinghouse for fascinating Ogden historical topics in his column, which has given me more than a few significant leads. I am indebted to Charlie for many sources I could not have imagined, as well as for his searches in the newspaper's archives.

For their cooperation, I would also like to thank Tracy Hansen, deputy Ogden City recorder; Greg Montgomery and Jannette Borklund of the City Planning Division (and Fred Aegerter and Jalynn Olsen Padilla, formerly of the same office); native Ogdenite Stephen Hales, archivist of the Rex Organization in New Orleans; Karen Carver at the J. Willard Marriott Library at the University of Utah; Glen M. Leonard; Kelli Garside McFarland; Larry Carr; Allen Roberts; and filmmaker Issac Goeckeritz for his interviews on

DVD with legendary Ogdenites, many now deceased. Thanks especially to Robert Peery King, whose inspiration launched this project.

My editor, John Alley, often kept the project from derailing and gave me the confidence to persevere.

And finally, my husband, Joseph Plocek, makes everything possible.

CHAPTER ONE

OGDEN ENVY

There is no rivalry between Ogden and Salt Lake City except a generous one....Ogden has one advantage: Its people are wickeder than ours, and wicked people as a rule are different from those who get all their punishment in this world.

—*Salt Lake Tribune*, June 21, 1889

During its first century, 25th Street loomed as a decadent specter in the consciousness of generations of Ogdenites. In 1911 Reverend Frederick Vining Fisher of Ogden's First Methodist Church condemned it as "one of the most disgraceful gateways to a city on the continent." A furloughed sailor visiting in 1937 called it "the worst hell hole from Panama to Nome, and I've been in all of them." Children were taught to avoid it. "My sixth grade teacher warned us about 25th Street and how you took your life in your hands if you dared to visit it," recalls former Ogden City councilwoman Dorrene Jeske. Yet others managed to find memorable amusements on its tainted blocks. "When I was overseas in the army in the early 1960s," says Tom Owens, "more than one old soldier from World War II would find out I was from Ogden and launch into fond memories of their wild and crazy nights on 25th Street."[1]

By the twenty-first century, the specter had vanished in tandem with the railroad passenger service that had once inflated the street's fortunes with customers and cash. Ogden has embraced the afterglow of all that decadence, promoting it heavily in outreach to tourists. Few persons still living can recall the street and its pulsating energies during World War II, let alone in its earlier eras, when men invariably toted weapons and amused themselves by belting back endless rounds of straight whiskey. Ogdenites of the baby-boomer generation and younger may well wonder what the fuss is about, and—if the street was so bad—how it got that way.

If Ogden had not lain smack dab in the path of the transcontinental railroad, 25th Street could not have existed. In its infancy, the city struck visitors as merely a poky Mormon settlement on the stage road into Idaho and Montana.[2] Until the first locomotives steamed into town on March 8, 1869, its future had not aroused public curiosity.

On that day, citizens from miles around packed their picnic lunches, donned their holiday attire, and came to town in buggies, by horseback, or on foot. One Ogdenite recalled "thousands and thousands" milling about, climbing on "high bluffs and every commanding elevation." Whoops and yells erupted when sharp-eyed spectators finally spotted Union Pacific tracklayers in the distance, hammering and clanging their way along the Weber River toward the city limits.

By 5:30 p.m. the rails were laid to a point even with present-day 24th Street. Mounting a makeshift public stand, Judge Franklin D. Richards struggled to project his prepared remarks over the crowd's exuberance. The local militia fired off a salute, a prearranged signal to three Union Pacific engines, which had remained out of sight, to chug to the front of the stand.[3] Their shrill whistles mingled with the militia's cannonading and may have exceeded previous city records for pandemonium. Many frightened children and not a few adults, according to witnesses, fled in terror at their first-ever sighting of a cacophonous locomotive. Some ran to their homes. "Swamps didn't hinder the fleeing citizens one bit," recalled one witness. Children "ran pell-mell through a nearby slough, ruining their Sunday clothes." Some hid so well that it took their parents hours to find them.[4]

Only a decade earlier, as the U.S. Army prepared to march into the territory in the so-called Utah War, the Mormons had abandoned Ogden and their other northern cities and planned to burn them. But when the rails reached Ogden in 1869, not only did the Mormons stay put, but they organized this jubilant celebration. Eastern pundits had predicted the railroad's advent would undermine the Mormon Church; the *Chicago Republican* even published an editorial entitled "Mormonism Doomed."[5] Judge Richards, however, scoffed at rumors that Mormons did not want the railroad—with its rough, lawless elements and legions of camp followers—to intrude upon their isolation. "Such prejudice," he said, "is unfounded...our labors along the line [demonstrate] our great desire and anxiety to see the completion." The railroad would multiply trading opportunities and allow the world's finest intellects "to visit our mountain homes and to form a true estimate of our character and position."[6]

However, Mormons who expected the railroad to introduce "swarms of scalawags" and "bummers, gamblers, saloon and hurdy-gurdy keepers, border ruffians, and desperadoes generally" were quite right.[7] Those influences arrived, in fact, well in advance of those first locomotives. In February 1869, a local man complained that "considerable whiskey now walks through Ogden." He had seen two drunken men fighting on Ogden's bench and heard a young teamster's account of being beaten up by railroad graders just north of town for refusing to give them a ride. The observer believed that "these and other occurrences are the results of a free use of bad liquor."[8]

Such pastimes already existed in Ogden but only in mild doses. Minutes of Ogden police meetings from the early 1860s record occasional arrests for public drunkenness or gambling. That was about the extent of sin in Ogden until 1868, when Central Pacific crews from the west and Union Pacific laborers from the east began closing in. Stagecoaches connecting the railroads' terminal points passed regularly through town, carrying "considerable whiskey" and promoting other vices. In August 1868, perhaps for the first time, the police had to be on guard for "some loose women in our town that would bear watching."[9]

That first trickle of intemperate teamsters and

graders soon became a deluge of Gentiles: railroad employees and hungry and tired train travelers whose expectations of hospitality were different, to say the least, from those of Mormon culture. Investors and entrepreneurs flocked to Ogden to fulfill those expectations. The shortest route to town from the railroad depot came to be known as 5th Street and, after 1889, 25th Street. Unique among Utah's byways, boulevards, and territorial turnpikes, 25th Street was the red carpet to Ogden and its wealth of diversions, libations, and anonymous encounters.

The railroads infused Ogden with not only vice but cash. "Before 1863 there was no regular commerce in Ogden," noted historian Edward W. Tullidge, and even after merchants established stores on Main Street in the years following that, transactions often took the form of barter.[10] The benefits of a cash-based economy were being felt by December 1868, as recorded by a *New York Times* correspondent in Salt Lake City: "Notwithstanding the dull and cheerless state of the weather this Christmas Eve, in consequence of the comparative abundance of greenbacks the present holiday is likely to be as merry a one to most of the population of this territory as any that has occurred."[11]

Once Ogden became accustomed to circulating currency, the progress of "pay cars" over the rails from Omaha or Sacramento was monitored with the same breathlessness once reserved for the circus. "The pay car of the Central Pacific came in last night," noted the *Ogden Junction* of October 8, 1873, "and paid out two months' wages.... Gold eagles were plentiful about dusk."[12] The hosannas so engendered continued for decades. The day after a big railroad payday in December 1909, "[Ogden's] Christmas shopping crowds [were] nearly twice as heavy as they had been before," noted the *Salt Lake Herald-Republican*.[13]

Compounding the payroll stimulus to Ogden's growth was the money travelers spent at the depot for food, lodging, and services pertaining to the unavoidable transfer between Union Pacific and Central Pacific trains. In the spring of 1877, magazine publisher Frank Leslie, on a cross-country excursion, recorded "the wildest confusion and noisiest bustle" at Ogden: "Whole pyramids of Saratoga trunks topple along the platforms, baggage expressmen wrangle and swear over the transfers, anxious tourists struggle in and out among the labyrinthine mazes of baggage and are knocked right and left." Peering into a hotel dining room, Leslie observed "Chinese waiters flying about for dear life, with plates and dishes piled on their clean, white-shirted arms, and a hungry crowd pursuing them with a multiplicity of orders."[14]

By 1881, with four rail lines converging at the depot, Ogden had become the avatar of the Utah beehive. To arrive at dinner time was sheer chaos. An Englishman described stepping off his train to the clanging and banging of gongs and an "uproarious and confused babel" from rival hotel runners haranguing customers with promises of the hottest and tastiest food and lowest prices. "So passionately did they address us, and so violently did they abuse one another, calling each other by the very choicest of American epithets," the gentleman said, "that I thought there was going to be a free fight." If one runner promised magnificent meals for seventy-five cents, a competitor countered with a sixty-cent deal, only to be undercut by a third, who practically gave dinner away for fifty cents with good wine thrown in and "young ladies to wait."[15]

To give travelers relief from such scenes is precisely why hotels and restaurants were built on 5th Street, a short, but sensible, distance away. The street soon came to play a critical role in getting railroad and depot emoluments into general circulation. A Weber County sheriff in the early 1890s mentioned his wish to clean up the street to the U.S. marshal, but the marshal replied,

> The railroads that run into Ogden are all doing a lot of construction work. That means that every week hundreds of laborers come in here with their wages. They spend a lot of it on Fifth Street. But those people down there [saloon keepers, gamblers, prostitutes] that get that money are all liberal spenders and when they get a dollar they spend it. So the rest of us then get a chance at it.[16]

Fifth Street was renumbered 25th Street in 1889, the year sometimes identified by historians as the watershed when the street assumed its opprobrious reputation. A new Liberal Party city government was accused of relaxing ordinances regulating vice and inducing purveyors of gambling, prostitution, and unbridled consumption of liquor to stampede to Ogden.[17] However, a review of the intricate political and economic circumstances of 1889 reveals a more complicated story. The elements that made the street notorious had already thrived there for a decade or more. What actually happened in 1889 is that 25th Street made its debut as a perennial bugaboo in Ogden politics.

Although the majority of Ogden voters were Mormon and belonged to the People's Party, its plurality had waned throughout the 1880s as Congress, determined to stamp out plural marriage, passed laws disenfranchising polygamists and, later, all Utah women.[18] Congress also created the Utah Commission to supervise all elections, federal and territorial, in a manner favoring non-Mormon voters.[19] A concurrent surge in Ogden's non-Mormon population preceded the municipal election of February 11, 1889. These shifts in demographics enabled the Liberal Party's first major victory in Utah's history; seated a prosperous merchant, Fred J. Kiesel, as mayor; and ushered in an all–Liberal Party city council.

The unprecedented Liberal Party sweep did not sit well with the People's Party. Immediately the Mormon newspaper, the *Deseret News,* insisted the victory came only through "what we have good reason to believe [were] fraudulent means."[20] The incumbent Mormon prophet, Wilford Woodruff, later asserted, "At the Ogden election...large numbers of names of resident voters were stricken from the registration lists. Hundreds of non-residents were imported and the election was carried by the Liberals by open fraud." Consequently, added Woodruff, "vice flourished."[21] More recently, one historian assumed that the "major contributor" to the Liberal Party victory was fraud and "the inability of the Mormons to obtain redress of grievances."[22] However, as the Utah Commission noted at the time, the People's Party neither brought specific charges to the commission's attention nor offered any proof.[23]

That the Liberal Party made its own accusations of fraud has been ignored. A syndicated dispatch from Ogden on election day said the People's Party had started "a system of intimidation," arresting Liberal Party members before they had a chance to vote and taking them to jail. U.S. Marshal Frank Dyer "at once stopped the arrests until the voter had a chance.... After this the election passed off quietly."[24]

Two nights after the election, celebratory banners stretched across 5th Street from the Chapman House to Thompson's Tavern as trainloads of joyful Liberal Party members from Salt Lake City and Park City marched from the depot past a bonfire at City Hall to a victory rally at Lester Park. Attorney Abbot R. Heywood, a future Ogden mayor, told the assembly, "We have been charged with fraud. I deny it. Had it not been for the intimidation of the People's Party we would have had two hundred more votes."[25]

Although Mayor Kiesel took office pledging to conduct city business "without partisanship or discrimination," his new government's first major initiative was anything but conciliatory. One of its first actions was to pass a unanimous ordinance setting aside the city block that for decades had been home to the Mormon Tabernacle "for use as a public square." The council believed the church had never secured legal title to Tabernacle Square. Despite forceful protests from the *Ogden Standard* that even the U.S. government had backed away from confiscating Tabernacle Square under federal anti-polygamy law, this ordinance remained on the books for five years.[26]

An election in August 1889 for justice of the peace of the Ogden precinct brought another defeat to the People's Party. Its incumbent candidate, Thomas D. Dee, lost to the Liberal Party's Samuel M. Preshaw, a carpenter and undertaker. For this setback, the People's Party had a remedy. The solidly Mormon county court, under authority conveyed by territorial law, dissolved the Ogden precinct, which comprised the entire city. In its place, the court created four precincts and appointed a new justice of the peace for each: Judge Dee, two other Mormons, and Judge Preshaw. Whether the precinct shake-up was in response to the Tabernacle Square ordinance is not recorded. But the Utah Commission interpreted the action as the result of "the intense aversion they [the People's Party] have to anything not under their own control."[27]

A native of Ludwigsburg, Germany, Frederick J. Kiesel (1841–1919) was mayor of Ogden from 1889 to 1891. He had run unsuccessfully against incumbent mayor David H. Peery in 1885. *Photo courtesy of Special Collections, Stewart Library, Weber State University.*

Following the Ogden City Council's blindsiding action on Tabernacle Square, the People's Party became vocal about the Liberal administration's perceived failings. Twenty-fifth Street was the ideal bludgeon. "Gambling and prostitution have been permitted to flourish there unchecked," the *Deseret News* stated. The *Salt Lake Herald,* a newspaper reflecting Mormon views, said that

Ogden prostitutes had grown brazen enough to post signs on their doors, but "this was a little too much for the Liberal authorities, and some time ago the women were notified that they must remove the signs, though otherwise they were not interfered with."[28]

Liberals retorted that venues of vice had been on 25th Street before 1889 "in all their pristine glory." John W. Metcalf, the Liberal Party chief of police, said thirteen houses of prostitution had been "run on the quiet" while the People's Party still held power. "For nearly a year before the election," said the *Salt Lake Tribune*, "[Ogden's] police never molested a gambling house nor the female resorts, and it was as easy to procure a drink on Sunday as on any weekday. Gambling existed in the days gone by and so did lascivious conduct."[29]

A grand jury tried to investigate the People's Party's allegations of lapsed enforcement but could not obtain testimony. The next move came from an unexpected quarter: U.S. Marshal Elias H. Parsons, who under federal antipolygamy law had the same powers as a local sheriff. Parsons sent his deputies to Ogden on August 15, 1889, to give gamblers and prostitutes five days to close their operations or be arrested. Within twenty-four hours, some forty tin-horn gamblers abandoned Ogden, followed by numerous trollops.[30] After the warning period, Deputy Marshal Arthur Pratt arrested half a dozen gambling proprietors and dealers who failed to close; most were tried and fined.[31]

The marshals' actions provoked as much outrage among Liberals as the Tabernacle Square ordinance had stirred up in the People's Party. The *Ogden Daily Commercial,* a Liberal newspaper founded soon after Kiesel's victory, published a rebuttal of the People's Party's accusations.[32] Ogden, it said, was "peaceful, orderly, and well-regulated" and "almost free" of the evils the People's Party accused it of harboring. Furthermore, for every gambling house or "chippie *bagnio*" in Ogden, there were twice as many running full tilt in Salt Lake City. A second Liberal newspaper, the *Daily Union,* fumed that the marshals' intrusion was a Salt Lake scheme and asked, "Why do they not enforce the law in their own city? Because they see an advantage in forcing Ogden to pull down its blinds."[33]

Although national political parties had not yet officially organized in Utah, ninety-two members of the Weber County Republican Committee signed a petition to Marshal Parsons, demanding that he remove Deputy Pratt from supervision of Ogden. Parsons replied that he stood firmly behind Deputy Pratt and expressed surprise "that a Republican committee in Utah is willing to go on record in such a manner."[34]

Parsons's rejection of the petition did not placate Abbot R. Heywood, the Republican chairman, who now assured the marshal that he and his cosigners wanted law, order, and peace. The People's Party, Heywood asserted, "claimed to have the same desire, and yet having the government of the city since its inception, their efforts resulted in only transferring crime to the streets and the back yards and the back rooms, and worst of all to the quiet houses of good citizens." Heywood reminded Parsons that he owed his appointment as U.S. marshal to a Republican platform—drawn up in preparation for statehood—that called for federal appointees to be chosen from Utah residents. "Yet you send to take charge of northern Utah [Deputy Pratt] who hasn't a dollar's interest of any kind therein, who moves here to remain while in office only, and whose desire would seem to be to exhibit to the people here how little he cares for their opinions."[35]

If the number of Ogden's vicious establishments increased after the 1889 election, a more plausible explanation is the city's greatly expanded and diversified population. An economic boom had taken root in the spring of 1887, prompting the founding of a chamber of commerce in April, attracting investors from outside the territory, and bringing welcome improvements to 25th Street, including graveling and new buildings.[36] By 1890 territorial governor Arthur L. Thomas could report that Ogden was "the most prominent railroad center between Denver and San Francisco.... No other city in the West has increased so rapidly in population during the past ten years; and, so far as I can learn, it is likely to continue." The governor cited census figures showing Ogden's population had more than doubled from 1880 to 1890, from 6,069 to 14,919.[37]

In fact, 1889 may have been Ogden's banner year for non-Mormon immigration. Among the notable Gentiles who arrived that year were Belle London, eventually the most successful madam not merely in Ogden but in all of Utah; Pat Desmond, proprietor of the Ogden River Resort; Augustus B. Patton, lawyer and eventual president of the Ogden Chamber of Commerce; and "Colonel" William Hope Harvey, gifted real-estate promoter and prime organizer of Ogden's enigmatic Mardi Gras celebration of July 1890. These four came from Colorado.

Also seeking their fortune in Ogden in 1889 were Edward A. Reed from Wyoming, developer of the stately Reed Hotel; Henry Bigelow from Nebraska, founder of the Ogden State Bank; Denny Smyth, native Irishman and Laramie-based Union Pacific engineer, who later owned and operated 25th Street's European Hotel; and Olin A. Kennedy from Iowa, a reporter for the *Ogden Daily Commercial* and valuable Ogden historian.[38]

In framing the 1889 debate on 25th Street's morals, the People's Party employed terms of horror and revulsion toward the street's activities. The reality, often overlooked, is that from the street's inception, Mormons played important roles in the businesses denounced by their party. Many saloons were Mormon owned and operated. The preeminent madam, Belle London, purchased the real estate that became Electric Alley from prominent Mormon businessman David H. Peery Jr.[39] Stephens Brothers, a family construction company whose reputation as builders extended back to the Mormon temple in Nauvoo, Illinois, erected the various dwellings in Electric Alley.[40] Rosetta Davie, twentieth-century heiress to Belle London's legacy, was descended from English and Danish pioneers and baptized a Mormon when she was eight.[41]

Ogden's Liberals, for their part, suspected a conspiracy by Salt Lake City interests to retard and injure local business, especially after the U.S. marshal's office invaded their police department's turf. Some Liberals called for a boycott of the anti-Mormon *Salt Lake Tribune,* which had supported the marshal's move.[42] Competition and jealousy between the junction and capital cities had existed from Utah's earliest years. "Salt Lakers, perhaps sensing betimes the certain rival destiny between Ogden and [themselves]," observed historian Edward W. Tullidge, "were enviously prone to stigmatize with the name 'Ogden Hole' one of the most notable places on our Territorial map."[43]

Brigham Young, the Mormon prophet and former territorial governor, had declared in 1868 that if the Union Pacific did not pass through Salt Lake City, it would be "an insult to the citizens of the territory."[44] But the Union Pacific routed its line through Ogden, provoking a severe case of envy in the capital city.[45] Young boycotted both Ogden's celebration welcoming the Union Pacific and the Golden Spike ceremony at Promontory Summit—two months later on May 10, 1869—to commemorate the transcontinental railroad's completion.

When the Southern Pacific announced plans in 1901 to build the Lucin Cutoff west from Ogden across the Great Salt Lake, shortening its route to San Francisco by forty-three miles, Salt Lake City schemed to dissuade the railroad and lobbied hard to get the line rerouted through its city, despite the logistical absurdity. The city claimed a cutoff would obstruct navigation on the lake and—when that argument fell on deaf ears—threatened to boycott the Southern Pacific.[46] Ogden's newspapers responded with scathing derision, suggesting that commercial air balloons could easily glide over the Ogden-Lucin bridgeway and Salt Lake would gladly furnish the hot air to inflate them.[47]

To celebrate the Lucin Cutoff's imminent construction, Ogden declared a holiday on St. Patrick's Day in 1902 and planned public events on a scale unseen since the first locomotives steamed into town in 1869. The same jubilation—cannons firing, steam whistles blowing, dignitaries' speeches, and parading schoolchildren carrying banners—was on display, but this time 25th Street, a mere path along the edge of a swamp thirty-three years earlier, anchored the proceedings as the site where the parade formed, Utah's grandest dignitaries were escorted into town from Union Station, and the speeches issued from the upper balcony of City Hall. Ogden's triumph over Utah's capital city was cleverly condensed onto a banner displayed prominently in the parade: "We're going to have the cutoff/Said Salt Lake with a shout/We're going to sidetrack Ogden/And then their pipe went out."[48]

On its face, 25th Street was not a phenomenon to faze a world-wise traveler. Its dens of iniquity and means of regulating them differed little from those in other American cities. Names of saloons (White Elephant, the Club, the Mint); unofficial tolerance of brothels so long as unwritten rules were followed; and the fees and fines collected on the street that filled the city's treasury were the same as in Denver, San Francisco, and Fort Worth. World War II stories from 25th Street carried a certain shock value, but so did the wartime ambience in Seattle, Detroit, Baltimore, Miami, Honolulu, or other cities.[49]

What did set 25th Street apart from other American vice districts was its ironic emergence in the heart of a Mormon city. Nowhere else was there such a configuration of contenders: a dominant, but beleaguered, religion fighting to retain political control of a city whose economic lifeblood, the railroad, was leveling the playing field. While the street's incompatibility with its Mormon host was chronic, it rankled especially during the nineteenth century when the Mormon Church was resisting federal efforts to quash polygamy.

"There is no understanding Utah without realizing that neighbor, for sixty years, was at neighbor's throat," wrote Ogden native Bernard DeVoto. The conflicts became a "first-rate religious war" in which the Liberal and People's parties conducted a "protracted, desperate, side-splitting battle for supremacy."[50] Irreconcilable political differences were the "fundamental division in late nineteenth-century Utah," wrote historians John McCormick and John Sillito. "Virtually every aspect of the territory's life...became entangled in that division."[51] In such a context, the decadent pastimes along 25th Street were always somewhat more threatening to locals than in other cities.

Twenty-fifth Street's location at the nation's major railroad junction assured its proximity to events and phenomena that—if not entirely unique—animated and enriched the tapestry of Ogden's history. All coast-to-coast travelers, no matter their distinction or high rank, had to pass through Ogden, bringing an impressive array of rulers, potentates, tastemakers, and celebrities to the city. Many U.S. presidents stopped in Ogden long enough to smile and acknowledge cheering crowds, but during the Progressive Era, three allotted time to become acquainted.

William Howard Taft probably saw more of Ogden than any other president. As soon as his train arrived on Sunday, September 26, 1909, he was whisked away to Ogden Canyon, chauffeured by Denny Smyth, proprietor of 25th Street's European Hotel, in Smyth's Packard. From the canyon, the presidential motorcade proceeded to Lester Park, where Taft spoke for fifteen minutes. The following day Ogden was humming with rumors that Taft had been "indisposed" by Smyth's high speeds of thirty-five miles per hour in the canyon, although Smyth said he drove as directed by the Secret Service. Two years later, in a brief speech at Union Station, Taft recalled "your beautiful city and going through that wonderful canyon" but said nothing about Smyth.[52]

Theodore Roosevelt, hoping to reclaim the presidency as Progressive Party candidate, arrived in Ogden on September 13, 1912, to address his party's Utah convention. Waiting at Union Station for Roosevelt was Denny Smyth, whose car had been painstakingly decorated as a bull moose, symbol of the Progressives. But Roosevelt "overlooked" Smyth's car, according to the

On September 26, 1909, President William Howard Taft rode through Ogden in Denny Smyth's 1908 Packard Model 30 seven-passenger touring car with Smyth at the wheel. The Packard was directly in front of Smyth's European Hotel at 242 25th Street (not visible) when this photo was snapped. In the upper left is a rare view of the Central Hotel at 224 25th. *Photo courtesy of Union Station Archives.*

Salt Lake Tribune, and "rode up from the station in a tiny little machine." Whether Taft had warned Roosevelt about Smyth is unknown. Roosevelt made an open-air speech at 25th Street and Grant Avenue, the same spot where he had spoken while president in 1903.[53]

Woodrow Wilson, on a promotional tour for his proposed League of Nations, had only an hour to see Ogden from an eleven-car motorcade, but as his driver turned east on 25th Street from Wall Avenue, loud cheers erupted from not only crowds lining the street but people standing on the roofs of buildings or perched precariously on the cross arms of telephone poles.[54]

Occasionally trains came to Ogden in dire circumstances. After the San Francisco earthquake of April 18, 1906, Edward H. Harriman, president of both the

Union Pacific and Southern Pacific, offered free passage out of California to destitute survivors. When the first relief train arrived, Ogden was ready. A hastily assembled local relief committee fed train after train, each bearing hundreds of refugees. Harriman projected that from ten to fifteen thousand victims would pass through Ogden.[55]

Certain natural advantages of 25th Street's location were not mentioned in polite company. Paul Kinsie, director of field studies for the American Social Hygiene Association and an expert on prostitution, wrote,

> The location of some cities seems to make it easier for men to become customers. Up to the early 1940s Ogden, Utah, was a popular locale for prostitution because it was a rail junction. Men could visit a brothel between trains, and indeed might plan their travel to permit a layover in Ogden. Some natives would enjoy driving their cars to Ogden's 25th Street on Saturday night to watch the prostitutes and their clients.[56]

One of the railroad's most enduring legacies in Ogden is the coalescence of an African American community in the blocks near Union Station. While the largest gains in the city's black population came during World War II, multitudes of traveling Pullman porters and other railroad workers had been stopping in Ogden between assignments for decades. Businesses catering to their needs located on 25th Street, most particularly the Porters and Waiters Club.[57] The club began as a boarding house, but its eventual inauguration of live music gave Ogden an enviable tradition of jazz performances it otherwise might have missed.

Saxophonist Joe McQueen, an Ogdenite since 1945 and resident headliner at Porters and Waiters, was well known in America's midcentury jazz fraternity. As McQueen explains it, "Musicians from New York coming to Salt Lake, they'd be talking to other bands and were told, 'If you get out there and you want to have some fun, go to the Porters and Waiters Club. Go and get hold of Joe McQueen.' " Jazzmen called him in the wee hours and said, "Man, we just got off a gig. I know it's late and everything, but we'd like to have someplace to go." The rousted McQueen then met the touring players at Porters and Waiters, where the upstairs bar was still open. "We'd start a jam session [downstairs], and in an hour's time, the club would be damn near full."[58]

After an evening's engagement at Lagoon or Salt Lake City's Rainbow Randevu, Duke Ellington's orchestra, Count Basie's band, and other groups preferred to drive to Ogden and improvise with McQueen than stay in Salt Lake. Count Basie liked Ogden because he could visit a childhood friend who lived there, and Paul Gonsalves, the great tenor saxophonist with Duke Ellington, was enamored of an Ogden woman and often lingered in town after the rest of Ellington's players departed. Gonsalves, who had rocked the 1956 Newport Jazz Festival by playing a herculean twenty-seven-chorus solo on Ellington's "Diminuendo and Crescendo in Blue," may have surpassed that marathon during a late-night Ogden session. McQueen was leaving Porters and Waiters to chauffeur someone to Salt Lake as Gonsalves launched into a solo. When McQueen returned, Gonsalves was still playing. "I asked, 'Is he playing again?' and they said, 'No, he's still playing.' Oh, my gracious. I couldn't believe it when they told me he was on the horn all this time,"[59] McQueen chuckles.

Exterior view of the Porters and Waiters Club at 127 25th Street with its neon sign and street-level glass-brick façade, circa 1959. On its right is the separate Porters and Waiters Café. *Photo courtesy of Kelli Garside McFarland.*

Joe McQueen. *Photo courtesy of Union Station Archives.*

Jack McVea, a rhythm-and-blues saxophonist, brought his Black and White Records studio band to Utah for holiday engagements. "[McVea's men] would always want to go and jam after they got through with their gig," McQueen recalls. "It didn't matter what time you started a jam session; you could always have a crowd. People stayed up all night anyway. These places down on 25th Street used to be open twenty-four hours a day, just like their own Las Vegas."[60]

That 25th Street influenced the development of Las Vegas is an unsung aspect of its history. It is well known that an Ogden-born banker, Parry Thomas, supervised the Bank of Las Vegas's financing of many notable casinos, and Young Electric Sign Company, manufacturer of those casinos' spectacular neon signs, originated as the Thomas Young Sign Company of Ogden.[61] But Las Vegas also had to implement measures to deal with the crime that inevitably accompanied gambling. They turned to Harman Peery, a five-term Ogden mayor during the 1930s and '40s, for guidance. "Wilbur Clark [of the Desert Inn] quizzed Harman on how he had handled vice on Twenty-fifth Street," recalls a grandson.

> Harman told Wilbur, "You'll have drunk calls and attempted murders every night, and you've got to have the force to deal with it." He recommended an assessment on the casinos to fund a special vice squad.
>
> Harman was treated like a God and a visionary when he went to Las Vegas. They'd seat him in the bar and powwow with him for hours and ask how he ran the city. His room and admissions to shows were comped at the Desert Inn. It couldn't have been for his patronage because he never gambled. Harman thought gambling was foolish. He's also the one who

The Kokomo Club at 216 25th Street has been in business for more than sixty years. "...then Ogden, which I dug, Jap hipsters, crazy bum street with Kokomo Bar at foot of which white-capped mountains rise—a town I'd heard about some, I can see it's something," wrote Jack Kerouac in *Visions of Cody. Photo courtesy of Special Collections, Stewart Library, Weber State University.*

Despite the reputation of 25th Street's vicious establishments, most of its storefronts were legitimate businesses. William Kent had a barber shop at 234 25th in the early twentieth century. *Photo courtesy of Anna Stone Keogh.*

told Wilbur he needed a big highway sign for the Desert Inn. Wilbur said no one in Las Vegas could manufacture such a sign, so Harman sent Young Electric down there.[62]

Over the course of its history, 25th Street experienced three separate heydays. The first lasted from 1880 to 1905, when the street epitomized the rip-roaring, trigger-happy, Wild West town. Saloons, novelty theaters, and opium dens overshadowed adjacent Mormon granaries, cooperative stores, and Catholic parish buildings. Shootings and murders were common. The tenderloin district called Electric Alley sprang up just behind the street, ruled by Belle London.

Then, in the twentieth century, the Progressive movement gradually engulfed the entire country, stirred up by ministerial associations, antisaloon leagues, and politicians. Utah was caught up in the momentum, and its legislature outlawed the sale and manufacture of liquor two and one half years before nationwide Prohibition went into effect. However, in spite of hundreds of arrests, fines, and jailings for trafficking in liquor, the Prohibition years on 25th Street became their own variety of heyday because finding a drink in Ogden was never easier than between 1917 and 1933.[63] You could scarcely toss an egg on the street without hitting a bootlegger or speakeasy.

Prohibition's repeal in 1933 kicked off 25th Street's third and grandest heyday, an era when organized crime figured prominently. The notable Rosetta Davie reigned with gentility over 25th Street harlotry and narcotics traffic. An irrepressible mayor, Harman Peery, kept Ogden solvent during the flatlining economy of the Great Depression with infusions of license money from gambling syndicates. Forces both inside and outside

John V. Brunetti's Wholesale & Retail store on the ground floor of the Denver Hotel at 161 25th Street. *Photo courtesy of Special Collections, Stewart Library, Weber State University.*

Ogden eventually deflated this third heyday. During the 1950s, elected officials and sheriff and police departments cracked down on 25th Street's vice with unprecedented determination. But the steady decline in railroad passenger service, which also intensified during that time period, proved to be the greater drain on the street's energies.

While the earliest contenders polarized over 25th Street were Mormon and Gentile, the identities of its partisans and detractors shifted many times over the years. Those who favored the street generally had business interests there; those who wanted to reform it most often had political aspirations, spiritual constituencies, or both. The street has always had an oversized influence on the city's reputation and given it a turbulent, but unforgettable, ride. Onward, then, to the saga of the life and times of Ogden's rowdiest road.

Successful goose hunter at Armstrong Sporting Goods store at 302 25th Street in 1939.
Photo used by permission of the Utah State Historical Society.

CHAPTER TWO

OGDEN HOSTS

Maybe they call it Larimer or Trent or Mission, but every western town that ever amounted to anything has a 25th Street. It usually staggers up the hill from the depot or the river boat landing and, the opinions of the Civic Adornment League notwithstanding, it is still the most legitimate lane in the whole downtown mess.

—Frank Tinker, *Salt Lake Tribune*, September 15, 1963

Like many early Utah settlements, Ogden was platted with exceptionally broad thoroughfares. As laid out by territorial Governor Brigham Young, Mayor Lorin Farr, and surveyor Henry G. Sherwood in the summer of 1851, Ogden's streets were ninety-nine feet wide.[1] But none had been named at the time of the Union Pacific's arrival. Some had descriptive appellations, such as the Tithing Office Street (today's 24th Street) or the State Road (now Washington Boulevard).[2] What the early settlers may have called 25th Street has been lost to history.

The city council finally named Ogden's north/south streets on December 12, 1870.[3] Only Wall (street, then, instead of today's avenue) has kept its original name. Not surprisingly, today's Washington Boulevard received the premiere designation of Main Street. Lincoln and Grant avenues were christened Franklin Street (after Judge Franklin D. Richards) and Young Street (after Brigham), respectively. The numbering of the east/west streets may never have been formalized. In the 1870s, present-day 24th and 25th streets were designated 4th and 5th.

Fifth Street's march towards its ultimate notoriety did not start with a bang. In the 1850s, the south side of its 300 block, familiar today as the beautiful City Hall Park, was a swamp where settlers' domestic animals sometimes got stuck and had to be pulled out. It was also a breeding ground for ducks and consequently a hunting mecca for boys with bows and arrows. Schoolchildren who lived east of State Road had to walk counterclockwise around the swamp to get to the Second Ward School, located on Young Street just south of 5th.[4] Other than the unimposing Seventies Hall, built before 1862, the street had no notable landmark until the railroads gave Ogden an economy.[5]

Strange as it may seem today, when the Union Pacific first began running trains through Ogden, early in 1869, the city had no station and was not even a stop. The closest station was Taylor's Mills (present-day

Eli Sheldon Glover's 1875 birds-eye view of Ogden shows the relationship of 5th Street to the depot.
Photo courtesy of Union Station Archives.

Riverdale), three miles away by stagecoach.[6] However, if a conductor happened to be in a good mood, Ogden-bound passengers could persuade him to stop his train due west of Tithing Office Street, where Mormon bishop Chauncey West's hotel, the Ogden House, was located.[7]

But after the U.S. Congress set the junction of the two railroads "at or near Ogden" on April 10, 1869, entrepreneurs could not rush to the city fast enough.[8] That spring a *New York Times* reporter found construction booming and real-estate prices and rental rates soaring "almost to comparatively fabulous prices....Lodging accommodations are yet not abundant." Another correspondent told Salt Lake City's *Deseret News* that Ogden was "a changed place...hotels, restaurants, chop houses, boarding houses, and 'meals at all hours' are literally jammed and crammed. About the only chance for the travelers now is to roost on the fence and board with themselves."[9]

At the depot, the railroads did most of the construction. The Union Pacific and Central Pacific jointly built two large freight sheds. Otherwise most of the buildings—baggage house and engine houses, telegraph office, and the Junction House passenger depot and eating house—belonged to the Union Pacific.[10] The Junction House was a ramshackle, one-story affair, not remotely like the two grand Union Stations that serially adorned the depot grounds in future decades. According to historian Milton R. Hunter, it was built of wide boards and painted red, with barely enough room to accommodate a station master, ticket vendor, and a few waiting passengers and their bags.[11]

Meanwhile, Brigham Young and Mormon businessmen had broken ground in Ogden on May 17, 1869, for the new Utah Central Railroad, which connected Salt Lake City to the transcontinental line. By December 1869, the Utah Central had completed its own passenger depot and engine house at the west end of 5th Street and laid switching tracks across Wall Street down the middle of 5th toward Franklin. If a resident had spent most of 1869 away from Ogden, "he would be apt to fail to recognize it," said the *Deseret News.*[12]

As the railroads hastily erected their buildings at the depot, "hunters of the almighty dollar" set up shop alongside them, noted the *Deseret News,* hoping to sell "forked lightning," "forty rod," and other spirituous liquors. But the three railroad lines, Ogden City Council, and Mayor

Lorin Farr publicly disapproved of saloons at the depot, fearing the "demoralizing" effects on railroad employees, and the council granted no licenses there. For the time being, would-be saloon keepers in shanties and tents could offer only food or billiards.[13]

Although the depot was dry, thirsty customers could buy all the liquor they wanted on Main Street. While the Ogden City Council maintained strict control over who could sell liquor, it never prohibited forked lightning outright.[14] Throughout this period, there were frequent protests that municipal governments in Utah required higher liquor-license fees from Gentiles than from Mormons.[15] A roving Denver reporter who visited Ogden in 1869 noted that "several saloons and fire shops do away with Mormon exclusiveness by paying the demanded licenses."[16]

But at Ogden's depot, "no [liquor] license is likely to be given," the *Deseret News* predicted.[17] The city, however, must have needed money, for one year later, the council approved four saloons at the depot; the terms were one hundred dollars per month and bonds to maintain orderly houses. Consequently, booze began to flow like the Ogden River.[18] A *Deseret News* correspondent complained that Ogden was "up with the spirit of the times" and "can boast of our petty thieves, burglars, man-slaughterers, murderers, and jail breakers. These are some of the fruits we have reaped...since the advent of 'civilization.'" After a man who tried to break up a fight was shot to death, the normally unflappable *Corinne Daily Reporter* commented, "These little episodes seem to be growing frequent in Ogden."[19]

As eager for liquor as some local customers appeared to be, the need for lodging in Ogden was even more critical. The first two hotels at the depot—the Pulaski House and Junction House—went up in 1869. Fred J. Kiesel, a future Ogden mayor, built the Pulaski House as one of his earliest local business ventures. As an old man, Kiesel recalled its lengthy roster of prominent guests, including U.S. senators, General Philip Sheridan, and Presidents Stanford and Huntington of the Central Pacific Railroad.[20]

The Union Pacific built the Junction House. Before trains had dining cars, they stopped at regular intervals so passengers could eat, and the Junction House was the railroad's official restaurant and inn at Ogden. At first it failed to impress. "From Omaha to San Francisco...the [railroad] restaurants are, well, endurable," noted an itinerant reporter. "They certainly might be bettered at some points, especially the important one at Ogden."[21]

One of Ogden's earliest notable hoteliers, Major Gabriel S. Erb, rehabilitated the Junction House's reputation. A Pennsylvanian and Civil War veteran of Chickamauga, Lookout Mountain, and Andersonville prison, Erb had kept a hotel at Quincy, Illinois, before coming west.[22] He ran the Junction House with two business partners: William M. Chapman, his brother-in-law from Quincy; and Dr. C. S. Nellis, an Ogden physician.[23] Soon the press was calling Major Erb a "prince of hotel men" and "one of the most courteous landlords on the Pacific roads."[24] One of his public relations triumphs was his celebration of the summer solstice of 1872, a moonlight dance for the public on the Union Pacific's platform, specially planed and leveled for the occasion.[25]

But misfortune struck a month later as straying sparks from the Junction House's faulty chimney caused both it and a nearby Wells Fargo office to burn in twenty minutes flat. Fortified, perhaps, with the same adrenaline he had known while charging up Lookout Mountain,

West front of the Union Depot Hotel, facing the Central Pacific railroad tracks. Men in the photo who were still alive nearly half a century later told Olin A. Kennedy that the date was probably 1884, not 1871. The lower floor housed a passenger waiting room, baggage room, dining hall, and freight offices. The second floor had rooms for overnight guests. *Photo courtesy of Special Collections, Stewart Library, Weber State University.*

Major Erb rushed into a nearby restaurant, the Chicago Bakery, and demanded to borrow its stove so he could continue serving food to incoming trains. The proprietor said he would sell his stove but not lend it. Friendly persuasion failing, Erb summoned his African American hotel runners and kitchen workers as a show of force. The Chicago Bakery proprietor rallied his patrons, and railroad workers and curious passersby joined the ensuing melee. Erb, Dr. Nellis, and William Chapman all sustained injuries, and Erb was arrested.[26]

But if Erb lost the battle of the bakeries, he ultimately won the war. Within six months, the Union Pacific and Central Pacific jointly rebuilt the ruin as the Union Depot Hotel, and Erb invited dignitaries from Corinne, Evanston, and Salt Lake City to a grand ball launching the new quarters.[27] He remained at the Union Depot Hotel until 1877, when he moved to Salt Lake City to manage the prestigious Walker House.[28] But he remained keenly interested in Ogden, later serving from Salt Lake as secretary of the Ogden Electric Light Company.[29]

An uptown alternative, the White House, at Main and 5th streets, had been built by Mormon pioneer Robert Burch.[30] When the rails reached Ogden in 1869, Burch's hotel was operating as the Lester House after proprietor Lester Herrick. Its name and host had changed to the White House and John Davies, respectively, by the end of the year, and the following spring, proprietorship passed to a young merchant seeking his fortune in the West, Simon Bamberger, who nearly half a century later became Utah's governor.[31]

Running the White House turned out to be an unlucky venture for Bamberger. He had difficulty keeping a business partner. He earned minor notoriety when one of his guests, a San Francisco reporter, got roaring drunk and threatened to shoot some of the other boarders. Bamberger lost his temper and struck the reporter, causing him to fall and break his nose. A local alderman fined both men ten dollars.[32]

One guest, a traveling salesman, must have thought the White House's bathing facilities were inadequate because he attempted to take a bath in the Weber Canal just east of the hotel. A spout for filling street-sprinkling wagons had been rigged, and as the salesman stepped under it, a revolving power wheel knocked him in the head, and he might have drowned if a night watchman had not observed the mishap.[33]

The last straw for Bamberger came when a small-pox epidemic besieged Ogden from May to October. At its peak, there were eighty-nine cases, quarantined by the city marshal at Farr's Grove (now Lorin Farr Park).[34] Word of the epidemic spread rapidly around the country, and Union Pacific passengers were barred from entering Ogden.[35] Bamberger threw in the towel and moved to Salt Lake City, where he bought a hotel at Second South and Main and named it the White House.[36]

Now anchored at one end by the Pulaski House and Union Depot Hotel and uptown by the White House, 5th Street began to sprout boarding houses and inns. It was a safer place than the chaotic depot, where moving trains were a constant hazard to buggies and pedestrians.[37] Ogden City Council minutes record hotel licenses issued for 5th Street without mentioning precise locations; two of the early ones were Thomas Scally's Arcade Hotel and Adolph Landt's Delmonico.[38] The Globe Hotel, built by Mormon pioneer John R. Poole, stood at the northeast corner of 5th and Young (present-day Grant Avenue). In June 1873, Poole redecorated and refurnished the Globe's rooms with new spring mattresses. The improvements failed to stave off unsavory publicity whenever thieves or prostitutes—most notably "Ten-Cent Annie" and four gentlemen found in her room—were apprehended on the premises.[39]

A third hostelry at Ogden's depot, the Junction Hotel, was built by George Loomis but significantly renovated and enlarged by William M. Chapman (who may have fallen out with his brother-in-law, Major Erb) and Thomas Scally in 1873.[40] Two stories tall with twenty rooms on the top floor, the Junction Hotel greeted travelers' eyes when they rode the Utah Central into town. From the west-facing second-floor porch, mingling guests enjoyed the view of the Weber River and slept comfortably in private quarters appointed with spring beds and walnut furniture. Downstairs a barber shop, billiard room, and barrooms flanked the central dining room. Chapman and Scally had reputations as attentive hosts "constantly on hand to attend to the welfare of their numerous guests." However, after 1875 the Junction Hotel vanishes from the historical record and may have burned down.[41]

William Chapman and Major Erb were only the first in a succession of ambitious and refined hosts attracted by Ogden's business potential. In November 1873, the Pulaski House got a new proprietor, Mills H. Beardsley, who promptly renamed the hotel after himself. Beardsley, from Akron, Ohio, had come west to manage a Salt Lake City hotel before setting his sights on Ogden.[42] He soon became widely recognized, both as a solicitous host and skilled marksman in Ogden's hunting club. "As a hotel man, Beardsley can't be beat and has friends wherever he goes," raved the *Corinne Daily Reporter*.[43]

In May 1874, Beardsley set the depot abuzz when one of his laying hens produced an egg with strange raised inscriptions on the shell. Some of the characters resembled Greek letters, while others were indecipherable, but the words "Mars," "Nephi," "death," "war," and the year 1879 were distinct. "These figures might have been carved *in* an egg shell by an expert," said one of the many Beardsley House guests who examined the mysterious oval, "but it does not seem possible that they could have been *raised* [italics in the original] by human hands." Some guests wondered if the hen was predicting war and desolation within the next five years.[44]

After running his eponymous hotel for three years, Beardsley moved to the Union Depot Hotel early in 1877 when Major Erb relocated to Salt Lake City.[45] Replacing Beardsley were two hotel men new to Ogden: Jake Keeney, from Malad, Idaho, and his partner, Amos Zeigler; the inn operated as the Keeney House through 1884.[46] This hotel's multiple identities have stumped

A view facing south from the Ogden depot in spring 1877. In the center, the Union Pacific Railroad tracks are on the left with the Central Pacific tracks on the right. A Utah Central train is heading west to cross the Weber River en route to Salt Lake City. Mills H. Beardsley ran the two-story Beardsley House from 1873 to 1877. *Photo from* Frank Leslie's Illustrated Newspaper, *December 15, 1877.*

The Beardsley House became the Keeney House when Jake Keeney took over management in June 1877. To its immediate south is the Chicago Bakery. *Photo courtesy of the Church History Library, Church of Jesus Christ of Latter-day Saints (Charles W. Carter Glass Negative Collection).*

The two-story Utah Hotel on the far right, circa 1871, had previously been run as the White House by Simon Bamberger. Its prime location on the southeast corner of present-day 25th Street and Washington Avenue has always had a hotel. *Photo courtesy of Special Collections, Stewart Library, Weber State University.*

Alvin D. Shakespeare operated many hotels in Ogden. He was the original proprietor of the Broom Hotel. *Photo courtesy of Golden Spike Lodge No. 6, Ogden, Utah.*

historians, who don't realize that the Pulaski House, Beardsley House, Keeney House, Chapman House, and Acropolis were all names at one time or another for the same structure.[47]

Meanwhile, the White House at 5th and Main, after performing so poorly for Simon Bamberger, had become the Utah Hotel.[48] Taking over management in 1875 was Alvin D. Shakespeare, an Ohioan like Beardsley and an equally prominent name in Ogden hospitality. A jack of many trades, Shakespeare was the first charter master of the Weber Masonic Lodge, a mining company officer, saloon and billiard room proprietor, and census taker in 1880.[49] To distinguish the Utah Hotel from its rivals at the depot, Shakespeare launched an advertising campaign branding it as a "strictly first-class" alternative. "Strangers visiting Ogden," he announced, "will find this hotel the best one to stop at, away from the depot, and free from the noise of the railroad."[50]

Whether at the depot or removed from its hubbub, Ogden's early hotels enjoyed an enormous advantage over their Salt Lake rivals. Since all railroad connections had to be made in Ogden, travelers could get several extra hours of sleep by lodging there instead of forty miles south in the capital city, a fact the Ogden hotels promoted to the hilt. "By coming to Ogden on the previous evening," noted the Utah Hotel's advertisements in Salt Lake newspapers, "travelers avoid the annoyance of rising at four o'clock to take the morning train at Salt Lake City."[51]

Fifth Street got its largest hotel of the 1870s when Thomas C. Chamberlain built his namesake inn on the approximate site of today's Ogden Blue printing and supply company. George Lashus, a former Central Pacific Railroad engineer at the Golden Spike ceremony of May 10, 1869, bought the Chamberlain Hotel in 1881. The following year—in violation of a covenant not to compete—Chamberlain built the

Before his namesake hotel was built, John Broom's property on the northwest corner of 5th and Main streets was occupied by nine small rental properties described as "permanently dangerous firetraps." *Photo courtesy of Special Collections, Stewart Library, Weber State University.*

View of the Broom Hotel's south side fronting 25th Street. *Photo courtesy of Special Collections, Stewart Library, Weber State University.*

Central Hotel on the north side of the next block. The Central Hotel had no sign indicating its name. Thomas Chamberlain sent his hotel runners in carriages to the depot, where they deceptively called out "new Chamberlain Hotel" and then transported confused patrons to the unmarked Central, while George Lashus waited in vain for them to arrive at the real Chamberlain Hotel. Lashus sued and won five thousand dollars in damages from Chamberlain, an award affirmed by the Utah Supreme Court.[52]

By 1880 Ogden realized that its supply of hotel rooms was inadequate and damaging its business potential. "Mr. Shakespeare," said the *Ogden Junction,* "is compelled to turn away daily from five to twenty-five persons for whom he has not room, and Mr. Beardsley is put to his wits' end to provide for the masses that stop with him." Entrepreneurs with dreams of investing in Ogden had abandoned the city and gone to Salt Lake "because of crowded hotels here."[53]

John Broom, a self-made Ogdenite, had the solution. Broom had arrived in Weber County in 1851 as a Mormon convert from England, although he later abandoned that faith for spiritualism.[54] Starting as a farmer in Marriott, he grew sugar cane and boiled it down to make molasses. He also made sewing needles, brewed beer, and grew the first crop of apricots in the county.[55]

In 1861 Broom was selling molasses to U.S. troops camped near Fort Bridger, Wyoming, en route from their Utah post, Camp Floyd, to fight in the Civil War. Nearby Broom found the charred remains of army supply wagons burned four years earlier by Mormon raiders in the Utah War. He loaded his wagon with the scrap iron, later trading it to Jonathan Browning, patriarch of the famous family of Ogden gunsmiths, for a prominent Ogden lot at 5th and Main. Broom built nine small commercial structures on the lot, which fattened his wallet with rental income.[56]

Now prosperous enough to sell his Marriott farm and move to Ogden, Broom ran unsuccessfully for the city council in 1871. He spent a few years in San Francisco, where he made a fortune in gold-mining stocks. He started hearing complaints about poor hotel accommodations west of Denver from railroad travelers. With a dream of a grand hotel on his Ogden lot similar to San Francisco's Palace, he moved back, gave notice to the tenants in his nine buildings—locally regarded as "permanently dangerous firetraps"—and began tearing them down on March 1, 1882.[57]

From its opening on January 15, 1883, the three-story Broom was considered the gem among Ogden hotels; all others were dismissed as mere taverns.[58] Its architect, J. C. Matthews of Oakland, California, specified nine double-bay window casings of California redwood supported by Corinthian columns in the top two stories and sixteen French plate-glass windows. Daylight flooded the building through seven crystal skylights in the roof. There were seventy rooms for guests, thirty-four of them on the top floor. The middle floor was home to the dining room, whose somewhat anatomical dinner menu offered ox heart, shoulder of mutton, and stewed kidneys, each accompanied by suitable condiments. At ground level, the billiard room and bar—opulent with solid walnut counters, marble countertops, inlaid French mirrors, and gilded pillars—were rumored to exceed all others west of New York City.[59]

The real story of the Broom, however, lies not in its glamour but the toughness of the hotel business. John Broom kept the title to his hotel but leased it to various proprietors, an arrangement seldom satisfactory to either side. Over the years, many of Ogden's veteran hotel men—in a succession resembling musical chairs—tried managing the Broom, but they were serial failures.

Presiding at the Broom's January 1883 grand opening was proprietor Alvin D. Shakespeare, who lasted eleven months before gambling debts forced him out.[60] Mills H. Beardsley replaced Shakespeare, refurbishing the still-young hotel extensively. One year into his tenure, Beardsley reduced weekly boarding rates to six dollars and meal prices to fifty cents while cheerfully telling the press that business was looking up. But a thirty-five-hundred-dollar garnishment from the Utah National Bank closed the Broom (temporarily) well before Beardsley's two-year anniversary. Subsequent proprietors were local druggist and saloon man J. W. McNutt; a businessman new to Ogden called Judge Gibbons; a San Francisco hotel matron named Mrs. Yowell, who signed a three-year lease but lasted only five months; and, from 1891 to 1893, Thomas C. Chamberlain, builder of Ogden's Chamberlain and Central hotels.[61]

Typically John Broom himself took control of his hotel between lessees, but after Ogden's Mardi Gras carnival in July 1890, he closed its doors suddenly without any announced reopening. The *Salt Lake Herald* called it a "surprising course pursued by the proprietor of the (alleged) only first-class hotel in Ogden," adding, "He emphatically denies that any Salt Lake influences were brought to bear."[62] Later, Broom explained, "I have leased it three times and got left each time. When I lease the building for five years and a man throws it up in eleven months it becomes disagreeable." However, the hotel reopened the following month.[63] Broom died in June 1893; after that his widow, Hester, ran the hotel.

The Chapman House, new on the scene in 1884,

The Virginia Hotel at 148½ 25th Street was originally built by Fred J. Kiesel as the Van Ness Hotel in 1912. *Photo courtesy of Special Collections, Stewart Library, Weber State University.*

could not compete with the Broom's grandeur, but guests could while away the hours on the second-floor veranda, taking in the flora and fauna of 5th Street. William M. Chapman, who had been running the Keeney House at the depot, recognized hospitality's future was on 5th Street, had the building moved to the middle of the north side of the 100 block, and renamed the hotel after himself.[64]

According to Ogden's most famous native author, Bernard DeVoto, the Chapman House was a favorite watering hole for barons of industry and frontier riff-raff alike, from mining magnates to migrating mavericks with names like Rattlesnake Bill. Its sumptuous menu, created by Chef "French Pete," might have exceeded the Broom's.[65] Featured dishes included turtle soup, mountain trout, Columbia River salmon, oysters San Francisco, antelope steak, shoulder of venison, beef Chicago, breast of sage hen, prairie chicken in cream, quail, mourning doves, Canada goose, candied southern yams, and potatoes O'Brien. "One was expected, not to make a choice from this ecstasy, but to down it all from the first to the last," DeVoto deadpanned. The Chapman House's libations menu, of equally impressive length, tempted tenants with cocktails named for railroad presidents and Indian chiefs.[66]

After just one summer season on 5th Street, Chapman sold his hotel to the partnership of Molinelli and Jenness, two gentlemen reputed to be shrewd businessmen.[67] But after only two months, the partnership transferred the Chapman back to its namesake, who then hired William Wadley to run the place. After Chapman died in 1893, the hotel retained his name until the same man who had built it at the depot in 1869, Fred J. Kiesel, purchased it in 1902.[68] The prosperous former mayor announced a new three-story hotel on the Chapman's site called the Van Ness. Kiesel was apparently too sentimental about the old building to have it demolished; instead, he supervised its removal to the center of the block, where it ended its days as a boarding house, the Acropolis, inhabited by Greek tenants.[69]

Kiesel's term as mayor coincided with completion of Ogden's long-awaited Union Station. Its grand opening on July 31, 1889, capped years of construction fits and starts. In the fall of 1886, the Union Pacific had petitioned the Ogden City Council to close the portion of 5th Street west of Wall Avenue so the station could be built there. The council approved the closing immediately, and, by the end of that year, the sandstone foundation had been laid. But legal and political problems delayed further construction from 1887 to 1888.[70]

The new station's potential for swelling the city's business traffic far beyond its current hotel capacity was not lost on Kiesel, who advocated development of facilities even bigger and grander than the Broom.[71] The *Ogden Standard* joined the crusade, editorializing, "Towns

Front view of Ogden's former Union Station, built in 1889. *Photo courtesy of Union Station Archives.*

east and west of us bid high for improvements, because they realize what vast advantages accrue from the possession of good hotels. If Ogden would have them, she must jump into the swim and breast the waters bravely."[72] The Chamber of Commerce amassed a bonus subscription of ten thousand dollars to induce a developer to build another landmark hotel. Capturing the stipend was real-estate investor Edward A. Reed of Cheyenne, Wyoming, a newcomer to Ogden.[73]

The Reed Hotel was built on the site of the old White House at the just-renamed intersection of 25th Street and Washington Avenue.[74] Its façade combined red diamond sandstone and high-quality pressed brick. Transporting the sandstone from quarries at Thistle in Utah County presented a conundrum; many times during the first year of construction, stonecutters had to be furloughed while carloads languished on railroad sidetracks. Then, in July 1890, Reed fired an entire battery of stonecutters, saying they resorted excessively to gin and did poor work.[75]

Trackside view of the former Union Station (1889–1923). *Photo courtesy of Union Station Archives.*

As the Reed neared completion, two longtime hotel

Antique postcard showing the exterior and lobby of the Reed Hotel at 25th Street and Washington Avenue, completed in 1891. *Photo courtesy of Union Station Archives.*

men from Joplin, Missouri—W. A. McMillen and A. N. Deming—leased it and oversaw the logistics of decorating and furnishing.[76] After numerous postponements, the Reed welcomed its first guests on July 3, 1891.[77] With custom-made furniture and carpeting, state-of-the art steam heating, electric wiring, and swift elevators, the turreted, five-story Reed became an instant rival to the Broom, kitty-cornered across Washington and 25th.[78] En route to the Reed's grand dining room on the fifth floor, guests walked from elevators through a conservatory bedecked with rare flowers and exotic plants. Steward William J. Prosser, a veteran of Chicago hotels, had trained his waiters impeccably. At the tap of a bell, they filed in, bearing each succeeding course with care and precision.[79]

Although the Reed's façade and décor were widely admired, its first years were even rockier than the Broom's. Its lease was resold three times before proprietor Ben Locke closed its doors in May 1893, saying the Reed simply had not covered its expenses since the previous summer.[80] After weeks of closed-door conclaves, local businessmen pledged subscriptions to a minimum level of patronage, and the much-buffeted hotel reopened.[81]

But developer Edward Reed never knew of his hotel's struggles. Since late 1891, he had been confined to a California insane asylum.[82] Succession fell to the vice president of the Reed Hotel Corporation, Henry C. Bigelow, who—like Edward Reed—had come to Ogden in the real-estate boom of the late 1880s. Bigelow had founded the Ogden State Bank, whose offices occupied the Reed Hotel's first floor, and was considered Ogden's top financier. He remained hotel president until his death in 1923.[83]

Economic conditions during the 1890s did not favor hotels. When the celebrated Major Erb went bankrupt at Salt Lake's Walker House in 1892, a sympathetic press pointed out that the only "good hotel year" since 1887 in Utah had been 1890.[84] The nationwide Panic of 1893 hit Utah especially hard, prompting layoffs and wage reductions and exacerbating the effects of a hard winter on agriculture and of declining silver prices on mining. The territory's economy remained depressed for the rest of the decade.[85]

The architectural progress prompted by the railroad's arrival was not exclusive to 5th Street. Comparable development also enriched and populated 4th Street, one block to the north. Both thoroughfares fronted the depot grounds; both their fortunes were directly tied to railroading. However, they differed significantly at their west ends. From 4th Street, a boardwalk stretched diagonally (southwesterly) to the depot, giving pedestrians safer access than from 5th Street, where the Utah Central's tracks and any switching engines on them—plus a few small creeks and irrigation ditches—made passage

An 1892 view of 25th Street from Union Station. The unsightly empty lot on the left was the first impression train travelers had of Ogden until 1901. The white, windowed west wall of the two-story Chapman House is visible halfway up the block. The second storefront on the right is the short-lived Beardsley House, the third and last Ogden hotel to carry that name. *Photo used by permission of the Utah State Historical Society.*

challenging.[86] But after the Broom Hotel opened, Stephens Brothers built Ogden's first sidewalk along 5th Street's north side from the Broom Hotel to the depot.[87]

Rivalry between 4th and 5th streets simmered throughout the nineteenth century. In the opinion of Leo Haefeli, Swiss-born editor of the *Ogden Junction,* 5th Street had "the balance of power" in the 1870s because it was "the nearest and most convenient route to the depots." But Haefeli, writing in 1881, believed the power shifted toward 4th Street when—in short succession—the post office moved there from 5th Street in 1877, and the *Ogden Junction* office followed one

Sheepman Patrick Healy, president of the Commercial National Bank and developer of the Healy Hotel. *Photo courtesy of the Patrick Healy family archives.*

West side of the Healy Hotel, renamed the Earle in 1946. *Photo courtesy of Special Collections, Stewart Library, Weber State University.*

year later. Haefeli criticized the complacency among property owners on 5th, who failed to improve or raze their "tumble-down lumber shanties," while over on 4th, landlords were keeping up with modern times by building handsome brick structures.[88]

But three major developments snatched victory from the jaws of defeat for 5th Street. First, all of the good hotels in town were built on it. Second, the ornate Union Station went up in 1889 at its west end. Third, because of municipal expediency, 5th Street was paved in 1893, six years earlier than 4th.[89]

In public debates on paving Ogden's streets, the businessmen of 5th Street underscored its special appeal. They said that because it led from the depot to the principal hotels, it gave travelers their first impressions of Ogden. These businessmen successfully fought City Hall's plan to pave with rough stone blocks, which were "very hard on horses and vehicles, noisy and disagreeable," and, worst of all, drove trade to other streets. Smooth streets, they argued, "would give ease and comfort to strangers visiting our fair city, while a rough ride from the depot to their hotels would have the adverse effect." The businessmen also pointed out that stone blocks were porous and subject to frost and water damage. "It is very much of an experiment to put it down here," they noted. "We would suggest that if the city wants to make the experiment they pave Fourth Street."[90]

The last of the nineteenth-century grand hotels on 25th Street was the Healy, across Wall Avenue from Union Station. Patrick Healy, president of Commercial National Bank, purchased the lot for five thousand dollars in 1899, one-fourth of its asking price during the real-estate boom ten years earlier.[91] Before the first shovelful of dirt was turned in November 1900, the *Ogden Standard* sighed with relief that "at last the unsightly hole in the ground, the first place upon which the eye of a stranger rests when he leaves the Union depot to go up Twenty-Fifth Street, is to be utilized."[92]

The Healy's exterior, like the Reed's, was sandstone and pressed brick, but the hotel was two stories shorter. Thanks to its stone, steel, and brick construction, the Healy claimed to be "absolutely" fireproof; nonetheless, fire escapes were installed. Patrick Healy, who disapproved of dark hotels, built a one-story brick cigar shop adjacent to its east end on 25th Street to prevent any future tall building from casting shadows. Ogden's Boyle Furniture store beat out Denver and Chicago competitors to outfit the hotel. Guests slept on iron and brass beds with celebrated Ostermoor mattresses. The Healy boasted that no other hotel west of the Mississippi had Ostermoors, which cost fifteen dollars no matter how many were purchased.[93]

Befitting a hotel serving Union Station, the Healy had a railroad ticket office and railway mail-service headquarters, plus a barbershop, drugstore, and bar. Most noteworthy was its restaurant, called the Arcade Café, whose furnishings and fixtures—reportedly of unequalled splendor—came from Salt Lake City's premiere dining venue, the Merchants' Café at 155 South Main. Patronage at Merchants' had plummeted following a sensational love-triangle murder in one of its private dining rooms. Arcade proprietor Lee Murdock scooped up the Merchants' effects at auction. Perhaps to ward off any lingering curse, Murdock publicized that no private dining rooms were planned for the Arcade.[94]

Denny Smyth, owner of the three-story European Hotel at 242 25th Street, must have been inspired by

The one-story cigar shop Patrick Healy built just east of the Healy (later the Earle) Hotel to prevent any future tall buildings from blocking the light. To the right of it is the China Temple restaurant. *Photo courtesy of Special Collections, Stewart Library, Weber State University.*

A 1933 view of the C. F. Krauch Building at 236 25th Street and (on the right) a partial view of the National (formerly the European) Hotel at 242 25th. *Photo courtesy of Special Collections, Stewart Library, Weber State University.*

the street's increasingly grand hotels because in 1906 he ordered costly renovations to the fifteen-year-old structure. Frescoes on the lobby walls and ceilings were claimed to be the finest in the state. Most conspicuous to passersby was a new mosaic tile map of the western hemisphere inlaid in the sidewalk. The map, an eight-foot circle, depicted North and South America in pale colors, while the Atlantic Ocean and Gulf of Mexico were rendered in blue tiles. Alongside the map, framed in a parallelogram, was the logo, "European Hotel."[95]

Six months after the resplendent Reed Hotel's mid-1891 opening, Ogden's businessmen permitted themselves a victory lap in the form of a banquet honoring the proprietors. The evening's highlight was a series of eight toasts celebrating the territory of Utah, the city of Ogden, the railroads, the press, and other institutions. Mormon businessman Ben E. Rich's response to the opening toast to Utah could well have described 25th Street in microcosm. Rich contrasted the Mormon pioneers' view of "desolate, dreary" Utah in 1847 with the prosperity and magnificence attained after forty-five years of labor and investment. Five stories below the Reed's dining room, 25th Street, confident now with brick business blocks and fine hotels, hummed with entrepreneurial energy, and from Union Station, the sounds of moving trains and working crews echoed back toward the Reed. Out of nothing, the street had grown into an essential economic engine for Ogden in the post–Golden Spike years.

It was the evening's final toast, however, that pointed unintentionally toward 25th Street's most enduring legacy: "To our ladies, absent now, yet always with us; God bless them." In response Augustus Bosworth Patton—lawyer, real-estate man, and future Chamber of Commerce president—declared, "I pity the man who has lived to the age of thirty and has not loved an estimable woman." Somewhat cryptically, a guest speculated that "if Judge Patton would tell a tithe of what he knew about the ladies the assembly would not get home till morning."[96]

Among the many fortune seekers who prospered on 25th Street, some were women, and some of those women represented the world's oldest profession. From the street's earliest years, these ladies would alarm, perplex, enrage, delight, and help to define Ogden.

CHAPTER THREE

OGDEN HOSTESSES

How else could a spirited woman make her way... except through sex and assassination?

—Michael Dirda, *Bound to Please*

Sam McMillan was tired of selling ice cream for a living. Confident that he could pluck fortunes from the hurly-burly along 5th Street, he sketched out a new and remarkably simple business plan: blackmail. He decided to set up his wife, Clara Allen, as a prostitute. Once Clara had enticed an unsuspecting gentleman, Sam would burst into her room, fire his revolver over the canoodling couple, and threaten Clara's victim with public shame if he failed to fork over a wad of hush money.

Sam and Clara planned a regular night's work on January 16, 1880, but they didn't reckon on the marksmanship or fury of Clara's prey, Ed Morton, a local saloon man. Despite Morton's compromised position, his gun lay within reach as Sam made his usual rude entrance. Morton's bullets shattered Sam's lungs, abdomen, and skull above the right eye. Sam was a goner, unmourned by a town that considered him a disgrace and wished that his wife would disappear, too.[1]

Fast forward eighteen years. In the middle of a chilly night, three gun-toting men in black coats, slouch hats, and masks crept through the back door of the Senate Saloon at 113 25th Street. They surprised the porter and night bartender, ordering them to raise their hands. One robber guarded the swinging door in front, and another watched the back door, while the third rifled the money drawers.[2]

Sheriff Gilbert Belnap had already been keeping an eye on three suspicious drifters after a similar holdup at the Little Queen Saloon. Two nights after the Senate Saloon robbery, Belnap and his deputies apprehended the guilty trio inside Madam Kirk's house at 25th and Grant. The trio were George Allen, or Hatchet-Face George, whom police had told to get out of town one week earlier; Norman Curtis, recently released from the state penitentiary; and Donald McMillan, who an alert reporter realized was the son of the late blackmailer, Sam McMillan. Young McMillan had been "raised with a knife and gun in his hands."[3]

The McMillan family crime saga spanned the transformation of crude, muddy 5th Street into bustling, metropolitan 25th Street. When Sam McMillan launched his blackmailing spree in the winter of 1879–1880, the street and its skyline were works in progress. While the north side of its block nearest Main Street was already finished, the majority of lots on the other two blocks leading to the depot remained vacant. A few boarding houses and hotels had materialized, and construction of saloons was proceeding, but the street's sinkholes and muck were constant hazards to buggies and pedestrians.

By the time McMillan's son, Donald, and his gang were robbing saloons late in 1897, 25th Street, handsomely flanked by two- and three-story brick structures, would not have been recognized by his late father, and its paving in 1893 had alleviated the weather's ill effects on traffic.

The year 1880 launched 5th Street's first heyday as oasis of iniquity in the middle of a Mormon town. Lester Herrick had recently been elected mayor on a platform to reduce Ogden's high liquor-license fees. Herrick's new regime fueled not only a rush to build saloons but a corresponding rise in public drunkenness.[4]

Houses of ill repute had appeared on 5th Street well in advance of 1880. One month after Sam McMillan met his violent death, the crusading *Ogden Morning Rustler* ran a series of articles critical of prominent men who were patronizing the local working women. The series so disturbed the "advocates of the red-light district" that they dragged editor Charles S. King out of the *Rustler* office one night and tarred and feathered him.[5]

Ogden's first memorable madam, "Aunt" Fanny Payne, was in business on 5th Street by 1879. Payne's frequent appearances in police court, usually on charges of keeping a disorderly house or disturbing the peace, furnished ample material for the press. To gain competitive advantage over her rival, Ida Abels, Payne spread rumors impugning Abels's "sanitary condition." The aggrieved Abels stormed into Payne's house with a loaded pistol, but Payne had her own weapon ready. Each woman fired, but the prosecution could not prove that either was actually aiming at the other. Both were fined fifty dollars.[6]

Once in midsummer, Payne was in court on the same day as her Chinese neighbors, keepers of an opium den. The courtroom was stifling, and Payne disrupted the proceedings with loud complaints about her neighbors' odor. "We can't stand too much of this stuff," she wailed. "Too strong, too strong, these opium eaters are!" The court's windows were thrown open, and Payne was placated.[7]

The *Ogden Herald* reported a loud fistfight among four Irishmen in Payne's house, but she dictated a letter to the editor (marked with her *X*) emphatically denying the story. She insisted the men had fought across the street from her house, not in it, and claimed she had refused supper and a bed to one of them afterward. "I have none but respectable boarders at my house," she affirmed, "and no brawlers or bad characters need apply for lodging there."[8]

Prominent among the next wave of Ogden madams was Maggie Kirk, a close associate of the young robber, Donald McMillan. Kirk operated the Capitol lodging house on the second floor of 304 25th Street. Like Aunt Fanny Payne before her, Kirk never wavered in her insistence that she kept a respectable boarding house, in spite of her multiple arrests and trials. The first time police raided her rooms, they found opium-smoking paraphernalia hidden under the bedsheets, so she was convicted of

View of the north side of 25th Street's 300 block in the 1890s. The second floor of number 304 at the left edge was Maggie Kirk's Capitol lodging house. Two doors east at number 308 was Thomas Topham's Mint saloon. Ogden's federal building now occupies the entire west half of the block. *Photo courtesy of Special Collections, Stewart Library, Weber State University.*

keeping both a bawdy house and an opium den. Mayor William H. Turner pardoned Kirk conditionally and ordered her to leave town, but if she ever actually left, she was soon back in her old digs with a vengeance.[9]

When Donald McMillan's gang was captured inside Kirk's house in 1897, she, too, was arrested, as an accomplice. The police searched her rooms and unearthed both a steel device to pry open saloon money drawers and a missing gun from the gang's earlier robbery of the Little Queen Saloon. Kirk's lawyer convinced a justice of the peace to dismiss charges against her, but the police—frustrated that they had not nailed her—ordered her to vacate Capitol house, citing citizen complaints. They wanted her to move from 25th Street to Ogden's new tenderloin district, Electric Alley. Kirk refused and prepared to challenge the police order in court, backed by her landlord, a Civil War hero named Patrick Martin.[10]

But before Kirk could sue, police raided her house yet again, arresting her and six boarders, two of whom were known prostitutes. Those two ladies testified in court that Kirk's establishment was a brothel, as did Nick Bernardis, who ran a restaurant directly below Kirk's boarding house and bemoaned her reputation's chilling effect on his business. A jury found Kirk guilty, and she was fined fifty dollars.[11] Even so, she managed to hang onto her Capitol lodging house for almost two more years before moving, not to Electric Alley but 24th Street.[12]

Prostitution became common in the interior areas of Ogden's downtown blocks. In April 1890, a French woman was running a bawdy house inside block 24, while immediately to the east, block 25 contained Adobe Row (later Hudson Alley), a "pestilential dumping ground" and red-light district.[13] The legendary Electric

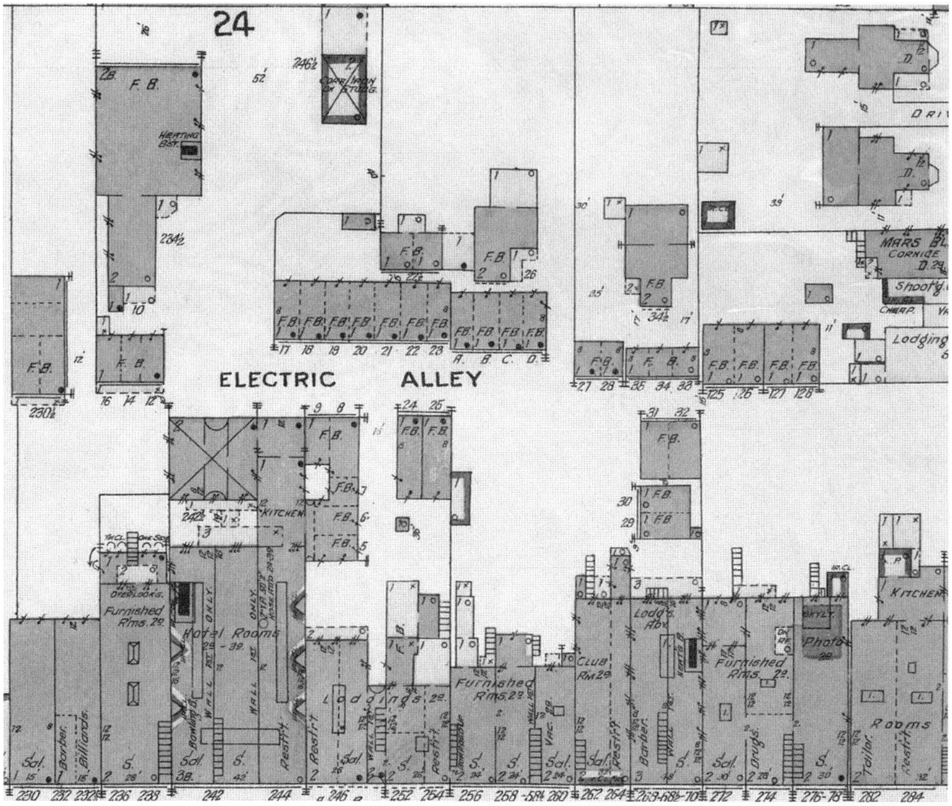

The layout of Electric Alley from the 1906 Sanborn map of Ogden's block 24. Belle London's parlor house, number 10, looms prominently at the upper left. Tiny apartments ("cribs") labeled F. B. (female boarding) flank the approach. *Photo courtesy of the J. Willard Marriott Library, University of Utah.*

Alley emerged inside block 24, where the Ogden Summit Hotel's parking lot is today (between 24th and 25th streets).

The moving force behind Electric Alley was the most famous and successful madam in not only Ogden's but Utah's history: Dora Bella Hughes, better known by her professional name, Belle London. Born in Kentucky about 1866, London may have worked in Denver before joining the throngs of fortune seekers attracted by Ogden's vigorous economy of the late 1880s.[14] She first came into view in May 1889, one of many inmates of houses of ill fame arraigned in police court.[15]

Six months later, London was proprietress of her own house, one of two Ogden bordellos raided by federal marshals on November 7, 1889. They arrested London, two female inmates, and Thomas Topham, a Union Pacific master boilermaker and recent arrival in Ogden. London and Topham married the following year, and her career as madam and real-estate magnate, in tandem with Topham's as saloon keeper, cemented their status as 25th Street's power couple over the next sixteen years.[16]

A location more convenient to the new Union Station would surely increase business, and in the spring of 1893, London announced plans for a grand parlor house inside block 24. She hired Stephens Brothers, a local firm that had already put up many 25th Street buildings, to construct the ten-thousand-dollar project.[17]

One year later, the name Electric Alley began popping up in local newspapers and may have originated with London.[18] The parlor house, known as No. 10 Electric Alley, glittered in the center of block 24, and rows of small cubicles for prostitutes flanked the alley.[19]

Once the big house was up and running, London began hosting semiannual "grand masquerade balls," open at first to the general public ("all friends invited") but later restricted ("ladies without invitations not wanted"). These entertainments lasted all night with sumptuous suppers served at 2:00 a.m.[20] The parlor house generated a constant stream of headlines: suicides, suicides attempted, murder suspects arrested, patrons robbed, or stolen merchandise pawned, not to mention London's monthly arrests and fines for keeping a bawdy house, part and parcel of Ogden's system for enforcing its vice laws.[21] London always furnished bail for herself and her women, then forfeited it as a normal business expense.

Although London and her husband, Thomas Topham, operated in the same block, they were busy people and appeared to lead quite separate lives, causing some to wonder whether the marriage was a genuine love match or just a convenience. London filed for divorce twice—in 1898 and 1902—but never completed the process.[22]

Lost among the sensation of their endless news items was one scene of domestic bliss. In 1900 Guy DuFlott of No. 2 Electric Alley married Laura Grognier of No. 5 Electric Alley in London's parlor house with Judge Joseph Hall, a staunch Mormon, officiating. The ceremony—for close friends only—was followed by a wedding feast and champagne toast, after which the newlyweds departed for their honeymoon at Thomas Topham's ranch on North Washington Avenue, just past Five Points, which became their marital abode.[23]

One of Electric Alley's wildest establishments was the Ice Palace, whose grande dames were Maggie Ferris, or "Hog-Faced Mag," and Alma Taylor, alias "Queen Lil." It had scarcely been open one month when Police Chief John E. Davenport ordered it closed. Its "recent holdups and other atrocities," reported the *Salt Lake Tribune*, "have cast such odium upon the place" that Davenport had no choice. The Ice Palace's premises, prior to its opening, had been "an old three-roomed rookery." With the abrupt closure, the building was expected to revert to its former identity, "a refuge for tramps."[24]

Ogden's madams tended to be prominent and notorious, but its rank-and-file prostitutes were highly transient, and little information about them survives. Some of them came from local families but sold sex under fictitious names. After the November 1889 raid that broke up Belle London's house on the river bottoms, for example, the *Deseret News* reported that the "well-known" parents of one girl "begged hard that her real name be not given to the public."[25]

A few sketchy histories of Ogden prostitutes emerge from court cases. Alice Umber, a courtesan in Maggie Kirk's house, was the "woman of interest" in the February 1896 trial of Henry Allen for the murder of William Wickham, Allen's rival for Umber's affections. A reporter described Umber as tall, blonde, winsome, and probably twenty-three years old and seemed surprised that "although she is a fallen woman, she does not appear dissipated."[26]

A brakeman for the Southern Pacific Railroad, Henry Allen had a wife back home in Pocatello, Idaho, but was smitten with Alice Umber at first sight and became obsessed with replacing William Wickham as the object of her attention. Allen's dealings with Umber illustrate the dangers prostitutes often faced. On a date at Hot Springs at the Weber/Box Elder County border, he became enraged when she had a drink with another man. Instead of driving her back to Maggie Kirk's, he forced her out of his buggy at the foot of the mountains to find her own way back to town. Later, he convinced her to go riding with him again, but once they were behind the oil tanks at the railroad depot, he pulled a gun and threatened to kill her if she didn't renounce Wickham. For her own safety, Umber moved from Maggie Kirk's to Belle London's house and never saw Henry Allen again until the preliminary hearing in his case.[27]

Lizzie Sloan, a Hudson Alley harlot, gained fleeting fame when she confessed to stabbing Dick Kerth, a hotel porter, during a drunken free-for-all in Eva Walter's bordello. But Sloan's confession was false. She lied to protect James Wims, the actual stabber, who was the piano player at Miss Coleman's house of prostitution and also Sloan's lover. A reporter who chatted with Sloan in her jail cell wrote that she was about twenty-four, blonde, and not bad looking but "of the lowest character...vile and corrupt." Years earlier she had disguised herself in men's clothes to join a band of cattle thieves hiding out in the mountains of Rich County, where she was captured and sent to Ogden's reform school. She had a husband named Tipton, but he was serving time in the territorial penitentiary for stealing horses.[28]

Lena Carter, originally from Salt Lake City, left home when her parents tried to force her to marry a man she didn't love. She came to Ogden in 1896 to work as Mamie Evans at No. 6 Electric Alley, where her "Venus-like figure and glossy auburn hair" were valuable assets. After certain young men found Carter irresistible, their prominent families complained to Ogden police, who ordered her to leave town. When she returned a year later, a tragic destiny awaited her. On April 24, 1897, she planned to catch a train to Butte, Montana, to get away from an unemployed actor, John Ross, who had become her jealous lover. But Ross followed her to Union Station and fatally shot her three times before putting a bullet through his own brain.[29]

Saloons, according to Reverend Samuel Blair of Ogden's First Methodist Church, were "twin sister[s] in crime" to brothels.[30] Some saloon keepers became almost as notorious as their counterparts, the madams. A prominent example was Belle London's husband, Thomas Topham. His saloon, the Mint, at 308 25th Street, had an elegant interior with carved oak and beveled plate mirrors. It boasted imported wines aged half a century and an array of the finest sherries, brandies, and ports.[31]

Business at the Mint was so good that Topham rarely purchased advertising. Its unique clientele encompassed sportsmen—especially boxers and wrestlers—whose gymnasium was located conveniently above the saloon.[32] Topham was a "giant" of a man, "well-known among sporting men" and "mixed up with everything of a sporting nature in the past ten years," noted the *Salt Lake Tribune*. He was "pleasant when sober" but "extremely quarrelsome when drunk."[33] Perhaps his nightly roistering with Ogden's pugilists prompted him to seek sparring partners, who sometimes happened to be customers who stood up to him.[34]

Topham's penchant for fisticuffs crossed the line one night when a local cigar maker, Charles Wessler, asked him to settle an old bill. Rather than pay up, Topham suggested Wessler "take it out in drinks." An argument followed, and Wessler—fifteen years younger than Topham but smaller—claimed that Topham knocked him down and jumped on him with both feet. Two days later, Wessler died of hemorrhaging in the lungs. At least two other men had leapt into the deadly fray, making it problematic to attribute the fatal blows to Topham. The county attorney chose not to try him, sparing him a murder conviction. Five years later, Topham pleaded guilty to knocking a man senseless for no better reason than that the unfortunate fellow had joked with him. Topham died of a stroke in 1906.[35]

A kindred spirit to Topham was Ogden River Resort owner Pat Desmond, who "when not intoxicated was of a friendly, kind-hearted disposition."[36] Like Belle London, Desmond came to Ogden from Colorado during the real-estate boom of 1889. The Ogden River Resort, on the west side of Washington Avenue just across the bridge, already had a reputation as a tough place before Desmond bought it. But despite his background as city marshal of South Pueblo, Colorado, Desmond only intensified his resort's bad reputation.

On the night of July 18, 1889, Desmond's wife made a cutting remark about Jack Wilson's wife, a dancer at the Novelty Theater on 25th Street. What began as blows between Desmond and Wilson escalated into a resortwide rumble. When the smoke cleared, Desmond had a black eye and swollen mouth, his son's finger was almost bitten off, and Mrs. Desmond had a broken arm. A bullet had grazed Jack Wilson's head, and he claimed Desmond was the shooter.[37]

The brawl was a public-relations disaster for the Ogden River Resort, and Desmond had to close it. He blamed the failure not on the unsavory atmosphere but on his bartender, Thomas Tod, whom he believed had been stealing from him. Desmond made a trip to Pueblo on business, and a few days later, the Ogden newspapers printed an incorrect rumor that he had been shot to death. Desmond was outraged and told acquaintances he would "fix up" Thomas Tod, whom he accused of starting the rumor.

On the night of February 28, 1890, Desmond and Tod encountered each other in the Capitol Saloon at 308 25th Street. Tod knew of Desmond's threats, and when Desmond's hand moved toward his pocket as if reaching for a gun, Tod shot him five times. Tod's murder trial—"one of the most important in the criminal history of Ogden"—featured as witnesses a battery of saloon keepers from the length of 25th Street who had seen the two men on the fateful night. Tod was convicted of voluntary manslaughter.[38]

George Wells, a cigar maker from Cheyenne, had a shop at 139 25th Street that he transformed into the O.K. Saloon in April 1903. Immediately the O.K. became a rendezvous and escape route for one of the most dangerous criminal gangs in western annals: twenty-five men strong, they robbed and murdered in groups of three or four along the Southern Pacific Railroad line from Ogden to Reno. After police surveillance showed that the same gang was responsible for a number of local saloon holdups in the autumn of 1903, George Wells was arrested on suspicion of aiding the gang by providing alibis and hiding their weapons. But by taking the witness stand in his defense, Wells convinced the jury that he had no prior knowledge of the gang or its activities and was acquitted.[39]

While Ogden's controversial saloon men exacerbated political squabbles over 25th Street's status and reputation, their Mormon counterparts generally flew under the radar, maintaining a low profile. James Hutchins, a prosperous farmer and justice of the peace in Slaterville,

In 1933 the former Novelty Theater housed the Pioneer Furniture Company (partially seen on the left) at 261 25th Street. The Novelty's street number was 263 25th. Later businesses in the building used 261 25th Street. *Photo courtesy of Special Collections, Stewart Library, Weber State University.*

bought the Little King Saloon at 332 25th Street in May 1890. (Its liquor license was previously owned by Pat Desmond.)[40] George H. Tribe and James L. Dee had saloons on Washington Avenue.[41] All three men sailed the Atlantic Ocean and crossed the plains with Mormon pioneer companies. Other local Mormon saloon men were J. Wesley "Chubb" Browning Jr. of the Fischer Beer Hall;[42] Allen Joseph Stout of Stout's Saloon;[43] and David K. Farley, owner of the Headquarters Saloon and later the Riverside Saloon.[44]

Mormon ownership also complicated public debate on Ogden's variety theaters. Historian David Nasaw described variety theaters of the late nineteenth century as barrooms offering free entertainment in adjacent halls for male audiences.[45] However, the Novelty Theater at 263 25th Street had grander aspirations, proclaiming itself "the largest and most complete theater building in the city...one-hundred percent better than the opera house." Admission was fifty or seventy-five cents, depending on seating.[46] Its regular stars were the singing-and-dancing Oatley sisters, stepdaughters of proprietor Frank Monroe, whose repertoire included "Break the News to Mother" and "A Bird in a Gilded Cage." Their dog, Tiny—with his own "fine soprano singing voice"—sometimes joined them.[47] The sisters seldom failed to evoke thunderous applause and a shower of silver dollars tossed from the first-floor seats and balcony boxes.[48]

However, the Oatleys lent a veneer of respectability to the Novelty that it may not have deserved. Variety theaters' true livelihood came from female "box rustlers," who peddled alcohol and cigars to men in the audience, particularly those who sat in private boxes in the balcony. "By rustling in the boxes," explained Novelty employee Lucia Watson in a court proceeding, "I mean selling beer there." Opposing counsel asked her if her business was also to sit on men's laps. "None of your business," Watson retorted. The same counsel asked another witness, Mabel Nolan, if she had been fired by the Novelty's competitor, the Lyceum, "for holding improper relations in the boxes."[49]

The Novelty and Lyceum theaters scandalized the *Deseret News*, which declared, "Bolder and more brazen

By 1952 the Novelty Theater had become the Labor Temple (partially seen on the left), its final incarnation until it burned down in February 1961. *Photo courtesy of Special Collections, Stewart Library, Weber State University.*

dens of vice never existed in Sodom and Gomorrah."[50] The *News* blamed the February 1889 advent of Ogden's Liberal Party government for "the establishment of 'stews' in disguise under the name of novelty theaters."[51] The *Salt Lake Tribune* retorted that both theaters were Mormon owned, the Novelty by the Stephens brothers and the Lyceum by Richard James Taylor and David Kay.[52] In a puzzling rebuttal, the *News* asserted, "That statement [of Mormon ownership] was made once before by a Liberal and proved to be false," even though William Jesse Stephens had just testified in court that he owned the Novelty.[53]

On July 10, 1889, a group of Nebraska newspapermen visiting Ogden were escorted by their local hosts into the Novelty Theater's nether regions. They were startled to observe a man coming down the aisle followed by a woman holding a six-shooter against his shoulder blade. The woman was warning the man—apparently her husband—never to let her catch him in "a dirty joint like this" again. No sooner was the couple out of sight than a box rustler appeared, sighing with relief that the pistol-packing woman had not arrived two minutes earlier while the rustler had been sitting on the man's lap. Later, as the Nebraskans bade Ogden adieu, one of them asked if the scene at the Novelty had actually been staged for their entertainment.[54]

The era of variety theaters in Ogden was relatively brief, owing to politics and fate. The Liberal Party city council, acknowledging public disfavor, enacted "An Ordinance to Promote Morality" on September 6, 1889, to prohibit female box rustlers. Novelty proprietor Frank Monroe protested that the measure would "virtually shut up the variety theaters" if enforced.[55] But eight days later, the Novelty Theater's brand-new building burned down, the result of arson. The conflagration destroyed scenery, furnishings, and effects, plus untold valuable props used in vaudevillians' well-honed routines. It also saved Monroe and his box rustlers from a planned arrest.[56] The Stephens brothers, who must have deemed the venture highly profitable, rebuilt the hall immediately, and—within two months—the Oatley sisters were again treading the boards.[57] But the city's

Frank Leslie's Illustrated Newspaper of August 2, 1890, published etchings of Ogden's Mardi Gras celebration, the Rocky Mountain Carnival, based on photographs by Charles Durbin Kirkland of Cheyenne, Wyoming. In this view, crowds at Ogden's new Union Station await the special train from New Orleans. *Photo courtesy of Stephen Hales.*

The Rocky Mountain Carnival's Arch of Welcome at the foot of 25th Street. *Photo from* Frank Leslie's Illustrated Newspaper, *August 2, 1890, courtesy of Stephen Hales.*

forbearance did not outlast the Liberal city government. The next mayor, William Turner, refused to renew the Novelty's license, and it closed at the end of June 1892.[58]

The booming economy that primed 25th Street for variety theaters also spawned a remarkable coalition of cultural opposites. In a grand scheme to lure legions of real-estate investors, William Hope Harvey, a gifted promoter new to Ogden, persuaded the Royal Host of New Orleans to cooperate in staging a summer Mardi Gras in Ogden, culminating on Independence Day. By official edict, the Royal Host declared a separate "dependency," the Kingdom of the West, in Ogden and prepared to send a royal court and entourage via special train, arriving on July 1, 1890.[59]

Harvey, "by all odds the most picturesque and original character of Ogden's 'Golden Age,'" according to the Federal Writers Project, had moved to Ogden in 1889 ostensibly to practice law, but his chief interest was real-estate promotion. He organized the Order of Monte Cristo as the local Mardi Gras association.

Seven-hundred men joined the order, two-thirds of whom had not lived in Ogden more than one year, according to historian O. A. Kennedy, who was himself a recent arrival and real-estate speculator in 1890. Their duties included forming costumed companies of cowboys, Arabs, and knights and drilling for the parts they played in pageants and parades.[60]

As the conduit from the new Union Station to the commodious Royal Palace in City Hall Park, 25th Street was integral to the Rocky Mountain Carnival. A newly built Arch of Welcome spanned the street just east of the station, festooned in royal purple and gold and imbedded with evergreen boughs and shields and battle axes of ancient heraldry. Elaborate displays of bunting and streamers covered the entire street, obscuring its business signs. The twenty-five-thousand-square-foot Royal Palace, on the site of today's Ogden Amphitheater, had fourteen-foot walls of Oregon pine but no roof. It hosted the King's Banquet, the masquerade ball of the final night, and other ceremonial events.[61]

When the much-ballyhooed train from New Orleans chugged into the depot, seemingly half of northern Utah's population was on hand to hail its arrival. "There had never been and has never been since such a crowd at the depot," wrote Kennedy. "Grant, Harrison, Roosevelt, Taft, Wilson—no president ever attracted such a throng." Clearing the way for Rex I, King of New Orleans; Rex II, King of Ogden; and their queens—all resplendent in robes and jewels—were the famed Louisiana Rifles, the military escort. In open barouches, the royals led a stately procession up 25th Street to the Royal Palace. William Hope Harvey, master of ceremonies for the five-day extravaganza, wore a yachting costume: gold-braided white cap, square-cut blue serge coat, and white duck pants.[62]

Among many local businesses—legitimate and otherwise—planning to capitalize on the influx of tourists was the Novelty Theater, which announced a special daily 2:00 p.m. matinée that wouldn't conflict with grand nocturnal events. Performers included the May Antonio Female Burlesque Company ("engaged at an enormous expense"); the "gladiatorial" acrobats, the Brothers Leondor; male and female trapeze artists; and singers, dancers, and change artists, all to complement the hometown favorites, the Oatley sisters. As a grand finale to this unmatched spectacle, a new burlesque, *Kings and Queens,* was staged especially for carnival week.[63]

After several days of tournaments, parades, balls, military reviews, and receptions, a Salt Lake reporter lauded the Rocky Mountain Carnival. While no city can duplicate the annual bacchanalia at New Orleans, Ogden's festivity "has not been a burlesque but a very creditable presentation." If it lacked the "frivolity" of New Orleans, its gangs of cowboys roping, tying, and riding and Native Americans "painted up in war colors and ornamented with all the [traditional] emblems" lent the affair a unique Utah spin. Signs of cultural disconnect appeared at various moments because the New Orleans folks weren't interested in the least in the Wild West exhibitions, while the Ogdenites were underwhelmed by the armored knights' jousting and tilting and would have preferred a baseball game. Utahns tended to take Mardi Gras too seriously, "failing to catch the spirit of mythology and fiction" and viewing the pageantry as "matter-of-fact realism," according to the *Salt Lake Herald*.[64]

Police presence during the carnival was boosted to one hundred, but the milling crowds along 25th Street still attracted a bumper crop of petty criminals and

J. D. GILL,

REAL ESTATE

BUSINESS, RESIDENCE AND ACRE PROPERTY. CORRESPONDENCE SOLICITED. | 2404 WASHINGTON AVENUE, OGDEN, UTAH.

REX OFFICIAL PROGRAMME

King Mercantile Co.,
[INCORPORATED.]
Manufacturers' Confectioners,
WHOLESALE DEALERS IN
FANCY GROCERIES AND FINE CIGARS
Manufacturing Agents.
Our specialty is manufacturing Fine Confectionery to suit the most fastidious. We will make a
SPECIAL RECEPTION
At our factory, and ask all strangers to call during the Carnival. We welcome you to inspect our purity.
Wall Ave., bet. 23d and 24th Sts., OGDEN, UTAH.

Rex Place.
On Motor Line and Harrisville Road. Ten Minutes' ride to Postoffice. Two Blocks from Butcher's and Grocer's.

We will place Lots on the Market, for Thirty Days only, for $100, on payment of $25 cash balance in monthly or quarterly payments, at 8 per cent. These lots are in clover and fruit trees, with water privileges. They are high and dry. They overlook the City of Ogden. We only place these lots on the market for thirty days at the above price. We will then make an advance of 50 per cent. They are selling lots beyond at present for $300 to $350.
CALL ON
H. B. WESTOVER,
Agent for Rex Place, 2451½ Washington Ave.

R. B. SHEPHERD,
Contractor and Builder
Residence, 239 Twenty-Second Street. Estimates furnished on application. Terms reasonable.

Iliff College Hill Addition
This beautiful Residence Addition is situated between the great Methodist University and the City. It is only ten squares from the center of the city, and occupies a commanding position, from which a magnificent view is obtained of Ogden, its unrivaled surroundings and the Great Salt Lake. It is laid off into small squares of 24 lots each, and especially platted with a view to making it a desirable residence locality for those desiring to live near the Methodist University. The completion of the University will see Lots in this most desirable locality sell for $1,000 each.
The Lots are 25 x 142 feet, To 16-foot Alleys.
$200 to $300 per Lot, According to Location.
TERMS—One-Third Cash; balance in 6 and 12 months.
Call on or address W. H. HARVEY, Owner, Room 4 Kay Bl'k, Cor. Washington Av. & 25th St.

WEDNESDAY'S
PROGRAM.

10. a. m.—At this hour will occur the Cow Boys' lasso practice and exhibition of fancy horsemanship on Tabernacle Square. Among the Cow Boys now here are many riders whose skill and expert work in horsemanship are well known, and which have given them a reputation all over this Western country. Tabernacle Square is on the corner of Washington Avenue and Twenty-First street.

The prizes for this exhibition will be conferred by the King on July 4.

2. p. m.—At this hour will occur the laying of the corner stone of the Utah Wesleyan University, of which Sam Small is President, with imposing and impressive ceremonies.

4. p. m.—The Royal Tournament on Twenty-Fourth street between Grant and Lincoln Avenues. In this tournament the twelve Knights will take part who were seleted on Monday for their pre-eminent

[CONTINUED ON SECOND PAGE.]

E. Stratford & Sons,
FURNITURE, WALL PAPER, CARPETS
WASHINGTON AVENUE
Our Goods are the Best Made.

S. H. CAVE. E. S. LUTY.
The Ogden Liquor Co
WHOLESALE
WINES, LIQUORS AND CIGARS.
We make a specialty of California Table Wines and Anheuser Beer, For Family Use.
Free and Prompt Delivery to any Part of the City.
2472 WASHINGTON AVENUE., OGDEN, UTAH.

KING REX II
—Said he was—
GOING TO MURDER
The Little Fat Music Man,
Chubbie Arnold
If he did not stop selling his
Pianos and Organs
So All-Fired Cheap.
Chubbie's headquarters are 24th street, near P.O. up stairs over Vienna Bakery.
Yours 10-Derly, CHUBBIE.

—THE—
OGDEN ABSTRACT CO.
(INCORPORATED.)
We furnish the only complete and reliable Abstracts of Title with plats to all lands in Weber county, including Additions and Subdivisions.
OFFICE:—First National Bank Building, Washington Avenue, Ogden, Utah.
C. C. RICHARDS, President.
JOHN HAMER, Manager.

Utah and Oregon Lumber Co
Wholesale and Retail Dealers in
LUMBER, DOORS, WINDOWS,
and all kinds of
BUILDING MATERIAL, &C.
130 Cor. Wall & 24th. OGDEN, UTAH.
John Seaman Manager.

OGDEN EQUITABLE CO-OP.
Keeps a Full and Complete
Stock of General Merchandise
They DIVIDE the PROFITS with their customers. It is the People's Friend. You can find anything you want in
DRY GOODS, SHOES, CLOTHING, GROCERIES, ETC., ETC.
BEN. E. RICH, MANAGER.

Official Rocky Mountain Carnival program for Wednesday, July 2, 1890. *Photo courtesy of Special Collections, Stewart Library, Weber State University.*

At the grand ball on July 4, 1890, King Rex II was unmasked as Major J. Henry Behan of New Orleans. *Photo from* Frank Leslie's Illustrated Newspaper, *August 2, 1890, courtesy of Stephen Hales.*

The queen of the Rockies was unmasked as Ogden's Minerva Anderson, daughter of the president of Anderson Pressed Brick Company in Harrisville. *Photo from* Frank Leslie's Illustrated Newspaper, *August 2, 1890, courtesy of Stephen Hales.*

prostitutes. Many women and elderly persons at the depot for the welcoming ceremonies reported handbags and wallets stolen. In the afternoon, a trio of pickpockets was caught on the street, while two thieves were arrested in front of the Senate Saloon for stealing diamonds. With the abundance of special carnival beer concessions, drunkenness was prevalent. The police blotter for the five-day event showed eighty-nine arrests.[65]

The strain of posing as New Orleans gave Ogden a collective hangover. Feverish publicity led merchants and realtors to expect fifty thousand guests, but except for the welcoming ceremonies at Union Station, the city was seldom crowded during the week. Food vendors lost heavily, and John Dwyer, the successful bidder for the King's Café concession on 25th Street, when closed down by creditors, shot himself. In all aspects, the receipts of the Rocky Mountain Carnival did not cover expenses. The royal train from New Orleans cost about three thousand, costumes cost four thousand, and a New Orleans advertising bureau hired for three months cost more than thirteen thousand dollars. Paying those expenses depleted the Order of Monte Cristo's treasury.

Many other creditors sued William Hope Harvey for damages. The litigation took years to resolve.[66]

The Rocky Mountain Carnival may have been the high-water mark of non-Mormon efforts to shape Ogden's character and destiny. However, the temporary transformation of 25th Street into a tableau of pageantry made no permanent difference in its quotidian squalor. Shortly before the carnival, a Salt Lake reporter deplored the abundance of inebriated "hard cases" on 25th Street who reclined on beer kegs in front of the saloons, and uncouth men who sat on fences lining the path to Union Station and insulted female passengers who were entering and leaving. After the carnival's end, newspapers lamented the return of "tough characters" to the two blocks between Grant and Wall avenues: "as crooked-looking specimens of humanity as exist in this country."[67]

The street was not for the fainthearted during its first heyday, roughly from 1880 to 1905. Multigenerational families of criminals, irrepressible hosts and hostesses of vice, and Mormon and Gentile businessmen alike reveled in the mix with little concern for the future. But 25th Street's crime and wide-open atmosphere—especially in Electric Alley—was soon vigorously challenged as Utah and the rest of the country were swept up in the Progressive reform movements of a new century.

CHAPTER FOUR

OGDEN SCRUBBED

The pulpits, myself amongst the number, have been as dumb dogs on the watchtowers of Jerusalem. The press has been silent, the police passive, and the backbone of the community needing repairs, whilst the moral cancer is eating away the very vitals of society.

—Father Patrick M. Cushnahan, St. Joseph's Church, February 1, 1906

At 10:00 p.m. on August 3, 1910, Mayor William Glasmann locked his office for the night, but he had miles to go before he slept. Glasmann and four visitors from the Ogden Betterment League—Mormon apostle David O. McKay, Reverend Noble Strong Elderkin of the First Congregational Church, and businessmen Heber Scowcroft and Herbert L. Griffin—strolled out of City Hall into 25th Street for a smelling tour of the gambling dens and bordellos.

The Betterment League had demanded for months that Mayor Glasmann see firsthand that illegal gambling and prostitution were operating full tilt in Ogden. The league advocated total suppression of gambling, prostitution, alcoholic beverages, and businesses operating on Sundays.[1] Glasmann, on the other hand, believed that suppression often backfired because it forced vice to retreat behind closed doors where it could not be properly regulated.[2] However, mayoral etiquette required him to hear the Betterment League's concerns.

Inside the Elephant House at 308 25th Street, the delegation found three hundred gamblers playing faro, craps, stud poker, and twenty-one. The Reverend Elderkin, a self-taught expert on straight flushes and aces back to back, explained the intricacies of these games to his inexperienced cohorts. The Elephant House's manager, former *Utah State Journal* editor Brigham Bowman, recognized his prominent guests and offered them lemonade on the house, which they declined.[3]

Instead, the group repaired to a nearby drugstore, where Glasmann bought a round of lemonades to settle a bet with Heber Scowcroft. Glasmann had wagered that the gamblers would be foreigners, but the crowd at the Elephant House turned out to be predominantly American as Scowcroft had predicted.

The gambling dens' doors were closely guarded, in some cases by former policemen. Thanks to Reverend Elderkin's youth and fleetness of foot, he outwitted and outran the guards at the Turf (2466 Grant Avenue) and

Mayor William Glasmann. *Photo courtesy of Union Station Archives.*

Heber Scowcroft (1868–1929) of the Ogden Betterment League. *Photo courtesy of Special Collections, Stewart Library, Weber State University.*

David O. McKay, Mormon apostle, principal of Weber Academy from 1902 to 1908, and president of the Ogden Betterment League. *Photo used by permission of the Utah State Historical Society.*

White Elephant (320 25th Street) houses and hustled his cohorts inside to observe the amusements. But guards at the St. Louis (286 25th Street) and Grill (264 25th Street) houses recognized them and barred the doors.

So the delegates wandered into Electric Alley, where they found women of assorted descriptions and dimensions standing or sitting in open doors and windows. An especially beautiful, dark-haired young woman pointed at Heber Scowcroft and cooed, "You look good to me; come on in." Scowcroft blushed deep purple.

A large Victorian mansion loomed before the delegates, and someone asked what it was. "That's Belle London's place," replied the street-smart Reverend Elderkin. A diminutive Japanese man answered their knock and welcomed them into a grand parlor glowing with light from an electric star overhead. Dropping a nickel into a player piano, the man announced, "The girls will be in pretty soon." The delegates fidgeted uncomfortably on plush divans, so Glasmann suggested they leave. As they filed out the door, the Japanese host embraced Glasmann and giggled, "You are the mayor."

Glasmann's nocturnal expedition with the Ogden Betterment League was widely reported,[4] so it should have surprised no one when the biggest raiding party ever seen in Ogden swooped down upon 25th Street's gambling dens just eight nights later. Reverend Elderkin, Heber Scowcroft, and two dozen other Betterment League volunteers were sworn in as special police officers and dispatched to the Elephant and St. Louis houses to block doors, staircases, and other means of escape. Officers and detectives seized tables, counted money, sealed bags of cash, and tendered receipts to proprietors.

Word of the raid flew across town, and by the time police unlocked the invaded resorts' front doors, large crowds had congregated on 25th Street to gawk as clusters of seized gamblers were marched to the police station. Altogether 450 men—some reputedly prominent—were caught in the dragnet. However, even an expanded police force was not large enough to ambush all five gambling dens at once. The Turf, Grill, and White Elephant houses got wind of the threat in time to empty and go dark before the police arrived. Their proprietors were arrested the following morning.[5]

For their criminal trials three weeks later, the apprehended proprietors retained some of Ogden's most talented defense lawyers, who punched gaping holes in the Betterment League's notions of cleaning up Ogden. They asked Heber Scowcroft, whose brother managed the Orpheum Theater, if he had ever tried to prohibit theaters from operating on Sunday in Ogden or opposed gambling at the Weber Club, to which he belonged. They reminded Reverend Elderkin of unspecified conditions in the First Congregational Church's basement. (Elderkin replied that those irregularities had been stopped "without any trouble.") The proprietors asked why Elderkin's reforming efforts did not extend to "three-ply criminals" in Ogden, such as industrialist David Eccles and banker James Pingree.[6]

The only men convicted were those whose names were on the gambling houses' rental agreements: Richard Tyree of the Turf and E. A. Smith of the Elephant.[7] The guilty verdicts, however, had less of an impact in the media than Reverend Elderkin's courtroom theatrics, particularly his loss of composure on the last day. Insisting that gambling houses on 25th Street were still operating in spite of the raid, Elderkin bitterly assailed Glasmann from the witness stand, claiming the mayor had "pulled the wool" over the Ogden Betterment League's eyes in persuading them to join a raid that was merely a farce.[8]

Ogden's great raid of 1910—whether farce or full-court press—followed five years of citizens' efforts to reform 25th Street and mirrored concurrent campaigns elsewhere in the nation emerging from the Progressive zeitgeist. While most conspicuously concerned with vicious pastimes, Progressives also aspired to enact worker protections, rein in corporate abuses, and dismantle corrupt political machines. The chief difference between these reformers of the new century and their forerunners—according to historian Michael McGerr—was a sudden interest "in compelling, not cajoling, people to change and behave."[9]

The year 1905 was a watershed in Ogden's tolerance of 25th Street; both ecclesiastical and political foes escalated their attacks. Ogden's ministers began weekly sermons against the street's decadence. "Pass along Twenty-Fifth Street any night," thundered Samuel Blair, reverend of the First Methodist Church. "You would be horrified to see young men pass through the saloon doorways, which are but an entrance to the regions of darkness."[10] Denunciations of Electric Alley enlivened the sermons of Father Cushnahan at St. Joseph's and Reverend Alfred Brown at Good Shepherd Episcopal.[11] Perhaps the key development of 1905 was the arrival at Ogden's First Congregational Church of Reverend Noble Strong Elderkin, fresh from Yale Divinity School and destined to be 25th Street's most relentless scourge.[12]

On the political side, 25th Street's chief adversaries were George Halverson, the district attorney, and Jedediah Dixon Skeen, a lawyer in private practice. Halverson and Skeen had gone to excellent eastern law schools, but both seemed to retain the farm boy's atavistic resentment of city slickers. Halverson's father was the polygamous Mormon bishop of Marriott. Skeen, a native of Plain City, was a born gadfly who at fourteen had petitioned the Weber County court to dissolve his school district.[13] Ironically, Halverson and Skeen seemed to care less about the street's debauchery than its usefulness as a pawn in their ongoing feud with William Glasmann, who was not only mayor but owner of Ogden's two newspapers, the *Standard* and the *Examiner.*[14]

In June 1905, Glasmann's *Standard* published withering criticism of District Attorney Halverson's professional ethics.[15] The following year—in a move interpreted as payback—Skeen sued, and Halverson coprosecuted, Ogden's city councilmen for approving overtime pay for themselves.[16] Mayor Glasmann retaliated by printing a list of criminal cases inexplicably dismissed by Halverson when he had been county attorney, all of which involved crimes less ambiguous than overtime pay. The dismissals included Belle London's husband, Thomas Topham, whom Halverson had failed to try for the 1899 beating death of Charles Wessler.[17]

Halverson and Skeen realized that 25th Street could be exploited as a political liability for Mayor Glasmann. On December 14, 1905, Halverson sent a letter to Glasmann's police chief, Thomas E. Browning, threatening him with arrest if he failed to enforce laws against gambling. So Browning and his police force immediately shut down the gambling establishments.[18] Two months later, under continuing pressure from Halverson, Browning ordered the madams in Electric Alley to close their houses and the prostitutes to leave town.[19]

However, because legal technicalities made it difficult to prosecute and convict offenders, the gamblers and prostitutes were soon back in business.[20] Skeen then sued to have Browning removed as police chief. But a district court judge ruled that Skeen had no authority to have Browning ousted. Later, the Utah Supreme Court agreed, saying the power to install or remove a police chief belongs exclusively to the mayor and Ogden City Council.[21]

Future state senator Rudolph Kuchler, wearing a straw hat in the doorway of his family's cigar shop at 348 25th Street, circa 1900. *Photo used by permission of the Utah State Historical Society.*

The campaign for saloon reform got a significant boost when the Mormon Church joined the debate. Since Utah's statehood in 1896, the church had remained neutral since its president, Joseph F. Smith, preferred to avoid the appearance of interfering in politics.[22] Utah had taken pains to enter the union as a normal state, declining to include prohibition of alcoholic beverages in its constitution despite the abstemious customs of its majority Mormon population.[23]

The Mormon Church's turning point came in October 1908, when it devoted its entire semiannual General Conference to temperance and vehement denunciations of alcohol.[24] Opponents interpreted the church's sudden "rage for Prohibition" as a political gambit to starve the Gentile-controlled municipal governments of Ogden and Salt Lake City of revenue.[25]

Neither Utah's Democrats nor the state's Republicans had included Prohibition in party platforms for the 1908 election, so the unexpected public clamor caught legislators convening for the 1909 session by surprise. The state chapter of the Anti-Saloon League delivered petitions signed by seventy thousand Utahns. The alcohol-friendly *Salt Lake Telegram* downplayed these petitions as originating "simply through obedience to the higher priesthood of the Mormon Church."[26]

That Utah did not go dry in 1909 was due in large part to Ogden's two Republican state senators, one of whom had a long family history on 25th Street. Rudolph Kuchler, thirty-eight years old, had been part owner of I. Kuchler and Sons, a cigar and tobacco business, located during the 1890s at 348 and after 1901 at 370 25th Street. From an early age, Kuchler had been a joiner, quickly working his way up to leadership positions in fraternal organizations and the local Republican Party.[27] The other senator, Civil War veteran Edmund T. Hulaniski, was local counsel for the National Brewers Association and a former county attorney.[28]

State senator Edmund T. Hulaniski of Ogden. *Photo used by permission of the Utah State Historical Society.*

Although new to the senate in 1909, Rudolph Kuchler had four years as a state representative under his belt, where he had earned a reputation for influence and "keen comprehension of parliamentary rulings." As Republican floor leader, he and a "dictatorial" speaker of the house had reputedly "handled that body at will."[29] As the Republican Party's candidate for mayor of Ogden in 1905, Kuchler—strongly backed by the incumbent, William Glasmann—was expected to win; his eleventh-hour loss was attributed to anti-Semitism and voter fatigue with the first Glasmann administration.[30] Once in the Utah Senate, Kuchler landed the plum chairmanship of the Committee on Manufactures and Commerce, "probably the most important committee in the legislature [in 1909]," surmised the *Salt Lake Herald,* because of its jurisdiction over Prohibition bills.[31]

During the fevered 1909 debates on Prohibition, a delegation from Ogden—headed by Mormon apostle David O. McKay, Reverend Guy W. McCreery from the Methodist Episcopal Church, and businessman Parley T. Wright—visited Senator Kuchler in Salt Lake and presented him with a petition signed by sixty-four hundred Weber County residents who favored statewide Prohibition. As an inducement to support the delegates' cause, Wright told Kuchler that they could finesse his election to the United States Senate.[32]

Kuchler reminded the delegates that if they brought all those who had signed the petition to the mayor and Ogden City Council, they could get all saloon licenses in the city revoked within twenty-four hours. "Why come here asking for new laws," Kuchler asked, "when you are countenancing and supporting men who fail in every particular to enforce the laws now upon the statute books?" Warning that closing 25th Street's saloons would lead Ogden's young men to seek their libations in dark alleys, "blind tigers," and "blind pigs," the senator shook his visitors' hands and ushered them out of his hotel room.[33]

The Utah Legislature of 1909 did pass a strict liquor-control bill, but Governor Spry determined that it contained unconstitutional provisions and vetoed it. All of the flawed provisions—called "jokers" by the Utah press—were attributed to Senator Kuchler's deft maneuvering. The original bill called for all Utah counties to be units that would hold local-option elections to decide whether to permit the sale of alcohol. But Kuchler insisted that cities with populations of more than twelve thousand—exclusively Ogden and Salt Lake—should constitute separate local-option units.[34] Governor Spry's veto message said this measure would create special classes of citizens and keep the law from applying uniformly across the state.[35] Brewers, saloon men, and their allies cheered the senator as their "hero of the hour." "For crafty legislative work," said his hometown newspaper, "Rudolph Kuchler stands preeminent."[36]

Despite this legislative failure, 1909 was a significant milestone in Utah's march toward aridity because many cities chose to go dry, including Lehi, Pleasant Grove, American Fork, Spanish Fork, Logan, and Provo (the latter two were Utah's most populous cities after Ogden and Salt Lake). They accomplished this by votes in their city councils, responding to citizens' petitions.[37] All Utah cities had authority under their incorporating charters to prohibit alcohol.[38]

Ogden's liquor interests clearly recognized the threat to their livelihood. They proposed an increase in license fees in hopes of suppressing the public appetite for Prohibition. During official debate on the proposal, Councilman Haymond J. Powers spoke against local "ministers of the gospel" (i.e., Reverend Elderkin) who "come into our city and after a short residence here, during which time they do not own a single foot of property, attempt to dictate to this council what its policy shall be." The council voted not to raise license fees that year.[39]

Glasmann's *Ogden Standard* warned the liquor interests that if they failed to clean up their act, Prohibition was inevitable in the next election. "There are too many saloons, too many dives, too many unprincipled men in the business," the paper declared.[40] The *Standard* also reflected local concern that saloon proprietors often seemed to get away with breaking the law.

At the same time that Senator Kuchler was working to keep Utah's large cities wet, Ogden's courts were deciding the fate of the proprietors of the Apex Saloon on lower 25th Street. Robert McGuire, John Garret, and "Dublin" Fleming had drugged and robbed an elderly customer, then kept him drunk and falsely imprisoned in a room above the Apex for an entire week. The day before Kuchler's joker amendments passed the senate, a judge threw out the complaint against the Apex men because the district attorney, Nathan J. Harris, had failed to state the time and place of the robbery.[41] The Apex, noted the *Deseret Evening News,* continued the tradition of "several saloons on lower Twenty-Fifth Street which are known to have had a hand in relieving men of their money during the days of the building of the [Lucin] cutoff."[42] Situations like these fed the outrage of Prohibitionists.

When Utah's biennial legislature convened in 1911, both its house and senate had overwhelming Republican majorities. In February Utah's all-Republican congressional delegation sent a telegram to the state party chair urging Utah legislators to enact a state local-option law.[43] The result was a statute little different from the vetoed 1909 measure, except that it authorized individual cities and towns to choose whether to permit the sale of alcohol, rather than lumping them together in their counties. The law set June 27, 1911, as the date of the first election where each town could vote on the question. Similar elections could be held every two years if sufficient petitioners in a given town requested them.[44]

Mayor Glasmann realized the vote in Ogden could be troublesome. The disreputable "dives" on 25th Street had made little effort to change their ways. Early in 1911, the keepers of the Owl (232 25th Street) and Ranch (on 24th Street) saloons—on trial for selling liquor to minors—were acquitted in twenty minutes flat on the unfortunate technicality of a printing error in the pertinent Ogden city ordinance. Their attorney was former state senator Hulaniski.[45]

Glasmann said he did not want to see the liquor question agitated every two years, nor did he want a religious war.[46] Without waiting for the mandated election, he submitted a new municipal liquor-control ordinance to the Ogden City Council, which restricted saloons to one room and prohibited all furniture, booths, curtains, or partitions for customers. It also barred all gambling, billiards, music, free lunches, obscene decorations, female employees, or connection to any room where prostitution might occur. In enumerating so many restrictions, the ordinance bore a strong resemblance to the state Prohibition bill of 1909 vetoed by Governor Spry.[47]

Because 40 percent of Ogden's business trade came from industrialists likely to avoid the city if it became dry, Glasmann felt he must preserve those interests.[48] Nonetheless, he warned the saloons that they must accept new restrictions or face the likelihood of being voted out of existence. The council passed the ordinance three weeks before Ogden's local-option election. It raised license fees, limited the number of saloons, and set their closing hour at 9:00 p.m. On June 9—the effective date of the ordinance—25th Street's saloons closed at the new hour without disturbances or protests.[49]

Some Ogden City Council members felt it was premature to pass the ordinance before the local-option election, but Glasmann anticipated its passage would placate undecided voters and keep Ogden wet. To dispel rumors that the ordinance was merely a political feint, the council pledged that it would not repeal the measure after the local-option election.[50]

The Ogden Betterment League, however, was not impressed. It conducted a spirited fight to persuade citizens to vote to become dry on June 27, importing a roster of noted temperance lecturers and running David O. McKay's position papers as paid advertisements.

"America," wrote McKay, "is moving westward, but as long as Twenty-Fifth Street of this city is what it is, the thousands of emigrants to the west will pass us by."[51]

On the opposing side, members of the Weber Club hastily created the Ogden Manufacturers' and Business Men's Association (mirroring a Salt Lake organization with the same name), headed by former mayor Edward Conroy and city recorder Carl Allison.[52] They were reacting to rumors of a conspiracy among Salt Lake City businessmen to keep the capital city wet while Ogden went dry. The Weber Club strung banners across Washington Avenue proclaiming, "The Word Has Passed to Vote Salt Lake Wet and Ogden Dry—Will You Do It?"[53]

On the eve of the June 27 election, competing wet and dry events on 25th Street collided unpleasantly. As those favoring wet status were leaving a rally in front of city hall, they noticed former Salt Lake police chief and ardent Prohibitionist Brigham F. Grant addressing a large crowd from an open car at Washington Avenue. They hooted and heckled Grant, disrupting his speech for more than an hour until Ogden police arrived and restored the peace.[54]

The Ogden vote was 4,713 for remaining wet to 3,051 for becoming dry. The total of 7,764 votes was the largest ever cast in a city election up to that time. Ogden voted to remain wet by a slightly larger plurality than Salt Lake did.[55] Mayor Glasmann, however, viewed the results pessimistically and warned that if saloons failed to obey the new ordinance, disgusted voters would elect a Prohibitionist city hall in the mayoral election four months later. Reacting to reports of saloons selling alcohol after 9:00 p.m. in secret locations and restaurants serving whiskey on Sundays in coffee cups and teapots, Glasmann offered a one-hundred-dollar reward for evidence leading to the conviction of any offenders.[56]

From 1911 through 1915, the Prohibition question remained relatively quiet in Utah, especially in Ogden. Mayor Glasmann's liquor-control ordinance had successfully reduced the level of nuisance from the saloons. A few Utah cities—taking advantage of the state's local-option law—held elections on liquor control in 1913 and 1915, but Ogden did not.[57]

Official tolerance of prostitution appeared to decline significantly following the municipal election of November 7, 1911, where Ogden's form of government changed to a three-person commission (including the mayor, ex officio).[58] Thomas E. Browning, police chief for the previous ten years, was soundly defeated for city commissioner by his cousin, Samuel Browning, which was a repudiation of Ogden's longtime philosophy of regulating vice through monthly arrests and fines. "Since the beginning of commission government," Samuel Browning later said, "we have assessed no fines and made no attempt to derive revenue from such a source."[59]

Acting on the Ogden City Commission's orders, Police Sergeant Orson Hyde Mohlman went from door to door in Electric Alley on June 10, 1912, informing the madams and prostitutes that they had five days to settle their affairs and leave town.[60] Two months later, the police conducted a follow-up raid on Belle London's properties: No. 10 Electric Alley and the Palace and Fashion rooming houses at 264½ and 268½ 25th Street. The city commission seemed to mean business, and in spite of occasional minor arrests in the ensuing

Belle London. *Photo courtesy of Special Collections, Stewart Library, Weber State University.*

Ogden Police Chief Thomas E. Browning. *Photo courtesy of Special Collections, Stewart Library, Weber State University.*

months, Electric Alley's years as an open-air bazaar for whores and johns were over.[61]

There was considerable public skepticism, however, that the new policy applied to Belle London, who had spent comparatively little time in Ogden during the previous four years. Recruited in 1908 by Salt Lake City's mayor to develop and operate a tenderloin district, the Stockade, in the capital city, London had turned over the management of No. 10 Electric Alley to a woman named Nina Bond.[62] The Stockade closed in September 1911 after London was tried and convicted of pandering and sentenced to eighteen years of hard labor. Her conviction, however, was overturned on appeal.[63]

That London was able to resume her old life in Ogden seamlessly may be a measure of the power and grudging respect she had acquired over two decades. After the official closure of Electric Alley's establishments, the *Ogden Evening Standard* reported inquiries from citizens wanting to know if Ogden was secretly allowing London to run her grand parlor house while officials were chasing less-influential operators out of town. London had had numerous audiences with Public Safety Commissioner Samuel Browning recently, as she had done previously with former mayor William Glasmann. "That old slam, Bill and Belle, must now be changed to Sam and Belle," the newspaper taunted.[64]

Although documentary evidence of London's clout never found its way into official records, the public perception was that her influence had long and powerful tentacles. During a March 1909 debate on brothels in the Utah House of Representatives, the delegate from Bingham provoked a collective gasp by asking, "Isn't it a fact that Belle London runs politics in Ogden?" "I will admit," replied James B. McCracken of Ogden, "that she exerts a great influence in politics." As evidence of London's power, McCracken cited her ability to "default the [ten-dollar] bail" on herself and sixty-five prostitutes by writing a check for $660 in lieu of personal appearances.

A representative from Washington County then asked if McCracken owed his seat to London's influence. "I desire to state," retorted Republican McCracken, "that the sixty-six votes controlled by the person in question went to support the Democratic ticket." The chamber roared with laughter.[65]

Circumstantial evidence does indicate London's influence among the Ogden police. Chief Thomas E. Browning traveled to Salt Lake to testify as a character witness for London in her 1911 Stockade trial. "She has always been very fair with the officers," stated Browning, adding that her reputation for truth and veracity was "good." He said he did not know if London "was interested in" (i.e., owned) Ogden brothels. As historian Jeffrey Nichols reports, Browning perjured himself because he had personally arrested London in Electric Alley many times.[66]

In November 1909, longtime desk sergeant Ben Ternes, responsible for collecting fees, resigned from the Ogden Police Department "to accept a more lucrative position." Unstated was the source of the irresistible salary that separated Ternes from the department: Belle London, who needed a clerk to manage her Ogden affairs while she ran the Salt Lake Stockade. Ternes worked for London for at least two years.[67]

London's power accrued from what she knew and what she owned. Her arsenal of private information, as noted, remains undocumented, but her wealth was a matter of public record. A planned 1913 tax assessment of 25th Street property owners indicated she owned more footage (206) on the street than any other private party except Patrick Healy. Her holdings outside of Weber County included a boarding house in Ely, Nevada.[68]

Assets of her Arcadia Land and Livestock Company—the last of many corporations she formed before leaving Utah—included twelve parcels in block 24 (Electric Alley and 25th Street frontage between Lincoln and Grant avenues), five rights-of-way in Electric Alley, and additional parcels, rights-of-way, and an irrigation ditch at her Arcadia farm. Property at the farm (formerly the Thomas Topham ranch on North Washington Avenue) comprised cattle, horses, purebred Belgian hares, geese, pigs, five thousand chickens, one thousand pigeons, farm machinery, and two pianos.[69]

Despite her unflagging prosperity, a businesswoman as clever as London could see that Ogden's hospitality to her operations was evaporating, and not necessarily because of opposition to prostitution. Stricter liquor control in Ogden was complicating her most profitable activity: selling beer at a dollar a bottle to customers.[70] The purpose of the August 1912 raid on No. 10 Electric Alley was not to prosecute prostitution but to seize illegally maintained liquor. Police confiscated nineteen bottles of champagne and forty-seven bottles of beer.[71]

Not long after her adopted daughter, Ethel Topham, graduated from Ogden High School in 1914, London sold everything and moved her daughters and staff to San Francisco. The Hellenic-American Club, a gambling enterprise, purchased No. 10 Electric Alley.[72] London's stately private residence on North Washington Avenue was sold to the Martha Society, a local charitable organization (and forerunner of the Junior League of Ogden), which turned the house into a children's nursery.[73]

Meanwhile, the relative success of Ogden's tough 1911 liquor-control ordinance was of no consequence to Utahns who were determined to have Prohibition regardless of social costs. Dry-promoting organizations

Gus Becker, John M. Browning, Archie Bigelow, and Matt S. Browning *(left to right)* constituted the Four B's, Ogden's renowned live-bird and trapshooting team. *Photo used by permission of the Utah State Historical Society.*

throughout the state merged in 1914 to form the Utah Federation of Prohibition and Betterment Leagues to exert greater influence on the Utah Legislature that convened in 1915.[74] No longer did Ogden have senators like Kuchler and Hulaniski to deflect and frustrate the groundswell for aridity that was now practically unstoppable.[75] However, among the lobbying forces opposing Prohibition that year, none was more credible than Ogden's Gus Becker, president of his family-owned brewery and, incidentally, a teetotaler.[76]

On March 2, 1915, a special afternoon train from Salt Lake City carried the entire Utah Senate—except for three unavailable members—and Governor Spry to the Becker Brewing and Malting Company on the banks of the Ogden River. The welcoming committee was Gus Becker himself, who conducted his distinguished visitors to the brewery bar. "Most" of the guests, according to the *Salt Lake Tribune,* "tested the Becker product." One senator drank a toast to the brewery's future success. Governor Spry lauded Ogden's manufacturing initiative

Becker Products company's advertisement for Becco, its near beer, ran in the *Salt Lake Tribune* on August 15, 1917, two weeks after Utah had gone dry. *Photo used by permission of the Utah State Historical Society.*

and said he wished the capitalists of Salt Lake were as inclined as their Ogden counterparts to reinvest their profits locally.[77]

Although the legislature easily passed a Prohibition bill in 1915, Governor Spry—repeating his action of 1909—vetoed it, maintaining that the people had elected him to enact local-option laws and not Prohibition. Because of the widespread support in Utah for Prohibition, Spry's veto signaled the end of his political career. The state Republican convention the following year failed to nominate him as its gubernatorial candidate.

The Democrats' nominee for governor was Simon Bamberger, whose sad proprietorship at Ogden's White House hotel back in 1870 was scarcely indicative of his brilliant future in business.[78] Now widely revered as the developer of the Lagoon resort in Farmington and the Bamberger Electric Railway connecting Ogden and Salt Lake, Bamberger ran as a drier-than-thou Prohibition candidate. Utahns—impatient with years of Republican inaction—swept Bamberger and his fellow Democrats into statewide offices in November 1916.

Gus Becker realized his days as a Utah brewer were numbered. His lobbying during the 1917 legislative session aimed to mitigate, rather than obstruct, a Prohibition law that was now a foregone conclusion. Testifying before the Utah Legislature, Becker requested forbearance in two areas: delaying the law's effective date to allow more time—as other states' dry laws did—for breweries to modify their plants; and defining as nonintoxicating all beverages containing no more than 2 percent alcohol.[79] The legislature—unmoved by the imperiled livelihood of the Becker Brewing and Malting Company's loyal and largely Mormon workforce—passed a stringent Prohibition bill making no concessions to either Becker's or any other liquor interests' concerns. Governor Bamberger signed the bill on February 8, 1917.[80]

The Utah Legislature also passed a companion resolution adding a Prohibition amendment to Utah's constitution, to be voted on at the next general election in November 1918. The rationale behind a constitutional amendment was to block forever the state legislature's ability to reinstate liquor traffic.[81] When the general election came, large pluralities approved the amendment, even in the formerly wet holdout cities of Ogden and Salt Lake.[82]

Even a man as resourceful as Gus Becker was temporarily stunned to be put out of business. On April 18, 1917, he sent a telegram to President Woodrow Wilson offering his fifteen-acre brewing operation to the government as a munitions plant since the United States had entered World War I only two weeks earlier. Although Becker briefly entertained the thought of closing the brewery, he soon devised a practical solution.

Because the neighboring state of Wyoming was still wet, Becker announced that a new brewery would be constructed in Evanston—only seventy-two miles from Ogden—by local contractor George Whitmeyer.[83] He also decided that—providing the government did not need it—the Ogden brewery would not close but retool to manufacture ice, soft drinks, and a new near beer called Becco. Idaho, already in the dry column, was becoming an avid market for near beer, and Becker was confident of Becco's sales potential. Refrigerated railcars would transfer thousands of gallons of beer at the Ogden brewery to Evanston once statewide Prohibition became effective on August 1, 1917.[84]

For several days before July 31, 1917—Utah's final day of legal liquor—25th Street was besieged with customers buying beer, whiskey, vermouth, and absinthe at fire-sale prices. By the evening of July 31, downtown Ogden was mobbed, and not only by longtime aficionados of grape and grain.

Men who had never before touched alcohol drank that day. Women, who could not legally be served in bars, crowded into restaurants with connecting saloons. Boys as young as fifteen staggered about the streets with bottles protruding from their pockets. Teetotalers who just wanted to ogle the spectacle elbowed their way along 25th and 24th streets and Washington Avenue. Reporters counted numerous parked cars with Idaho license plates. The Gem State had already gone dry on New Year's Day, 1916, and many Idahoans hankered to go dry once again in Ogden.

At 9:00 p.m.—Ogden saloons' normal closing time since 1911—church bells throughout the city began to peal, their chimes mingling with a long siren blast from the Southern Pacific Railroad. Saloons emptied out in a fairly orderly manner, and police reported only a few arrests of disorderly drinkers. Many customers had already caught the 8:30 p.m. Bamberger train for Salt Lake City, where bars remained open until midnight.

At 9:01 p.m., legions of carpenters began ripping out bar fixtures in 25th Street's saloons to convert them to the new wave of businesses: restaurants, soft-drink parlors, beer-free cabarets, and dance halls.

When the sun rose on 25th Street the next day, black mourning crepe hung from all the doors,[85] but the funereal trappings were more ironic than sad. It was about to become easier to get a drink in Ogden than at any other time in its history.[86]

CHAPTER FIVE

OGDEN PARCHED

When we smell liquor on the breath of officers of the law we can readily understand why Twenty-Fifth Street is a bootleggers' paradise.

— Alfred Gladwell, Burch Creek Justice of the Peace, September 18, 1924

The Prohibitionists had triumphed, serenely confident that drinkers would come to love an alcohol-free utopia. The first bootlegger arrested and tried in Ogden—proprietor Frank Prouty of the Weber Hotel[1]—got the maximum sentence of six months in jail, and municipal judge George S. Barker warned that other scofflaws could expect the same harsh treatment.[2] The *Ogden Standard-Examiner* predicted that bootleggers would silence their stills, rather than face trial before no-nonsense Judge Barker, and that Ogden would surely be bone dry within ten days.[3]

But the bootleggers had an almost insurmountable head start on the law. Long before Ogden's saloons and breweries were slammed shut, moonshiners were already making whiskey and smuggling it into dry Idaho.[4] Illegal stills bubbled day and night, concealed in barns in Slaterville and other western Weber County farm communities, sagebrush dugouts in Box Elder County, or even in Ogden Valley or elegant new homes on Ogden's east bench.

Twenty-fifth Street's saloons may have been retrofitted to sling soda pop, but thanks to eager bootleggers, their chief stock-in-trade never really changed after Prohibition became the law of Utah in 1917 or the United States in 1920.[5] The profits from illegal moonshine, combined with citizens' resistance to enforced compliance, ensured that the Prohibition years—though officially sober—would evolve into a booze-addled second heyday for 25th Street.

While plenty of American-born bootleggers supplied the street with hooch (or "moon," as insiders called it), Ogden's immigrant populations—as in most U.S. cities—found that making illegal libations could be a fast track to the American dream, outstripping the inadequate wages many were forced to accept. Prohibition historian Gus Russo notes that immigrants' affinity for the ales, wines, or whiskeys of their cultures created natural and avid markets after Prohibition was imposed. After long periods of barely earning a living,

The Weber Hotel at 166 25th Street was home to Ogden's first convicted bootlegger. At present it is the vacant Windsor Hotel. *Photo courtesy of Special Collections, Stewart Library, Weber State University.*

entrepreneurial immigrants could at last find "a clear road map to riches."[6]

For Ogden moonshiners, sugar whiskey was easiest to make because it required only fermenting sugar, water, and yeast, which was ready to distill after forty-eight hours. Although grain whiskey was cheaper to produce than sugar whiskey, its mash took almost two weeks to ferment enough to distill, and there was also the problem of disposing of the sediment without clogging city sewers and arousing suspicion. So grain whiskey was usually made by rural residents in canyons or desert places.[7]

Do-it-yourself wine also became popular in Ogden, usually made from raisins instead of grapes. The raisins were steeped in wooden casks until they were ready to crush. After being pulverized, they were left to ferment, then strained and bottled. The resulting concoction often registered thirty proof. In May 1919, police arrested two Italian men who were making wine on Pingree Avenue and wholesaling it to Roma Grocery at 168 25th Street. According to Ogden police, making wine at home reached alarming proportions, and the local supply of raisins could not keep up with the demand.[8]

Ogden's soft-drink parlors may all have been speakeasies, but their facilities were much less glamorous than their New York counterparts, whose clandestine culture of passwords and secret entrances became world renowned. Soft-drink parlors' true purpose was an open secret in Ogden, so there was no need for passwords. The only coded phrase regularly used was "give me a shot," which meant whiskey, please.[9] In 1925 a local bootlegger claimed Ogden had sixty-eight speakeasies.[10]

Twenty-fifth Street joints often employed lookouts to watch for police or federal Prohibition agents. Keeping liquor bottles at the bar was risky, so often a man in the crowd—known only to the bartender—hid a bottle in his coat pocket. When someone called for a shot, the bartender gave the wink, and the stooge approached the bar cautiously for the transaction. Police could not search an entire crowd of customers, so the stooge enjoyed a reasonable margin of safety.[11]

With Becker beer back on tap after Prohibition's demise, Louis Prantil presides at his bar at 201 25th Street, circa May 1935. *Photo courtesy of Joseph E. Prantil.*

A common means of avoiding arrest was to kick a bottle of booze through a hole in the floor so it would fall onto a strategically placed pile of bricks in the basement, shattering before police could capture its contents. If a hole in the floor wasn't available, a bartender might simply break the vessel over the nearest available hard surface, even a policeman's head—which is what happened when an officer tried to arrest proprietor Charles Deru of the Empire Club at 227 25th Street.[12]

Many restaurants on 25th Street also doubled as clandestine liquor outlets. When an Ogden officer surprised Mrs. Sayamo Matsumori in the kitchen of her American Noodle Parlor at 218 25th Street, she poured a bottle of moonshine onto the floor. The cop, spying a teapot on a table, removed its lid and realized it was full of whiskey. He seized it, but Mrs. Matsumori lunged at him, clawing, pinching, and hitting. When that strategy failed to loosen his grip on the teapot, she started pushing him toward a red-hot stove. Luckily for the cop, a backup officer was with him and grabbed hold of Mrs. Matsumori. She spent several hours in jail before rustling up her three-hundred-dollar bail.[13]

Perhaps the award for best hiding place on 25th Street should go to Louis Prantil, an Austrian who owned the Lincoln Cigar Store at No. 201. In the store's basement, police found a ten-gallon keg of whiskey concealed behind multiple sliding panels and trap doors and nestled in a hollowed-out space in the building's rock foundation. A lead pipe connected to an upstairs sink was used to fill the keg. A year later, the police were back in Prantil's store, which was now a confectionery. This time they uncovered a copper container hidden in a transom above a closet door; a rubber tube, hidden inside a wall, extended from it to a sink. The sink's faucet was rigged so it could draw whiskey from the copper container.[14]

Louis Prantil's grandson, Joseph, says his grandfather was a stone mason in northern Italy before emigrating first to Argentina, and then to America. "My dad told me that Sandburg Plumbing installed the plumbing in Grandpa's store," recalls Joseph. "Then Grandpa as a stone mason rocked it all up. The booze was made by all the Italian families in West Weber. I also heard that the way the city got rid of the booze was to flush some contaminant back into it through the plumbing."[15]

The Weber County Sheriff's Department appeared to get a leg up on the moonshiners when it recruited Deputy David F. Steele in the fall of 1922. Steele gained immediate renown for his ability to use his keen sense of smell to detect fermenting grain; he merely had to drive around the county with his window rolled down. As the sheriff's nose for booze, Steele averaged two stills per week, whether on 25th Street, in Roy, or hidden in thick clumps of oak brush above Burch Creek.[16]

As police enforcement of Prohibition laws gradually became more adept and bootleggers increasingly felt the squeeze, the quality of the booze got worse. Fraudulent "bonded" whiskey or gin with phony British-sounding labels made its way into the speakeasies, but the liquor was often concocted in Salt Lake City hotel rooms. Genuine-looking bottles and labels could be procured from California. The gin was actually ordinary alcohol mixed with oil of juniper, while the bonded whiskey was merely alcohol flavored with a dubious Scotch extract that tasted like burned shoe leather. Drinking these improvisations could be hazardous to your health because bootleggers sometimes stooped to using denatured alcohol, which was toxic.[17]

One of the tougher punishments for liquor violations was padlocking the premises for a year, even if the building's owner claimed no knowledge of the infraction.[18] But padlocking had its limits. The Imperial Club at 318 25th Street was a chronic trouble spot for Ogden police. It was padlocked late in 1932, not only for liquor violations but also illegal gambling and connections to a ring of automobile thieves. But the Imperial's clever proprietors built a partition that closed off its front and were soon back in business behind it with the convenient new address of 318½.[19]

The police often had help from the federal government. In the winter of 1928, two U.S. Prohibition agents disguised as lumberjacks swept methodically along 25th Street from Wall to Washington avenues, effortlessly buying flasks of whiskey in seventeen different soft-drink parlors. Getting this evidence was a cinch, reported the federal administrator, because Ogden was—beyond dispute—wide open. The federal agents launched immediate padlocking proceedings against the seventeen businesses and rounded up thirty-six owners, many of them repeat offenders. The next day pedestrians on 25th Street saw many "for rent or sale cheap" signs hanging in the shuttered windows.[20]

Often the moonshiner's chief adversary was not the police but the competition. In a lengthy anonymous newspaper interview, a soft-drink parlor man—recently retired from bootlegging—said that all of Ogden's larger distilling operations had consolidated under a local Greek kingpin, who showed no mercy to competitors or rebellious subordinates.[21] He disposed of rivals by tipping police about the stills' locations. At the retail level, if a soft-drink parlor refused to carry the kingpin's moonshine, it could expect to be raided. On the rare occasion when protection money failed and police shut down one of the kingpin's stills, he ordered his other stills idled for a while, and 25th Street suddenly became parched. Someone then had to rush to Salt Lake for an emergency supply of bathtub booze.[22]

The same soft-drink parlor man said he retired from bootlegging when he realized the numerous bribed officials on his payroll were consuming all his profits.[23] Given the political and logistical inconsistencies that hobbled Prohibition enforcement, authorities were bound to look the other way in exchange for cash. Congress exempted federal Prohibition agents from civil-service job protection, fearing that patronage jobs could fall into the hands of subversives who secretly planned to undermine the law. Although the agent's annual salary of eighteen hundred dollars was hardly enough to live on, the job "guaranteed you the lucky number in a fabulous sweepstakes" of bribery and blackmail, according to Prohibition scholar Daniel Okrent. A Justice Department official estimated that each of New York City's thirty-two thousand speakeasies "paid a beat cop five dollars a day to keep the taps and cash register open."[24]

In Utah the original 1917 bill to impose statewide Prohibition called for a state commissioner as its ultimate enforcer, but Governor Bamberger's objections—that a commissioner was redundant and too expensive—carried the day. Moreover, subsequent Utah Legislatures declined to fund any enforcement. Special Prohibition officers appointed by Governor Dern in 1929 and 1930 had to serve without pay. Enforcement was left to city and county officers, who earned less than federal agents. The situation was ripe for corruption.[25]

Orson Hyde Mohlman—formerly an Ogden policeman—was the largest man in the Weber County Sheriff's Department. During Prohibition Deputy Mohlman often conducted raids on speakeasies and distilling operations, and he was the star witness for the prosecution in many bootlegging trials. The sheer bulk of confiscated whiskey stills in the sheriff's custody eventually became unmanageable, so Mohlman—the department's giant—was handed a sledgehammer and ordered to smash them to pieces.[26]

The recently discovered diary of Mohlman's wife, Clara, paints a different portrait. Clara Decker Mohlman was a desperate housewife of the 1920s without love in her marriage or an independent means of support. On January 21, 1925, Deputy Mohlman telephoned Clara that he was joining friends from Salt Lake for dinner, after which he "rolled in at three a.m., tied up proper." Clara confided to her diary that her husband's "closest associates in these all night carousals" were Italian bootleggers, who phoned him every payday to request "a quiet little talk in the parlor with closed doors and drawn blinds, ooh-la-la piling up." "Never mind," wrote Clara. "Tomorrow he will be the Honorable Mr. Mohlman just the same."[27] The honorable Mr. Mohlman had only recently caused a minor sensation in Ogden by unscrewing a sewer trap pipe beneath a soft-drink parlor at 136 25th Street and siphoning out a quart of whiskey dumped by a panicked bartender.[28]

Two months later, Clara asked her husband for money for a new spring wardrobe, but he pleaded an empty wallet. "When I told him how much he did have," she continued, "my wonderful husband said I was a dirty sneak [and] had been ever since we had been married." But the next day deputy Mohlman coughed up the cash, perhaps because "he knew he had better hand me some money or I would tell him a few more things that I know about him." The allowance Mohlman reluctantly gave Clara covered her gleeful shopping spree.[29]

While Mohlman's renowned prowess with a sledgehammer explained the fate of whiskey stills, the question of where confiscated whiskey went persisted. Bernard DeVoto's memoir of Ogden in the 1920s—never published until 2012—reveals that police regularly delivered large quantities to the local American Legion post. DeVoto, the post's chaplain, and his chums shrewdly made Jack Littlefield, a veteran and adjutant of the Ogden police force, secretary/treasurer of the post, a salaried job. "We now had the inside track with the police department," DeVoto wrote. Endowed with "the privilege of the police," DeVoto recalled he could "drop in on any dive on lower 25th Street and ask for what I wanted." Littlefield reliably supplied the post with "fairly presentable liquor [but] not as presentable as later on when we made terms with the federal officers."[30]

To celebrate the January 5, 1921, opening of its new mill and grain elevators in Ogden, the Sperry Flour Company "brought in an enormous assortment of wonderful liquor from California in a box car," DeVoto reported. "Because of the dignitaries, a lot of them governors and senators, they supposed they wouldn't have to have protection. The federal boys held otherwise and, the afternoon of the party, took over the box car. They sold it back at a good price but they took out some of the finest for themselves and telephoned me." DeVoto requested half a case of champagne and two cases of whiskey, then dispatched a police sergeant to fetch it. He even claimed to have a police guard "whenever I got lit in public or attended a wild party, and night after night [I was] driven home in a police car."[31]

The cumulative failure of liquor abatement prompted Utah Attorney General Harvey Cluff to write a confidential letter to the Women's Christian Temperance Union of Ogden, confessing that Prohibition had "caused the bootlegger to flourish and the illicit still to spring up.... I am frank to confess that Prohibition in Utah is a farce and is developing a citizenry of sneaks and lawbreakers."[32]

Although Prohibition enforcement consumed the lion's share of police department man-hours from 1917 to 1933, gambling and prostitution persisted as significant concerns on 25th Street. The sudden appearance of illegal slot machines in dozens of downtown businesses in 1931 caused great excitement. Salt Lake found itself similarly infested. But while Salt Lake's machines accepted only trade slugs, the syndicate behind the operation felt brazen enough to install coin machines in Ogden.[33] That may have been because the Ogden police and Weber County Sheriff's Department each claimed slot-machine patrol was the other's responsibility.

Finally, in April 1932, the district attorney, David Wilson, supervised a raid of several 25th Street shops, confiscating fourteen machines. A judge ordered them destroyed and the money forfeited to the state, but the sentence hardly made a dent in the profusion of one-armed bandits.[34] Ogden did not rid itself of the machines for decades.

Prostitution in Ogden was closely monitored and vigorously suppressed during World War I. To minimize the incidence of venereal disease in drafted men, the U.S. War Department Commission issued a list of eleven model laws that cities should enact to curtail immoral behavior. President Wilson's order of January 17, 1918, banned "immoral resorts" within a five-mile radius of military installations.[35] Although Ogden had no nearby military camp in World War I, city government took the wartime admonitions seriously. Mayor Samuel Browning said that physical examinations of Ogden draftees were revealing an "astounding and alarming" situation. Police Chief Thomas Browning assigned two officers to keep "in constant touch with women of loose character." Judge Barker, noted for harsh sentences on bootleggers, was equally tough on persons arrested for immoral conduct.[36]

Groundwork for suppressing prostitution on 25th Street had already been done in the 1912 raids,[37] and Belle London's departure from Ogden around 1914 marked the end of gilded-age houses of prostitution in the city. Most wartime cases involved freelancers in second-floor walkups. Under wartime pressure, Ogden police arrested women not necessarily guilty of anything more serious than wearing men's clothes on the street.[38]

Late in 1924, word of London's death came from California.[39] After leaving Ogden with her adopted daughters, she had settled in San Francisco, where she bought a hotel and continued in the commercial sex business under a new name, Maxine Rose.[40] Later, she moved to a farm just outside the city—which may have been a replica of the Topham ranch in Ogden—and operated a small hotel for factory workers. She hired a Chinese man to run the farm. One day the hired man's car broke down, and London towed it to the street. As she was untying the rope, the man's car rolled forward and crushed her against her car, breaking bones and injuring internal organs. She died five days later of blood poisoning.

London's adopted daughter, Ethel Topham, graduated from the University of California at Berkeley in 1922 and taught school, then took over the farm and hotel after London's death.[41] Her other adopted daughter, Charlotte Hill, married a wealthy Los Angeles candy maker. A young Ogden man, Raymond Weaver Brown, who said he had known London through real-estate dealings, provided the details of her Bay Area life to the *Ogden Standard-Examiner* and revealed that during her long Ogden career, she had spent considerable money donating food, coal, and clothing to the poor.[42]

Prostitution after World War I often transpired in rooming houses, especially the Olive at 217 and Carlyle at 238 25th Street.[43] Some of the women were pimped by their husbands. Matrimony gave these men immunity from the Mann Act of 1910, which made it a crime to transport an unmarried woman across state lines for immoral purposes. "The man who marries a girl to escape Mann Act charges is one of the biggest problems police officers have to confront today," said Ogden Police Chief Curtis Allison.[44]

Ethel Elizabeth Jane Topham, adopted daughter of Belle London and Thomas Topham, part of Ogden High School's class of 1914. *Photo courtesy of Special Collections, Stewart Library, Weber State University.*

Quite apart from Prohibition and the elemental futility of enforcing it, the parched years of 1917–1933 brought unprecedented challenges and opportunities to 25th Street. World War I underscored Ogden's importance as a railroad center, and Union Station was the place where Ogden interfaced with the nation's war effort. At the end of each month, Weber County's latest quota of drafted men were treated to a farewell meal at one of the 25th Street restaurants. They then marched in formation to Union Station to catch trains to West Coast training camps. Crowds lined the street to applaud the men, then thronged the station to bid them farewell.[45]

The same restaurants that fed departing draftees observed the wartime meatless Tuesdays and wheatless Wednesdays initiative to support the government's food-conservation program. Even so, the City Café in the Healy Hotel offered trout, seafood, and four kinds of fowl on Tuesdays and cornbread in lieu of rolls on Wednesdays.[46]

Not a day went by without war-related news from Union Station. Police—acting on tips from faraway draft boards—arrested suspected draft evaders there. Trainloads of German prisoners of war came through en route to internment at Fort Douglas in Salt Lake. The Weber County chapter of the Red Cross established a canteen at the south end of the station for the convenience and comfort of all soldiers, sailors, and marines passing through.[47]

When news of the armistice reached Ogden at 1:45 a.m. on November 11, 1918, an informal committee of doctors, railroad officials, and journalists felt that any celebration should be postponed until morning since many Ogdenites had influenza as victims of the infamous 1918 world epidemic and needed rest. But at 5:00 a.m., the Southern Pacific Railroad whistle began blasting. Within minutes nearly every band in town—Southern Pacific, Ogden City, state industrial school, and Weber Academy girls—was marching. No one went to work or school. Twenty-fifth Street played host to thronging citizens throughout the day.[48]

On January 17, 1919—two months after the armistice that ended World War I—trains carrying the Utah National Guard's regiment, the 145th Field Artillery, which included about sixty Weber County men, were scheduled to stop briefly at Union Station en route to Logan for demobilization. Perceptive city officials realized that Utah families eager to see their boys would become an uncontrollable mob at the depot if no provision was made to review the troops. After a hasty exchange of telegrams with the regimental colonel, plans were set for a two-hour parade of all 1,174 men and forty-three officers. Returning soldiers from Ogden formed an honor guard, and—accompanied by three local bands—led the march. Citizens fanned out along 25th Street and Washington Avenue to cheer the victorious soldiers. Ogden had never before hosted a military parade of that size.[49]

The parade to cheer the 145th Field Artillery was only one of many processions improvised along 25th Street in the early months of 1919. Countless special trains carrying veterans to San Francisco's Presidio and other western points of demobilization passed through the Junction City. On March 20, four hundred men of the 67th Coast Artillery—veterans of the Battle of the Argonne Forest—marched up 25th Street as a strong wind buffeted its banner bearers. The commanding officer was shocked that few male spectators took off their hats as the flag passed, saying he had "never seen such a bunch of boobs." But he lauded Ogden's "splendid" Red Cross women, who served sixty gallons of coffee, one-hundred-dozen doughnuts, and sandwiches, as "our bright particular comfort all the way across the continent."[50]

Regiments of the U.S. Army's 91st Infantry or Wild West Division arrived at Union Station on April 19 as whistles from all of downtown Ogden's factories, shops, and engines blew. Perhaps chastened by the earlier "boobs" reference, the city fathers seemed determined to impress the Wild West Division and rolled out the red carpet. Officers were given tours of Ogden Canyon and feted at the Weber Club. After marching on 25th Street, the soldiers were taken to the sanitarium in Ogden Canyon for showers. The Red Cross women provided the usual feast, and a returning war correspondent from the *San Francisco Examiner* said, "I've heard of this canteen. Every soldier who has been through Ogden can tell you about this canteen." Soldiers remarked that

Ogden was the only place since they had left New York where they were "treated like real men."[51]

Unfortunately, Ogdenites were unable to cheer their native sons. The Utah men of the Wild West Division had been routed to Wyoming's Fort Russell for demobilization and did not parade with their fellow battalions on 25th Street.[52]

Competition with other cities to host military parades and exhibitions occasionally provoked Ogden's high dudgeon. In May 1918, the U.S. Committee on Public Information scheduled a trainload of decorated Belgian soldiers—heroes of the Russian front—to parade in Ogden, and the city plunged into lavish preparations. At the last minute, the Belgians were rerouted to Salt Lake for the capital city's Red Cross drive. While stopped at Union Station after the Salt Lake event, Belgian officers said they regretted bypassing Ogden because they knew it was the home of John M. Browning (half brother to Mayor Sam Browning), inventor of the Browning machine gun so essential to Belgian troops.[53]

In April 1919, the daredevil flying veterans of the French Lafayette Escadrille began a tour of western cities to drum up support for the Victory Loan program. But once again, Ogden lost the flyers' scheduled performance to Salt Lake at the last minute. Outraged, the *Ogden Standard* excoriated "whoever is conducting government publicity work in Washington" for "wiping Ogden off the map." The writer revealed he had made a full-scale investigation of the reason why the Belgian veterans were not allowed to parade in Ogden in 1918. "The Belgian minister in Washington was made to accept the odium," explained the writer, but the contretemps "was never explained to our satisfaction." Furthermore, he wrote, it made no sense to exhibit the daredevil flyers in cities such as Reno and Pocatello with much smaller populations than "the greatest intermountain railroad junction." From now on, the *Standard* determined to demand "the respect due Ogden."[54]

The plethora of parades only whetted Ogden's appetite for its imminent historical saturnalia. The Golden Spike Jubilee celebrated the semicentennial of the transcontinental railroad, which made Ogden an important city and 25th Street famous. The main event—an enormous parade up Washington Avenue on the morning of May 10, 1919—reflected a dedicated municipal effort to honor the panorama of Ogden and Utah history. Float after float represented such events as the Dominguez-Escalante expedition of 1776, migrations by Mormon pioneer wagons and handcart companies, the 1847 purchase from Miles Goodyear of land that became Ogden City, and the 1902 construction of the Lucin Cutoff.

Old men from distant towns in Utah and other states wrote to Mayor Samuel Browning, recalling their work in grading the Union Pacific and Central Pacific lines into Utah in 1868 and 1869. These men were designated "railroad pioneers" and given free transportation to Ogden and honored seats on a reviewing stand. The Central Pacific Railroad float featured three surviving Chinese men who had laid track at Promontory Summit. The Southern Pacific Railroad (successor to the Central Pacific) built a miniature replica of the Jupiter, its engine at the May 10, 1869, Golden Spike ceremony. Ogdenite George Lashus, a Central Pacific engineer who had been at the ceremony fifty years earlier, rode with the replica. Ogdenites of Japanese, Chinese, Greek, and Italian backgrounds contributed heritage-specific floats. The African American community created a float depicting southern cabins and cotton fields, underwritten

Built as the Hotel Bigelow in 1927, this prominent landmark on Ogden's skyline changed its name to the Ben Lomond Hotel in 1932. *Photo courtesy of Special Collections, Stewart Library, Weber State University.*

by William Weakley, secretary/treasurer of the Porters and Waiters Club on 25th Street.[55]

The Union Pacific Railroad mounted a relic exhibit in Berthana Hall on 24th Street, featuring a number of personal possessions and furniture belonging to Abraham Lincoln, honored for signing into law the Pacific Railway Act of 1862. The only relic from the actual Golden Spike ceremony was a section of fifty-pound iron rail salvaged from Promontory Summit. No overture to the Stanford Museum in California for a loan of the Golden Spike was recorded.[56]

Thanks to Utah Senator Reed Smoot's clout with the Army Air Service, the Golden Spike Jubilee secured a special stunt show by three Sacramento-based Curtiss biplanes. Of even greater interest was the biplanes' flight over the Sierra Nevada and Nevada desert, which at that time was unprecedented and perilous. The flights took several days and were tracked by the press. One plane crashed on takeoff after refueling in Carlin, Nevada, although its crew survived. The ensuing two-plane show over Ogden somewhat mollified those who were still miffed over the Victory Loan show snub.[57]

The present Union Station, newly completed in 1924. *Photo courtesy of Union Station Archives.*

Forces set in motion by World War I fostered the booming business environment of the 1920s. Locally those forces fueled the construction of notable buildings, whose prominence and architectural distinction have yet to be exceeded in downtown Ogden—Union Station, the Ben Lomond Hotel, and two others not on 25th Street but close enough to stoke its energy: Peery's Egyptian Theater, which opened on July 3, 1924, and the First National Bank tower, which followed on June 27, 1927. (For most of its existence, the tower was known as the First Security Bank building. Today Wells Fargo Bank's logo adorns its roof).

The current Union Station went up on the foundation of its 1889 predecessor, which had burned in 1923. The laborers who built it became some of the 25th Street speakeasies' best customers.[58] At its dedication on November 22, 1924, a Union Pacific official praised the joint efforts between his company and

Ogden to beautify the city. The railroad had recently launched a plan to pattern its buildings after famous structures in Europe, he said, and the design of Union Station was inspired by an old Italian church.[59]

The Ben Lomond Hotel began as a gleam in the eyes of Ogden businessmen, who became keen to replace the old Reed Hotel with a modern facility. At first they planned to keep the Reed name, but stockholders later voted to call it the Bigelow, honoring Henry Bigelow, the late Ogden financier and president of the Reed Hotel Company. In September 1926, the Ogden Chamber of Commerce hosted a flag-raising ceremony on the Bigelow's newly completed roof, and Governor Dern declared that Ogden had entered a new era in its history: "the skyscraper period." Former governor Simon Bamberger, who had operated the White House Hotel on the Bigelow's site back in 1870, was a special guest, making the final public appearance of his life. "Simon Bamberger got his start in Ogden," noted the Chamber of Commerce president, "and then he went south and gave Salt Lake its start."[60]

The Bigelow opened for business on March 3, 1927. Its board of directors voted in December 1932 to rename it the Ben Lomond to capitalize on the fame of Weber County's most prominent topographical landmark.[61]

Ogden was fortunate to acquire a skyline before the Great Depression crippled the national economy during the 1930s. Tax collections at the U.S. Treasury fell 60 percent in the first three years of the new decade, while requests for government spending on relief measures increased dramatically. When potential tax revenue from beer sales started to glitter as an expedient solution, the legal bastion of national Prohibition began to unravel late in 1932.[62]

Congress passed a joint resolution proposing repeal of the Eighteenth Amendment before Herbert Hoover left the White House.[63] Newly elected President Franklin D. Roosevelt requested—and Congress quickly passed—the Cullen-Harrison Act to legalize 3.2 percent beer, to take effect on April 7, 1933.[64] However, it applied only to states that were either repealing their Prohibition laws or had never adopted them in the first place. Utah was not one of these.[65] In August 1933, the Utah Legislature provided that beer would become legal in the Beehive State no earlier than January 1, 1934. Moreover, it made legal beer contingent on Utah citizens voting to repeal their state constitution's Prohibition clause in a special November 1933 election.[66]

The Cullen-Harrison Act set the stage for an ironic legal situation in Utah. Perhaps no Utahn had monitored beer legislation's progress in Congress more closely than Ogden's famously deposed brewery mogul, Gus Becker.[67] Legal beer, Becker realized, would decimate the market for Becco, his near beer, both outside Utah—states where beer could legally be consumed right away—and inside Utah, which would be deluged with illegal beer. His solution was to recruit influential Utahns to lobby the Utah Legislature to legalize brewing beer, but only for sale outside the state. The most influential Utahn of all—Utah Senator Reed Smoot—wrote to Becker saying he thought such an arrangement was "reasonable."[68]

State senator Ira Huggins, a Mormon bishop from Ogden who affirmed he was "just as dry as any member of the senate," sponsored the bill to allow Becker Products finally to resume manufacturing its renowned beer.[69] After the Huggins bill cleared the legislature, farmers who wanted to sell their barley to Becker Products and Mormon foremen and workers at the brewery urged

Gus Becker—featured sharpshooter and "successor to Buffalo Bill"—is the horseman behind the flag in the Labor Day parade of September 5, 1921, featuring the Wild West show. Prominent on the north side of 25th Street's 200 block *(right to left)* are the Creston Hotel, the three-story Fashion rooming house, and the three-story National Hotel (formerly the European). *Photo courtesy of Special Collections and Archives, Merrill-Cazier Library, Utah State University (Gustav Lorenz Becker photograph collection).*

Governor Blood to sign it. Blood affixed his signature on March 21, 1933; the effective date—contingent on an overhaul of Utah's statutory code—was expected in late June.[70]

With all deliberate speed, Gus Becker procured a federal permit to brew beer—effective on April 7—issued on condition that Utah law would be obeyed. Because making near beer, which Becker Products had done since 1917, involved brewing full-strength beer and then drawing off the alcohol, the brewery needed no advance groundwork.[71] Bolstered by an opinion from the state attorney general that exporting beer from Utah had never been illegal under the state Prohibition law,[72] Becker Products began selling beer in Wendover, Nevada, just across the state line, and Montana on April 7, 1933.

But the shipments came to a screeching halt when Governor Blood, who had not issued any state permit, saw an article in the *Salt Lake Telegram* describing the Becker brewery as a "hive of activity" as it loaded the Nevada and Montana orders. Blood informed the attorney general, who replied that these shipments violated state law since the Huggins bill was not yet in effect. A Denver-based supervisor of federal permits—in Utah for the Mormon General Conference—ordered Becker's brewery closed. The American Legion and Ogden and Salt Lake Chambers of Commerce pleaded with Blood to find a way to allow Becker Products to ship beer, but the governor replied that no state official could authorize a violation of the law, no matter how worthy the cause.[73]

Nearly 150 Becker Products employees were thrown out of work, and the brewery forfeited money on a year's worth of orders from Honolulu to Boston. However, the plant must have got permission to reopen in advance of the state permit because when Governor Blood finally granted it on June 26, Becker workers immediately began loading beer orders for eleven western states into waiting refrigerated railcars. "We have scrupulously observed the Prohibition laws, and everybody knows it," Becker commented. "We feel the Huggins bill was adopted because the lawmakers had confidence in us."[74] Later that summer, a state senator urging beer's legalization said the Huggins bill had made Utah "the laughing stock of the land," but Huggins replied that seven hundred dollars a day in revenue from other states gave Utah the last laugh.[75]

In proposing the repeal of national Prohibition, Congress directed that each state's decision must be made at a ratifying convention. In Ogden the Weber County League for Prohibition Repeal organized at the Ben Lomond Hotel to support a slate of pro-repeal candidates for Utah's convention.[76] Although pollsters in favor of remaining dry predicted Utah would not choose to repeal national Prohibition, they were wrong. On November 7, 1933, the Beehive State voted overwhelmingly for the list of pro-repeal candidates.[77]

For this nationwide effort to succeed, three-fourths of the state conventions, or thirty-six out of forty-eight, had to ratify the repeal amendment. Thirty-three states had already ratified before Utah's convention met on December 5, 1933, and Ohio's and Pennsylvania's conventions—meeting on December 5 as well—ratified earlier in the day. At 3:32 p.m. Mountain Standard Time, Utah became the thirty-sixth state to ratify, supplying the magical total needed.[78] Jubilant New Yorkers awaiting Utah's expected action gulped down fizzes and stingers the moment news of official repeal sailed across the telegraph wires.[79] President Roosevelt assured Americans that repeal would not bring back saloons and suggested that public drinking spots now be called taverns.[80]

The Prohibition clause of Utah's state constitution—in effect since 1918—also fell by the wayside in the November 7 election.[81] What did not change was Utah's 1917 statewide Prohibition law, which remained intact except for the modification to allow beer in 1934. Utahns were thus denied, for the moment, the benefit of their own convention's ratification of national repeal. Because the Utah Legislature met only in odd-numbered years, hard liquor could not be legalized earlier than 1935.

As Ogden's taverns geared up for legal beer in 1934, they failed to realize that—in addition to federal licenses—they must get city and state permits. New Year's Eve came, and not a single Ogden tavern had applied for a state permit, while only two had procured the city's. That did not stop beer from flooding the bar counters and restaurant tables along 25th Street at the stroke of midnight. (Actually, noted the *Ogden Standard-Examiner,* "many resorts have been dispensing both bottled and draft beer for months.") However, the punitive expense of three different licenses was unpopular with tavern keepers struggling to squeeze out a profit in the midst of the Great Depression.[82]

The draconian liquor-control law Utah adopted in 1935 gave the state, not cities, control over every drop of alcohol within its borders through a newly created state liquor commission. Hard liquor could be sold only at state liquor stores, and no person could purchase it without first buying a fifty-cent individual permit.[83] Ogden's first state liquor store, at 25th Street and Kiesel Avenue, had its grand opening on June 1, 1935. The good news was that legal booze was cheap, a move by the new state liquor commission to put bootleggers out of business once and for all. More than one thousand customers crowded the store on the first day. Its sales volume averaged twenty-five thousand dollars per month in 1935.[84]

One of the most jarring consequences of the 1935

In 1929 the Lyceum Theater at 269 25th Street (shown in the 1970s at its nadir) was designated as an exclusive venue for talking pictures. Despite such pretensions, the locals called it the Lice House. Today it is Wise Guys Comedy Club. *Photo used by permission of the Utah State Historical Society.*

Down the block, the Cozy Theater at 225 25th Street was remodeled in 1929 to be the local venue for silent movies. The building later served as the western half of the Star Noodle Restaurant and is currently vacant. The adjacent building on the right, Sorensen's Jewelers, was demolished during the late 1970s. *Photo courtesy of Special Collections, Stewart Library, Weber State University.*

law was the liquor commission's parsimonious allocation of draft-beer licenses. When beer became legal in Utah in 1934, Ogden granted licenses to fifty-one taverns. But in 1935, the commission announced it would restrict Ogden to a mere thirteen draft-beer licenses and decide who got them. The rationale was that illegal liquor sales most often occurred at taverns, so enforcement would become much easier if the number of searchable premises was reduced.[85] Putting taverns out of business and barkeepers out of work was apparently of no consequence.

The 1935 law ensured that Utah would continue to have speakeasies and bootleggers after Prohibition's demise and saddled the state with enforcement challenges it grapples with even today.[86] For the rest of the twentieth century, Ogden police spent a disproportionate amount of time patrolling 25th Street for illegal alcohol sales.[87] It cost Ogden far more to enforce state law on 25th Street, noted a city manager in 1966, than it could collect in license fees.[88]

Just as architectural landmarks of the Prohibition era—Union Station and the Ben Lomond Hotel—still dominate the city's skyline, political landmarks from that era still dictate Ogden's culture and nightlife. The legal impediments to public consumption of hard liquor were the single biggest factor in the reputation 25th Street acquired in its third and final heyday.

CHAPTER SIX

OGDEN FOLLIES

> They call them "pin-up girls" and think it's cute how "our boys," now that they're drafted, love to hang them in their wall lockers. And then close up all the whorehouses, every place they can, so our young men will not be contaminated.
>
> **—Private Prewitt in James Jones's *From Here to Eternity***

It was no accident that Harman Ward Peery's ascension as mayor of Ogden came in the same election that scuttled Prohibition. In the depths of the Great Depression, Ogden was desperate for an antidote. Peery was well known as the developer of the Egyptian Theater and other public entertainments, and while he was city commissioner, he had favored Ogden tradesmen over Salt Lake ones for public contracts.[1] The voters expected Peery's talents for rainmaking and publicity to get Ogden moving again, and he did not disappoint. Within months he founded the annual Ogden Pioneer Days rodeo, a cash magnet. His fame as the genial "cowboy mayor" burnished the city's image throughout the country.

Peery ran for mayor ten times between 1929 and 1949, winning half of those races—in 1933, 1935, 1937, 1941, and 1947.[2] His on-and-off mayoralty bracketed the era when 25th Street's wild reputation reached its zenith. One reason the street flourished during Peery's reign is that he believed it gave ordinary people access to entertainment usually enjoyed only by the rich in private clubs. He also believed that vice was most effectively regulated through licenses and fees.[3] Persistent mythology in Ogden holds that Peery received kickbacks from the street's rackets, but even his political enemies took pains to emphasize that he never profited personally.[4]

Peery's worldview was firmly in place from the time of his first mayoral campaign in 1929, when he pledged to fight for three things: a second daily newspaper in Ogden, an alternative Ogden boosters' commercial club, and a reduction of taxes.[5] Over the years, his 1929 platform never really changed. He disliked the *Ogden Standard-Examiner* and its owners, the Glasmann family, and felt an abiding antipathy for the Weber Club and Ogden Golf and Country Club. He believed property and other local taxes oppressed Ogden's working classes.

Like many Ogdenites of their time, the Peerys were Mormon pioneers, but from the time of their arrival in

Harman Peery in his final year as mayor in 1949 visits an historic, unidentified pioneer cabin. *Photo courtesy of Special Collections, Stewart Library, Weber State University (John David Eccles Collection).*

Utah, it was clear they marched to a different drummer. Their heritage was Virginian, and their patriarch, David H. Peery, had fought for the Confederacy during the Civil War. "The Peerys were liberals from the get-go," a great-grandson observes. "They freed their slaves long before the Emancipation Proclamation, brought them to Utah, and employed them."[6] David H. Peery, mayor of Ogden from 1883 to 1886, possessed exceptional entrepreneurial talent that subsequent generations of the family—most notably youngest son, Harman—inherited. At his death, David H. Peery's real-estate holdings were incorporated as the Peery Estate, and from an early age, Harman managed it.[7]

Despite their financial prowess, the Peerys were champions of the common man. Years before Harman held office, his older brother, City Councilman Harold Peery, favored enforcing rules and regulations as strictly in Ogden's private clubs as in its public saloons, despite his own membership in the Weber Club.[8] Harman was a founding member of the Ogden Golf and Country Club and built its first clubhouse, according to his grandson, "but he came to hate going out there after he realized it was another place for the elite to indulge in vices that ordinary people couldn't get in public. The country club set despised him because he ended up exposing all their vices."[9]

Opponents found little to admire in Harman Peery's political philosophy. Perhaps his greatest nemesis was Darrell Greenwell, an avid member of the Weber Club and Elks Lodge and executive editor of the *Ogden Standard-Examiner.* Greenwell told a friend that Peery's concept of tax reduction really meant lower taxes for the Peery Estate, while the mayor's slogan—"Money Going into the City Treasury Which Belongs There"—was a euphemism for licensing gambling enterprises. "This means," said Greenwell, "that wealthy tavern keeper Peery can pile up more gains when he as mayor authorizes himself to load his tavern with slot machines." Greenwell feared that as long as Peery was mayor, "Twenty-Fifth Street will continue to be the trademark by which the entire community is judged."[10]

The third and final heyday for 25th Street, which coincided with the Peery years, divided into three distinct periods. From 1935 to 1941, the dominant dynamic on the street was an uneasy coexistence with Utah's new liquor-control law. Then, during World War II, tension between military exigencies and soldiers' sexual appetites overwhelmed the street's established culture. Finally, the immediate postwar years—a prosperous time for Ogdenites—brought a brief gentrification to the street as middle-class customers patronized its clubs.

From its inception in March 1935, Utah's post-Prohibition liquor law created more problems than it solved. The new state liquor commission kept moving the goalposts in the number of draft-beer licenses it proposed to allocate to Ogden, announcing fourteen, then ten, then thirteen.[11] The stingy total would throw dozens of vendors recently licensed in Ogden out of business. Consequently, Ogden announced licenses would cost two thousand dollars. "Let these favored [thirteen] pets of the commission make a substantial contribution to the city treasury," Mayor Peery said. "We are badly in need of revenue and since we have lost heavily as a result of the state going into the liquor business we must find some other source."[12] After numerous complaints from vendors, however, the city reduced the fee to five hundred dollars per year.[13]

The law's most tangible feature—a new state liquor store at 25th Street and Kiesel Avenue—became a public nuisance with hordes of drunken, belligerent individuals congregating outside it on Saturday nights. "Even in the old bootleg days there was no such spectacle of public drinking," complained *Ogden Standard-Examiner* publisher Abraham Lincoln Glasmann. The refusal of state liquor commissioners to make an inspection tour of the store incensed Mayor Peery, who proposed moving it "to the state capitol where the idea of controlling the drinking activities of the people of Utah originated."[14]

The mayor's incessant complaints prompted the Utah Legislature in 1937 to return authority over beer sales to the cities.[15] Ogden immediately granted taverns an extra hour of operation until 1:00 a.m. and received seventy applications for new draft-beer licenses in the first two weeks. Within three months, the city treasury brimmed with a ten-thousand-dollar surplus from license fees.[16]

Juvenile delinquency on 25th Street was another major concern, especially during Peery's second term. The street had become a hangout for boys and girls playing hooky. Reform-school officials complained of a "revolving door" between the street and the classroom with truant youths loitering in taverns and pool halls to avoid being caught.[17] Boys under twenty-one found it was easy to lie about their age and get permits to buy liquor.

During a supposedly slow night on the street, an investigative reporter found drunken men and women patronizing the taverns with children in tow, underaged beer waitresses, minor girls canoodling with older men, prostitutes and pimps, fights that left teeth marks and blood, ripped clothing, trash strewn on tavern floors, and alley cats sniffing through garbage. After the beer taverns closed at 1:00 a.m., several clandestine liquor outlets opened for business.[18]

Only four months after extending taverns' closing time to 1:00 a.m., the Ogden City Commission voted—over Mayor Peery's objection—to roll it back to midnight, hoping to force juveniles to go home. Peery warned that Salt Lake's taverns stayed open until 1:00 a.m. and would draw business away from Ogden. He said a man who wanted a glass of beer at that hour ought to be entitled to have one and that, "when you criticize the Twenty-Fifth Street places, you're picking on the poor people. Why don't you go after the rich ones, too?"[19] This September 1937 vote was not the last

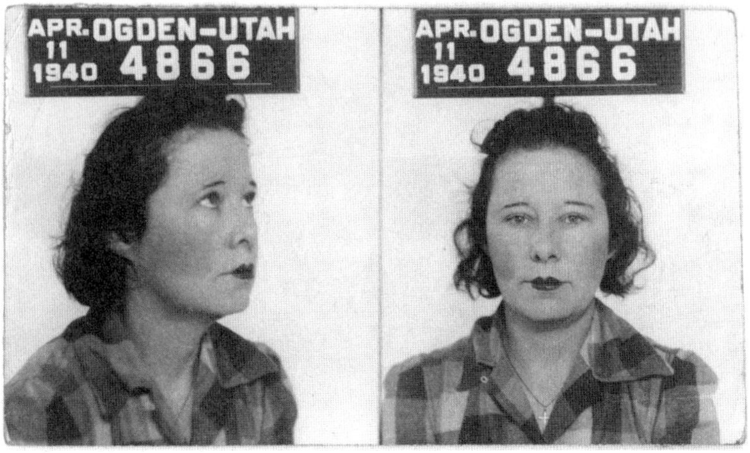

Betty Lou Miller of the Wyoming Rooms. *Photo used by permission of the Utah State Archives.*

The Wyoming Rooms above the Eagle Clothing Co. in 1952. This is the C. F. Krauch Building shown on page 29; its second-story façade and windows configuration were altered after damage from the 1935 National Hotel fire next door. *Photo Courtesy of Special Collections, Stewart Library, Weber State University.*

word on the tavern closing time; it was restored to 1:00 a.m. in 1942 and then bounced back and forth over the years, depending on the makeup of the commission.[20]

The best information on prostitution during Mayor Peery's first three terms comes from a contemporary Weber College Department of Sociology survey. When Peery was first sworn in, an estimated fifty to seventy-five houses of prostitution already existed along 25th Street and Grant Avenue, and each had to pay between thirty-five and sixty-five dollars per month to the police to operate. By the time the survey was completed four years later in May 1938, "about seventeen" houses of prostitution "known to police" remained in the same area, while several African American houses "unknown to police" were located around town. The cost of working as a prostitute in 1938 was a monthly fee of twenty-five dollars plus $2.50 for weekly health certificates.

Ogden city officials contacted by the sociology students denied the existence of brothels in town and forcefully declared that any houses of prostitution would be closed posthaste. The students learned what the real story was from members of the police force. LeMoyne Petersen, still in his teens when he worked on the survey, said former police chief L. M. Hilton told him that whenever the department closed the brothels, the number of rape cases in Ogden went up.[21]

By the time Mayor Fred Abbott took office in January 1940, even fewer houses of prostitution were in business. On March 6, 1940, Hugh O'Neil, project editor of the Utah Work Projects Administration (WPA) Historical Records Survey, made a personal-inspection tour of the eight "semilegal" houses he said existed in Ogden, four on 25th Street and four on Grant Avenue.[22] Each was on the second floor of a commercial building, and most had a parlor furnished with a few chairs, sofa, and phonograph. The small back rooms each had a bed, wash basin with Lysol, desk, and chair. Most employed two or three women between the ages of twenty and thirty, whose two-dollar fees were split evenly with the

Fire at Mecca Sporting Goods store, circa 1941. The vertical sign farthest on the left indicates the Wilson Rooms at 320½ 25th Street. Significant deterioration is evident in these buildings' upper floors. *Photo courtesy of Union Station Archives.*

landlady. Prostitutes in Ogden could not street-walk but had to operate exclusively out of established houses.[23]

Scenes of daily life during 1940 in one of those houses—the Golden Hotel—were revealed during the prosecution of Louise Wilson, its madam, for keeping a house of ill fame. An African American maid answered the door and introduced male customers to the women. The maid collected the fees and stored them in a drawer in Wilson's bedroom, where the money was divided at the end of the day. Police officers stopped by frequently to confer with Wilson, reminding her that the girls must report each week to the Ogden City Health Department's venereal-disease clinic.[24]

The clinic, established at the old City Hall in October 1939, was free and confidential.[25] Alta Roskelley, the clinic's nurse during 1940, said local prostitutes were mostly pleasant and cooperative. However, many of them asked Roskelley—who always wore her nurse's uniform in public—not to recognize them on the street. One of the clinic's doctors once told Roskelley, "Those women have the cleanest interiors that I have ever seen. It looks to me like they have used a rotary brush." Roskelley assumed the prostitutes were "exceptionally careful" when they came in and "tried to clean up as much as they could so they would not have a positive test."[26]

This was Ogden's public-health situation as war in Europe began to threaten the United States. President Roosevelt declared a limited national emergency on September 8, 1939, which prompted Congress to fund military installations and preparedness initiatives around the country. Millions of dollars were earmarked to make Ogden a major military center. The construction of Hill Field, initially estimated at eight million dollars, began on January 12, 1940, while groundbreaking at the Ogden Quartermaster Depot (later Defense Depot

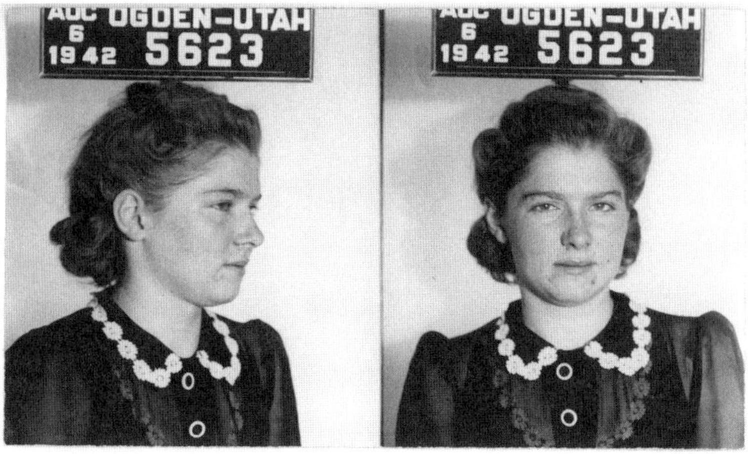

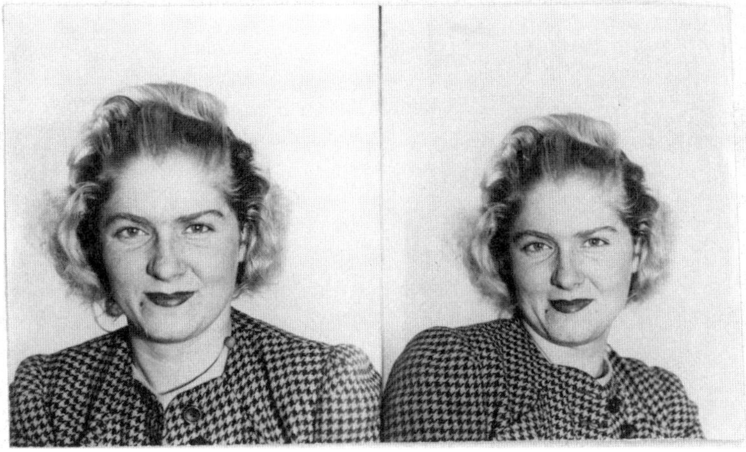

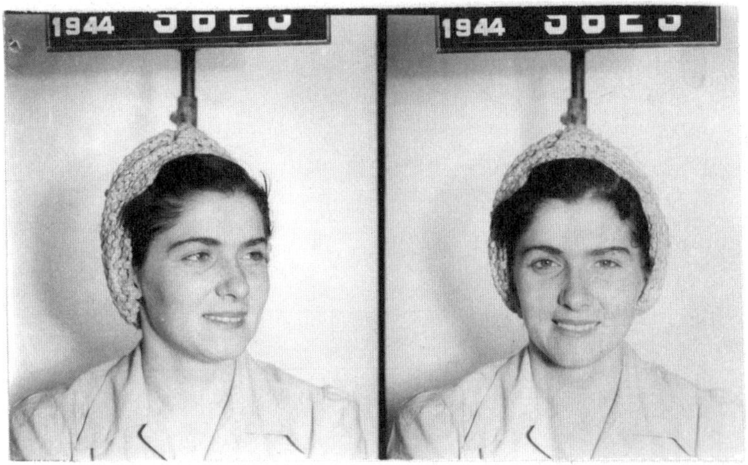

Shirley McCulloch seemed to have more mug shots (and makeovers) than any other young woman in Ogden during World War II. *Photo used by permission of the Utah State Archives.*

Miss McCulloch sometimes used an alias, Querida del Rosa. *Photo used by permission of the Utah State Archives.*

A more womanly looking Shirley McCulloch in 1944. *Photo used by permission of the Utah State Archives.*

Ogden), projected to cost eighteen million, followed on December 16, 1940. The existing Ogden Arsenal at Sunset, Utah, received an initial $6.5 million dollars for munitions and shell loading.[27]

As construction plans were unveiled, Ogden began to comprehend the impact of the workers arriving to build and operate the war plants.[28] Months before Pearl Harbor, the *Salt Lake Tribune* said Ogden already had a housing shortage even though defense employment was still nowhere near its projected peak. The Red Cross reported that families seeking war work were living in trailers along the Weber River, while Ogden's Employment Services office tracked an influx of single women from other western states who were moving into "cheap rooming houses in Ogden's questionable district." Juvenile court officers described a "local problem" of young women employed in beer parlors, cafés, and lunchrooms and at drive-in stands.[29]

The American Social Hygiene Association began surveying cities near war plants, including Ogden, to help the military avoid the loss of man hours to venereal disease it had suffered during World War I. "No sooner had the limited emergency been declared," wrote the association's director of field studies, "than the prostitution underworld saw an opportunity for fat profits." The director criticized cities that tolerated prostitution and issued health certificates, claiming they encouraged misrepresentations of the women's health status. He quoted a madam "in an important city in one of the Mountain States" (whose policy sounded a lot like Ogden's):

> Here's the set up: every girl has to be mugged [photographed] and fingerprinted. No more than three girls to a joint. Joints open at 9 a.m., close at 2 a.m. Girls can't answer hotel dates. No dating outside at all. All business must be done on the premises. No liquor or soft drinks can be sold. No window tapping or roping [accosting]. We're watched like criminals, treated like slaves. Can't even live in private apartments. Have to live in certain hotels.[30]

A memorandum from the Federal Security Agency's Division of Social Protection observed that Ogden collected anywhere from $250 to $1,000 per month in fines from prostitutes and used the cash to defray the cost of their medical examinations. In other words, noted the memo, Ogden's clinic depended "on revenue from persons engaged in prostitution, which is in turn the source of the disease it is hoped to eliminate."[31]

On November 11, 1941, federal and state public-health officials met with Mayor Abbott and urged him to close the approved houses of prostitution. They left feeling that Abbott had been "noncommittal."[32] However, they must have been more persuasive than they thought because one day later, Abbott ordered all the houses closed.[33] The mayor insisted he had merely taken the final step in a two-year crusade. The first had been "to chase juveniles and open solicitors off the streets"; the second was to prohibit women "exposing themselves from hotel windows clad in flimsy garments." In a related move that some probably thought counterintuitive, Abbott suspended the operation of the venereal-disease clinic.[34]

Abbott's closures must have relieved health officials since they anticipated trouble with venereal-disease prevention under incoming Mayor Harman Peery, who had just defeated Abbott for reelection. "Peery has been arrested two times for violation of the state gambling laws," warned a Division of Social Protection representative. "He has publicly stated that he believed in a wide-open town."[35] Peery was a popular piñata throughout his fourth mayoral term, 1942–1943, whenever officials needed to blame someone for rising venereal-disease rates in Ogden.

In February 1942, noted a confidential report from the Office of Community War Services, "it was already evident that [Ogden] was to be metamorphosed from a largely rural to a principally industrial community. All the problems of congestion and maladjustment attendant upon a suddenly expanded population were in evidence."[36] Eighteen months later, another government report from the Division of Recreation observed,

> Ogden has become the hub of one of the largest war ordnance areas in the nation. The thirty thousand civilian war workers at Hill Field, [Clearfield] Naval Ordnance, [Ogden] Arsenal, and [Ogden] Quartermaster Depot; seventy-five hundred troop personnel stationed at these plants; the Provost Marshal Training Camp, Weber College; and a war prisoner camp make Ogden look like a country town on circus day, twenty-four hours a day, every day.[37]

Thanks to this influx of jobs and workers, incomes in Utah exceeded the national average in 1943, probably the only year during the twentieth century when that happened, according to historian Floyd O'Neil.[38]

The sexual spectacle on 25th Street during World War II—while quite unlike anything Ogden had previously

The Club at 126 25th Street in 1952. *Photo courtesy of Special Collections, Stewart Library, Weber State University.*

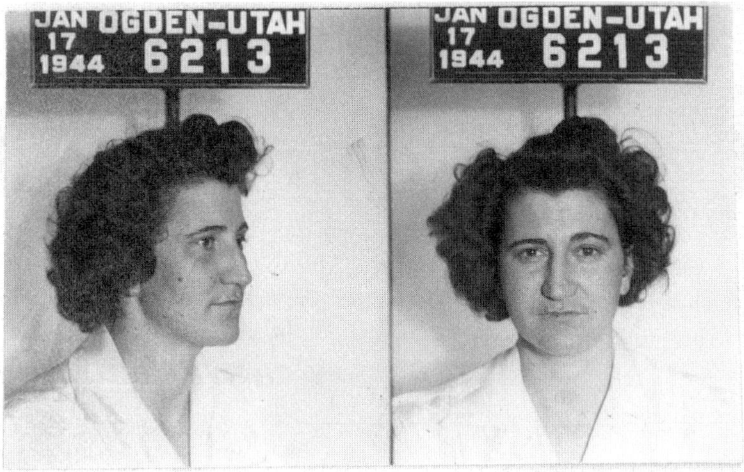

Irene White of Hill Field was arrested for prostitution in a parked car at 25th Street and Lincoln Avenue in January 1944. *Photo used by permission of the Utah State Archives.*

witnessed—didn't differ from the libidinous wartime atmosphere in other American cities near military camps.[39] Ross and Jack's, the popular all-night "burger-spud" diner at 362 25th Street, had to start closing at 10:00 p.m. despite a record business; after that hour, the soldiers and munitions workers became too boisterous and

Former Southern Pacific Railroad employee Jack Edwards stands in front of Union Station as a navy man in 1945. *Photo used by permission of the Utah State Historical Society (Hugh F. O'Neil photograph collection).*

propositioned the waitresses.[40] City policemen became very strict with their daughters after constantly finding soldiers and women in fevered entanglements in the street's doorways and parked cars.[41] The city's housing shortage (and possibly the abatement of brothels) aggravated public sexual behavior: during the warmer months, people without lodging slept in City Hall Park, where abundant shrubs and hedges provided the illusion of privacy.[42] The Ogden area provost marshal set up military police headquarters at 132 25th Street after a "thorough investigation" of optimal locations, but any Ogdenite knew the street was the prime spot for enlisted men who wanted to let it all hang out.[43]

Although the street continually teemed with servicemen on leave from Hill Field and the other area military posts, nothing could compare to the arrival of troop trains at Union Station, where they disgorged sailors and soldiers. At such times, said Tom Zito, a railroad car repairman, military police at Union Station threw up their hands at the futility of controlling such mobs. Zito once observed two "tough-looking sailors" standing outside The Club at 126 25th Street. One was telling the other, "I heard about this street over in Europe, and I would never have believed what I'm seeing now." Civilians were scarce on the street, said Zito, "because they had sense enough to get out of the way. There were just so many sailors coming out of those joints with bottles of beer in their hands, or whiskey, and gals. They would just go outside Union Station in the summertime and drop anywhere they could get a little sleep."[44]

As expected, the heavy pressure on military and public-health officials to minimize wartime venereal disease led to a few scrapes with Mayor Peery. On December 23, 1942, federal and state officials met with the Ogden City Commission to discuss a secret investigation by the U.S. Public Health Service. In just the previous week, the report said, six cases of venereal disease had been traced to 25th Street. As points of contact, the report cited three rooming houses: the Wyoming (238 25th Street), Golden (242½), and K. C. (250); and three taverns: the Pioneer (214), Town (227), and Falstaff (234), where waitresses solicited soldiers. The army mentioned its recent off-limits designation of Phoenix, Arizona, and threatened the same would happen in Ogden if the rate continued to rise.[45]

However, a police captain responded that he had checked these properties as soon as he received the report and found the rooming houses filled with defense workers, each with his own key. Nor could he verify "vice conditions" in the taverns. Mayor Peery expressed surprise to hear of these conditions in Ogden, pointing out that his predecessor, Mayor Abbott, had closed the brothels.[46] Peery speculated that the Public Health Service had launched its secret investigation after a recent "flare up" in Salt Lake City's venereal-disease statistics.[47]

The following summer, Howard Slutes, a Denver-based representative of the Division of Social Protection, heard from multiple sources that Ogden was "nearly wide open." The venereal-disease rate at Hill Field was higher than in the air corps as a whole. While the rate from exposures in Ogden was lower than in many cities, Slutes thought it was "high enough." Although Ogden had closed its brothels, surveys showed freelance African American prostitutes were earning up to $350 dollars per night. One of the army's biggest problems in Ogden was venereal-disease cases originating from "loose young white girls" picked up by enlisted men.

Because Slutes felt his agency was not getting cooperation from Mayor Peery, he organized a luncheon for Ogden's businessmen and club women where he and army officers candidly discussed the data from their surveys and urged the locals to demand official action. The agency also appealed to the *Ogden Standard-Examiner* for help in spreading the word. Without mentioning Peery by name, the newspaper had already editorialized about police forces that snickered whenever a city administration insisted it was doing all it could to suppress vice. It urged citizens to demand enforcement.[48]

Harman Peery would have scoffed at being labeled uncooperative. For Pioneer Days in 1943, he organized the biggest parade in the celebration's history; its theme was the sale of war bonds. The five-mile-long procession included every piece of military hardware that security allowed to be shown: guns, tanks, bulldozers, tractors, graders, sand washers, and water purification systems.[49] Top brass from Wendover Air Base, Brigham City's Bushnell General Military Hospital, and Ogden's four military installations were present on the reviewing stand. The climactic auction of war bonds at City Hall Park pulled in more than seventy-five thousand dollars, thanks to the persuasive powers of guest auctioneers Governor Maw, Utah Senators Thomas and Murdock, and Mormon apostle David O. McKay.[50]

After the Utah State Board of Health reported twenty-six cases of venereal disease in Ogden in September, the Division of Social Protection made another official visit. Acknowledging that Ogden's police force was understaffed, the representative urged the city to do more with less: organize a vice squad, hire female police officers, and patrol the parks more often to keep out the prostitutes. Mayor Peery calmly replied that the provost marshal's office had just told him there were only four new cases of venereal disease in Ogden in September and the city had no houses of prostitution. "The survey indicated Ogden had a wonderful record," said Peery. Nonetheless, he and the other commissioners pledged to step up enforcement of curfews and laws on room rentals and alcohol sales and expressed regret at any perception of noncooperation on their part.[51]

Gambling received much less attention than sexual conduct during the war, but under Harman Peery, it had always been essential for municipal solvency. When he first took office in January 1934, Ogden's bonded debt was nearly three million dollars, which cost the city five hundred dollars per day in interest, and tax collection prospects were projected to be less than 80 percent.[52] "Dozens of merchants," declared Peery, "approved [my] plan to pay Ogden City, instead of syndicates, to operate slot machines." By month's end, the plan had enriched Ogden by six thousand dollars, but the windfall was short lived. County Sheriff Amasa Hammon—who in previous years had shown little interest in regulating slot machines—began confiscating and destroying them, and merchants became skittish about having them.[53]

Just before the war, the Utah WPA Historical Records Survey's Hugh O'Neil reported that Ogden had no wide-open gambling houses. You could find discreet stud and draw-poker games at the Elks and Knights of Columbus meeting places (both private) and The Club (126) and the Lincoln Street Cigar Store (201) on 25th Street. The poker games, said O'Neil, were held "on a sort of secretive basis and in the event the police arrive at the establishments, the games are temporarily discontinued."[54]

But during the war, gambling became pervasive enough in Ogden to foreshadow Las Vegas. Darrell Greenwell maintained that Mayor Peery avidly recruited gambling to Ogden for its ability to channel a considerable portion of the area's military payroll into the city treasury. Peery's prize recruit, said Greenwell, was Jack Meyers, whose Playdium pinball-machine emporium was on the ground level of the Eccles Building.[55] From Peery's point of view, Ogden's treasury in 1943 was $7,250 richer from licensed amusement devices, a welcome boost to its ability to cover increased wartime costs.[56]

Raids were uncommon during most of Peery's wartime mayoral term. However, on September 6, 1943, deputy sheriffs and police—tipped off that dealers with marked cards were cheating customers—surprised the poker players at the Mecca (338) and Pioneer (214) taverns on 25th Street. They confiscated all cash, cards, chips, tables, stools, and slot machines. The *Ogden Standard-Examiner* reacted by accusing city officials of "pampering and petting" the rackets and suggesting the raid happened only because the state attorney general intervened.[57]

An intimate look at Ogden's gambling rackets came in the November 1943 murder trial of Paul Erz, proprietor of the Grill Tavern at 264 25th Street; he had shot Robert Savich, a thief and ex-convict. The Grill's back room was a haven for stud poker and twenty-one, while its upstairs was a flophouse. Erz and Savich had once been drifters together, and Erz had taught Savich how to cheat at card games and beat slot machines. Subsequently Erz barred Savich from the Grill. When Savich abruptly entered the tavern early one morning brandishing a gun, Erz shot him. The jury believed Erz had acted in self-defense and exonerated him.[58] However, the trial made it clear that on 25th Street, it would be difficult to find a card or dice game or a pinball machine that was not rigged.

Mayor Peery failed to gain enough votes in the primary on October 19, 1943, to advance to the general election. Earlier in the month, the Ogden area council of post and station commanders sent the mayor a letter demanding action to reduce Ogden's rising venereal-disease rate. Peery asked for an immediate meeting, but the day following the primary, the council told him no meeting was necessary. In a strange twist of fate, Ogden had no reported venereal-disease cases in October, but in November the number shot up to thirty-nine. Colonel Lilburn D. Fator, commanding officer at Hill Field, was furious. In a late November meeting, Fator gave the Ogden City Commission an ultimatum to correct the situation within five weeks or face a military off-limits designation.[59]

Most of the November cases were traced to two offending houses at 101 West Binford and 254½ 25th Street.[60] The previous month, soldiers had found both these houses closed. "If we can get temporary closure, why not permanent closure?" asked a medical officer. Another Hill Field man alleged that Ogden police had relaxed their cooperation because the city court would not try cases unless soldiers testified, which was contrary to military policy. Judge J. Quill Nebeker was asked to explain. "Unless the prosecution proves its case," said Nebeker, "it is just as much my duty to protect the defendant."[61]

Mayor Peery responded to the debate on closing ramshackle homes and storefronts that supposedly harbored prostitutes by insisting that "most of the vice in Ogden is being carried on in our main hotels," by which he meant the Ben Lomond.[62] He may have been troubled as well over wartime disregard for women's civil liberties. Historian Karen Anderson observes that the pursuit of "sex delinquents" and "morals violators" by federal and military officials (and city police departments) during the war invariably focused on women, never men.[63]

The Ben Lomond Hotel's elite status did have its perks during the war. Although the Ogden City Health Department said 10 to 15 percent of daily war-plant absences could be attributed to poor restaurant sanitation, the War Production Board in Salt Lake City was denying requests for adequate dishwashing equipment. Several underperforming Ogden restaurants had been declared out of bounds. But the Ben Lomond—noted the Office of Community War Services—"has obtained dish-washing equipment while Ross and Jack's across the street has been denied similar equipment, though the need is perhaps greater."[64]

Kent Bramwell, a thirty-one-year-old Red Cross official, replaced Peery as mayor. In the first few days of Bramwell's term, the new administration agreed to all the expansions of the police force—including a vice squad and policewomen—that Mayor Peery had said revenues would not support. New ordinances mandating early juvenile curfews and midnight closing for taverns were proposed at once. By February Ogden's venereal-disease rate had fallen considerably. Hotels became "more vigilant in attempting to curtail the amount of promiscuous sex activity." The Division of Social Protection recommended federal aid for the Ogden Police Department's budget.[65]

On the other hand, if Ogden's voters had envisioned a city government less tolerant of gambling under Bramwell, the rackets did not. Playdium pinball magnate Jack Meyers approached Bramwell on behalf of gambling proprietors to discuss financial incentives for keeping the heat off and gave the young mayor six hundred dollars for a vacation to California.[66] Less than three months after taking office, Bramwell shocked the city by resigning abruptly, joining the navy, and becoming virtually incommunicado.[67] He had realized that his underworld contacts would be revealed and cause a major scandal.

Responding to public pressure to investigate Bramwell's brief and baffling turn as mayor, Utah's attorney general recommended that a grand jury be impaneled. Because it had authority to investigate any local crime, the grand jury eventually indicted not only Bramwell and Jack Meyers but also Harman Peery and former police chief Rial Moore. They charged Peery and Moore with conspiring to allow various games of chance to operate in Ogden, collecting money from the proprietors, and monitoring these operators to make sure they paid.[68] The grand jury found that sixty-five establishments were part of this program. It identified Ogden Policeman William W. Richardson Jr. as the officer who arrested gambling-game operators once a month and saw that they paid bail to the department's desk sergeant but never made any other arrests.[69]

After fighting the indictment for seventeen months, Peery and Moore pleaded guilty in the Second District Court on November 20, 1945, to permitting pinball and slot machines to operate, stipulating that the devices had been licensed by Ogden City. Both the judge and district attorney stated for the record that neither Peery nor Moore had profited personally from those operations. They were fined two hundred and one hundred dollars, respectively.[70]

All histories of Ogden include the Bramwell case (and his eventual acquittal)[71] and the Peery indictment. What they fail to mention is that, back when Prohibition was still in force, Mayor Ora Bundy and Police Chief Albert Wilfong were indicted—not in state but federal court—for conspiring to violate Prohibition laws by approving soft-drink-parlor licenses for bootleggers. Judge Tillman Johnson saw no evidence of conspiracy and directed a verdict of not guilty.

As Judge Johnson saw it in 1933, Ogden's policy was to arrest bootleggers and fine them. Federal prosecutors attempted to show that making bootlegging a source of city revenue was conspiracy. However, policy was not conspiracy in Johnson's view. He said everyone knew that 90 percent of Ogden's soft-drink parlors were speakeasies, and he could not send Bundy and Wilfong to jail for conspiracy just because they knew that fact.[72]

In Harman Peery's case twelve years later, perhaps a different court might also have concluded that policy was not conspiracy. Meanwhile, venereal-disease rates in Utah and at its military installations rose sharply in 1945—doubling from the previous year—even though Peery was no longer in office to be chastised for not cooperating.[73]

When Peery announced his candidacy for mayor in 1947 after four years out of office, the *Ogden Standard-Examiner* was horrified. In the campaign's final two weeks, publisher Abe Glasmann and editor Darrell Greenwell printed caustic editorials. They warned that racketeers were rushing to Ogden and gearing up for business in case Peery was elected, and that other cities were maneuvering to steal one of Ogden's military installations with its huge payroll. "Would a return to Peery government help us in the fight to hold [our depots]?" Greenwell asked. "I don't think so, recalling the way Peery roiled the military in 1943."[74]

Buried beneath the editorials and additional expressions of distaste from the Ogden City Recreation Council, Weber County branch of the Utah Safety Council, Weber College officials, eight stake presidents, and others[75] was a low-key letter from Ogdenite Joseph Mumford. The letter said 25th Street had always been 25th Street no matter who was mayor or what campaign promises were made. Peery, wrote Mumford, was the only mayor ever to force racketeers to take out licenses and pay fines—not into some politician's pocket but into the city treasury—and the only one ever to lower property taxes. "I am a railroad man," declared Mumford, "and most railroad men feel as I do."[76] With assistance from multitudes of Mumfords, Peery was swept back into office for his fifth and final term.

Chastened, presumably, by his experience with the grand jury, Peery said, "My orders are for police to confiscate gambling devices whenever they're seen." He stressed that membership clubs and public taverns would be treated equally.[77]

An indication that Peery meant what he said was the experience of Edward Joseph "Eddie" Doherty, perhaps 25th Street's most-wanted criminal of the late 1940s. Doherty arrived in Ogden in 1943 as a thirty-three-year-old ex-convict who had "never done an honest day's work in his life" but wanted to make a new start. Working double shifts as a bartender at the Calico Cat at 272 25th Street, Doherty soon developed a "business-like" and "dependable" reputation. His earnings and connections enabled him to purchase scarce wartime commodities such as safety pins and bobby pins, which he resold to retailers. With excellent credit, Doherty opened his own novelty shop, Lucky's, and by 1946 owned three other 25th Street businesses: the Calico Cat, Pioneer Tavern (214), and Hy Land Hotel (278½).[78]

Doherty's parole officer (former Ogden police chief Hilton) called him "the greatest example of rehabilitation" he had witnessed in twenty years of police work. After Jack Meyers of the Playdium was indicted and forced out of business, Doherty—with Hilton's approval—paid five thousand dollars for the Playdium's amusement devices, reaping handsome profits from their operation and rental.[79] Sadly, Doherty eventually reverted to his criminal ways and conducted illegal gambling operations at Lucky's and prostitution at the Hy Land Hotel and Wyoming Rooms.

A view in 1933 of 214 25th Street. In the late 1940s, it was the Pioneer Tavern, one of Eddie Doherty's establishments on the street. The building, renumbered 216 25th Street, is now the Kokomo Club. Partially visible on the right is the three-story New Central (formerly the Central) Hotel, which burned in 1936. *Photo courtesy of Special Collections, Stewart Library, Weber State University.*

A view of 270, 272, 274, and 276 25th Street in 1933. Eddie Doherty's other establishments, Lucky's and the Calico Cat, were at 270 and 272. *Photo courtesy of Special Collections, Stewart Library, Weber State University.*

During Mayor Peery's final term, the new police chief, Maurice Schooff, and the county sheriff staged four separate raids at Lucky's, dramatically breaking into concealed rooms with crowbars and sledgehammers. In one of the raids, Schooff personally tussled with Doherty on a floor strewn with shattered glass fragments for the key to Lucky's backroom. Once inside the room, police found customers clinking glasses and making merry but drinking nothing stronger than beer. Nor was there any sign of gambling. Schooff was certain Doherty had been tipped off.[80]

Doherty was a determined racketeer. "You can smash down my doors, but I'll put up stronger ones," he warned. "We are on opposite sides of the fence. You have your job and I have mine."[81] What finally sent him to federal prison early in 1950 was a conviction on interstate transportation of stolen automobiles.[82]

The gamblers and social drinkers arrested in Lucky's backroom reflected a change in 25th Street's demographics since the end of World War II. It was now socially acceptable for wives to accompany husbands in many establishments that were formerly off limits to them. A number of private, state-chartered clubs began springing up along the street. "Ogden had five really good years after World War II, with trains constantly coming in and out," recalls Robert Peery King. "The trains were bringing people in, relocating them to Ogden, bringing soldiers back from the Pacific, allowing them to regroup. Salt Lake was jealous of Ogden's vitality even after the war."[83]

During his final year as mayor, Peery hosted an event that seemed auspicious at the time but was actually a sobering harbinger of Ogden's future. The occasion was a banquet at the Ben Lomond Hotel to introduce Arthur Stoddard, new president of the Union Pacific Railroad, to the business community of northern Utah. Eighty-six-year-old John Farr was an honored guest and provided historical continuity. As a boy of five, he had watched the first Union Pacific engines steam into Ogden on March 8, 1869.

Rumors were flying that Ogden faced displacement as the Junction City and would be shunted onto a minor spur line, and that the Lucin Cutoff was being abandoned. Contributing to this fear, the Union Pacific's flagship streamliner, the City of Los Angeles, was now bypassing Ogden for Salt Lake. The ulterior motive for the banquet was gauging the Union Pacific's future attitude toward Ogden. Stoddard reassured his audience that Ogden was important to the Union Pacific and the railroad would remodel its local commissary and help the city acquire new industries. The icing on the cake was his announcement that the City of Los Angeles would resume its Ogden stops in two days.

But Stoddard's real message lurked in the statistics he cited, which were important to the entire country, not just Ogden. Passenger and freight rates had risen by 30 and 50 percent. Railroad taxes had skyrocketed by 170 percent and wages by 100 percent. Pressure to control costs would soon force railroads to implement significant cutbacks.[84]

What was really stymieing the railroads was competition from other forms of transportation, whose costs to individual travelers were falling as rail fares rose. Airline travel was faster, while automobile travel—aided by interstate freeway construction in the 1950s—allowed people to go almost anywhere, not just from one railroad station to another. All of these factors were drastically altering the nature of railroad commerce, the font of Ogden's viability since 1869.

Citizens' increasing mobility—through automobiles—and their increasing immobility—through television—meant they no longer saw downtown Ogden as essential for shopping or entertainment. Twenty-fifth Street endured for a few more years as northern Utah's chief source of guilty pleasures. However, stricter laws and more determined enforcement removed the street's attraction for the middle class, leaving it to deteriorate into a skid row.

In the immediate aftermath of the banquet for the Union Pacific president, however, Harman Peery was overjoyed that the elegant City of Los Angeles was again including Ogden on its itinerary. Many evenings he ensconced his five-year-old grandson in the passenger seat of his car, drove to Farr's on 21st Street for an ice cream cone, and then continued to the 31st Street overpass just in time to wave at the westbound City of Los Angeles as it approached Union Station at 6:20 p.m. The grandson recalls that the streamliner always blew its whistle in response, and the engineer announced to passengers that the mayor of Ogden was personally welcoming them. As soon as the City of Los Angeles passed, the two jumped back in the car and sped to Union Station, where Peery greeted the disembarking passengers and personnel. "He knew all the train people, engineers, conductors, porters, by name," remembers the grandson. "We were really seeing the last hurrah of passenger service in Ogden."[85]

CHAPTER SEVEN

OGDEN BLUSHED

She was simply a girl for whom love was a delightful experience and if her admirers wished to express their appreciation with gifts of pesos to buy presents, so much the better.

—Donna Mathewson, *Bananas Have No Bones*

Of all the scarlet women to inhabit 25th Street during its third heyday, none is more enshrined in legend than Rosetta Ducinnie Davie, proprietress of the Rose Rooms from 1948 to 1950. Gifted with alluring beauty, poise, and an eye for high fashion, Rosetta was a celebrity on the street, in the courts, and in the press.

In partnership with her suave husband, William Snede Davie—a dedicated bootlegger, gambler, and burglar—Rosetta presided over an empire of forbidden delights. The Davies were best known for four plush operations: the Rose Rooms at 25th Street and Lincoln Avenue and the Benevolent Hand Club in Farmington, both houses of prostitution; the Key Club, a miniature casino at 200½ 25th Street; and Club Zebra, a speakeasy at 225½ 25th. Each emporium's décor reflected Rosetta's passion for fabrics with jungle animal stripes or—in homage to her pet ocelot—spots.[1]

The Davies knew how to attract customers, and the gentlemen fought to get in. On weekends they lined up at the Rose Rooms' entrance at 205 25th Street in a queue that snaked all the way to Grant Avenue. An intercom buzzer opened the entrance door, and at the top of the stairway, a maid welcomed customers through another door fitted with a peephole. A cover charge admitted gentlemen to a waiting room where illegal liquor abounded and beautifully dressed women mingled . The ladies sat with customers and conversed but without any obligation. Rosetta circulated graciously and inquired if her young women tempted the visitors: "Can we help you out? Anything can be arranged." A third door led to bedrooms fitted for clients' pleasure. The bedrooms—deliberately narrow to squeeze in a maximum number of customers—lined the west side of the building, some with windows looking out onto Lincoln Avenue. The usual fee was five dollars.[2]

Public sensation that she was, Rosetta Davie was only the most visible half of the Rose Rooms' story. Its landlords, Louis and Giuseppina Prantil, owned the building for nearly six decades. Rosetta and the Prantils appeared to have little in common, but they shared a

If the lines to get into the Rose Rooms were as long as old-timers remember, they would have extended past the Helena Hotel and the Seven-Up Bottling Company. *Photo courtesy of Special Collections, Stewart Library, Weber State University.*

Rosetta Davie. *Photo courtesy of Kelli Garside McFarland.*

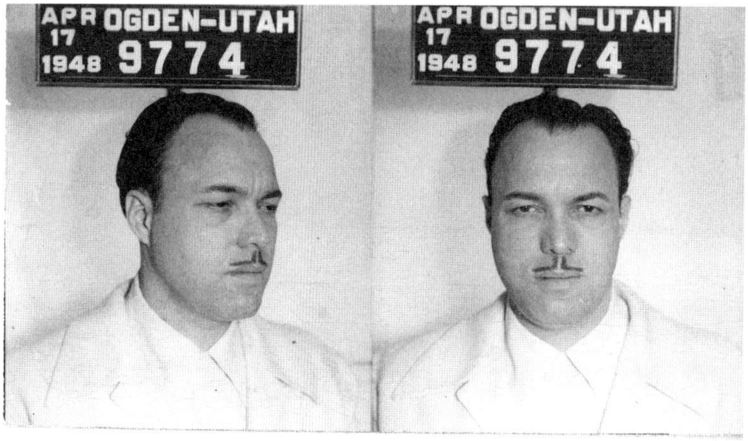

William Davie. *Photo courtesy of Kelli Garside McFarland.*

fierce determination to prosper in the face of relentless legal obstacles.

The Prantils were Austrian immigrants of Italian heritage. Their first known real-estate venture in Ogden was the Ray Hotel at 2456 Grant Avenue; they assumed its management in April 1923 after the previous landlady was convicted of pandering.[3] Here Louis Prantil learned the hard way that illegal liquor must be well hidden. (His subsequent ingenuity in concealing liquor was described in chapter five.) The vice squad was onto him and brought crowbars to tap on the Ray Hotel's walls, ceilings, and floors until a hollow sound in a hall floorboard led them to a cache of twelve pints of moonshine. Louis's defense in court was that Giuseppina was really the Ray's manager and the moonshine was not his. A jury deadlocked on his guilt, but rather than face a second trial, he pleaded guilty and paid a fine. His lawyer may have advised him that—as a persistent bootlegger with previous convictions—this was the easiest way out.[4]

The reputation of 205 25th Street was even worse than the Ray Hotel's. In 1919 the Ogden City Commission denied a rooming-house license to the Bamberger Hotel—then occupying 205's second floor—after Police Chief Thomas E. Browning's negative assessment. "This particular house," wrote Browning, "has been in bad repute for some time and is confined principally to the housing of Austrians and other foreigners. It has been reported that women of not the best character frequent the place."[5]

When the Prantils bought 205 in September 1923, its second floor housed the Troy Hotel. The first-floor tenant—the Harris Drug Company—was making ends meet through copious sales of paregoric: one hundred

The Prantils befriended a burro while visiting Argentina. *Photo courtesy of Joseph E. Prantil.*

Giuseppina and Louis Prantil. *Photo courtesy of Joseph E. Prantil.*

gallons in seventeen months when a normal drugstore might dispense two gallons in a year. A grand-jury indictment on narcotics violations shuttered Harris Drug, saddling Louis Prantil with a storeroom full of merchandise and fixtures. Another drugstore moved in, but within one year, its proprietor was arrested for employing no registered pharmacists and having a flask of whisky on the premises, which police could only reach after moving half a ton of coal away from a door.[6]

Frustrated by his tenants' poor records, Louis decided to run his own enterprises: a confectionery and cigar shop.[7] He also owned and operated the Utah Hot Springs on the Box Elder County line, where he was suspected of selling booze to minors. Authorities set up a sting operation where teenage boys purchased alcohol from Louis with marked bills. His name—he told the arresting officers—was Louis Smith.[8] Throughout the Prohibition years, he was arrested time and time again, avoiding convictions as a persistent violator by hiring good lawyers.[9]

The Troy Hotel gave way to the Rock Springs Hotel, which operated from 1929 until the February 1946 death of its proprietor, Alexander DeCorso.[10] The search for a new tenant led the Prantils—rather fatefully—to two sisters, Ada ArZella and Birdena Jackie Beveridge, whose business skills and flair for publicity forever altered and dominated public perception of 25th Street.[11] Each sister had multiple monikers, but Ada became most widely known as Rosetta Ducinnie Davie.

Ada was born in Benecia, California, on November 28, 1918. Her parents were John "Jack" Beveridge, a railroad man, and the former Midora Gladys Wilkins, a sixteen-year-old Mormon whose pioneer forbears emigrated from England and Denmark.[12] Midora preferred to be called Donna, and Ada eventually started calling herself Rosetta. Her sister, Birdena Jackie, or Birdie, was two years younger.

During the early 1930s, the sisters attended Salt Lake City schools while Donna worked at a beauty salon. Her

The Prantils' Lincoln Confectionery at 205 25th Street in 1933. The Rose Rooms occupied the second floor from 1948 to 1950. *Photo courtesy of Special Collections, Stewart Library, Weber State University.*

The building at 2512 Lincoln Avenue (once known as the Bamberger Depot) with the former Rose Rooms adjacent on the left on the second floor in 1952. *Photo courtesy of Special Collections, Stewart Library, Weber State University.*

favorite clients were professional wrestlers, including Salt Lake's Leo Papiano ("the Grecian Bone Crusher"), whose nails she polished.[13] In 1937 Donna acquired a new husband, Ogden widower Paul Mathewson.[14] She and her daughters were very close. Ada relied heavily on her mother and Birdie in future business ventures.

Both sisters migrated to 25th Street during World War II, not as ladies of the evening but married women.[15] Birdie was the first to take a spouse. Her husband, William J. Leatherwood, had a lengthy Ogden rap sheet as a thief and accessory to arson. By 1944 Birdie was a divorcée with two sons, living at 2512 Lincoln Avenue, adjacent to the future Rose Rooms.[16] Ada—giving her name as Rosetta Ducinnie—married Chester Shaw Frost, a burglar and drug addict, in September 1941. That marriage lasted four months.[17]

In January 1945, under her legal name Ada ArZella Beveridge, Rosetta married Michael Seaman of 205 25th Street (then the Rock Springs Hotel), which apparently became their home.[18] In March 1947, she had the marriage annulled, claiming Seaman was a bigamist.[19] Seaman remained in Ogden and—not long after the annulment—struck Birdie during an argument. She sued him, asking five thousand dollars in damages for permanent injuries.[20] Seaman filed his own suit against Rosetta, claiming he had her promissory note for sixty-five hundred dollars and she had stopped making installment payments.[21]

The Prantils and Rosetta (giving her surname as Seaman) signed a five-year lease for the second floor of 205 25th Street on January 3, 1947. Later, Rosetta apparently assigned the lease to Birdie. The sisters may have operated the second floor as an ordinary rooming house for the first year. Classified ads for "clean sleeping rooms" at 205 25th Street, a "private rooming house," appeared soon after Rosetta's March 1947 annulment of her marriage to Michael Seaman. There was still at least one male tenant at the end of 1947.[22] Not until May 1, 1948, did the name Rose Rooms blaze into public consciousness based on a scandal at the Weber Wildlife Federation's "jollification" party inside the Ogden Livestock Show Coliseum.

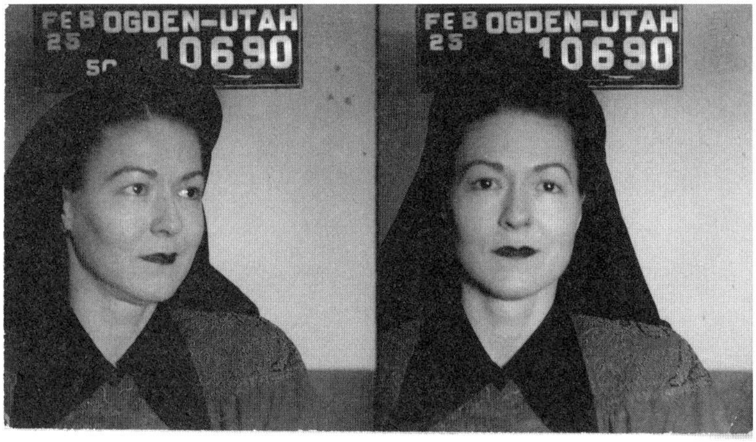

During a November 12, 1948, raid on several 25th Street rooming houses, Velma (or Thelma) Waldman was arrested for operating the Wilson Rooms at 320½ 25th. She was arrested again on February 25, 1950, on the same charge in the same house. *Photo courtesy of Kelli Garside McFarland.*

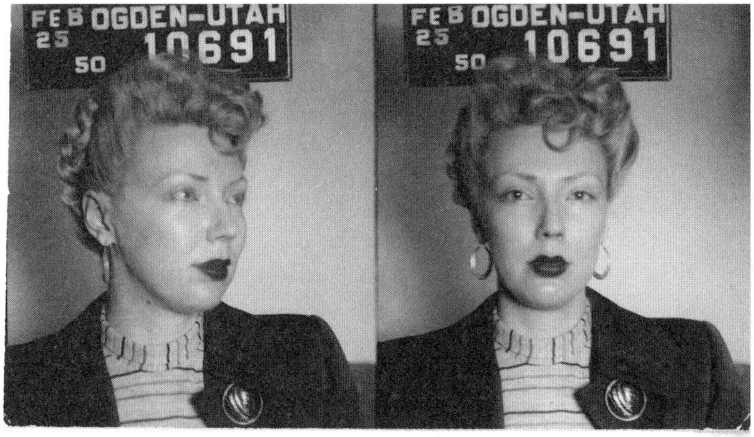

Mickey Wilson was arrested in a February 25, 1950, raid on the Wilson Rooms. *Photo courtesy of Kelli Garside McFarland.*

Over the years, the Wildlife Federation's annual jollification had offered saucy entertainment for male audiences. Kicking off the 1948 show, the Dorianaires—Weber College's renowned barbershop quartet—attempted the old razzle-dazzle, but the stag-minded audience had different expectations. Three female strippers hired as the grand finale had stoked the crowd's unruliness by passing around matchbooks bearing the Rose Rooms' logo and address. The matchbooks' reverse side had a picture of a woman in scanties and the slogan, "Come Again Soon." The strippers had also written their names in ink on the matchbooks.[23]

Weber College straw-hatters Laurence Burton and Dean Hurst—in a song-and-patter routine—summoned all their charisma to break the proverbial leg, but the wildlife buffs hurled bottles on the stage and hollered "bring on the girls!" Police hurried to the Coliseum and arrested not the bottle throwers but the strippers.[24] Three days later, the Ogden City Commission punished the Rose Rooms by revoking its rooming license.[25]

Right after the Wildlife wingding, both William and Rosetta Davie made their debut in the headlines as notorious local personalities. Exactly what led William Davie to Ogden—if not Rosetta—is unknown. Born in 1908, he was ten years older than the age he consistently gave to Ogden police. He was the son of an American doctor and Mexican mother, and his uncle, José, was a Catholic priest in Mexico. Birdie later recalled that both her mother and Rosetta "liked things with a Mexican slant."[26]

Davie became a public figure following an attempted burglary of a Firestone tire store on Washington Boulevard. A policeman arrested him as he tried to carry off a bundle of merchandise. He gave his address as 205 25th Street. (Perhaps he and Rosetta were already married.) The burglary case was ultimately dismissed for insufficient evidence.[27]

An arrest inside the Rose Rooms launched Rosetta into the news, not on a morals charge but on possession and distribution of narcotics. An undercover agent purchased opium, papine (a morphine sulfate), and bichloride of mercury from her with marked bills. She gave her name as Rosetta Ducinnie, not Davie. Authorities said they hoped Rosetta's arrest would help them identify leaders of a local narcotics ring, but they never determined who her source was.[28] Much later an acquaintance revealed Rosetta's drug supplier was Dr. Roger Brown, an Ogden physician.[29]

When the Ogden City Commission reconsidered its revocation of the Rose Rooms' license, it was not Rosetta—who had a previous engagement (a preliminary hearing on her narcotics charge)—but Birdie who showed up to plead their case. "I don't feel I should be penalized at my rooming house because of some girl tenants," Birdie argued, displaying matchbooks from other 25th Street rooming houses that invited patronage.[30] Despite Birdie's eloquence, the Rose Rooms' license was never restored.

Authorities raided 25th Street's rooming houses many more times in 1948, especially the Rose Rooms. On November 12, they arrested Jean Taylor, one of the Wildlife Federation strippers, for operating the Rose Rooms while Rosetta was in jail.[31] The following month, four women at the Rose Rooms told police they were part of a California-based prostitution ring that sent women deemed too old for Los Angeles to the Intermountain West. In the same raid, Rosetta—freshly paroled from her narcotics conviction—was booked for violating that parole.[32] Despite these numerous raids, Police Chief Maurice Schooff said he had been assured the Rose Rooms was now strictly a private residence, and visits by police had not uncovered evidence of prostitution.[33]

As Rosetta stirred up one scandal after another, her mother's marriage was collapsing. The timing of Paul Mathewson's divorce action against Donna in October 1948 suggests a certain discomfort with his stepdaughter's notoriety.[34]

Discomfort also suffused the county attorney's office as it monitored the raids. On December 21, 1948, the office sent a notice to Giuseppina Prantil, who was newly widowed, citing the Rose Rooms as a public nuisance and threatening an injunction if she did not correct the situation. A second notice followed on February 8, 1949, informing Giuseppina that the nuisance was continuing. Thus goaded, Giuseppina filed a complaint against her tenants, Rosetta and Birdena, demanding an end to prostitution at the Rose Rooms.[35]

William Davie, meanwhile, further blackened the Rose Rooms' reputation through an ill-advised public scrape. Sol Kaplan, a clothing salesman who lived kitty-corner from the Rose Rooms in the Milner Hotel, told police that William knocked him down in the post office, punched him in front of the American Eagle Café at 260 25th Street, and chased him across Washington Boulevard. The press reported no specific provocation for the attack but implied that Kaplan had called Davie a pimp. When Chief Schooff and an officer appeared at the Rose Rooms looking for William, three prostitutes solicited them.[36]

In spite of Giuseppina Prantil's lawsuit and William Davie's indiscretion, the Rose Rooms tried again to restore its license in July 1949. By then, however, the house's mere existence was so politically perilous that even jaded Mayor Harman Peery voted with the Ogden City Commission to deny its license and start injunction proceedings against Giuseppina and Rosetta.[37] The city commission asked Chief Schooff to confiscate the Rose Rooms' sign, but he refused, reminding them the city

William Davie's Key Club operated on the second floor of 200 25th Street from 1949 to 1950. *Photo courtesy of Special Collections, Stewart Library, Weber State University.*

could be liable for damages.[38] Finally, the state filed an injunction against Giuseppina Prantil, Rosetta and William Davie, and Birdie Nance on July 28, 1949.[39] District Judge John Hendricks dismissed the case against Giuseppina on October 4, but two weeks later, he issued a temporary restraining order that theoretically padlocked the Rose Rooms for one year.[40]

But the Rose Rooms blithely ignored the injunction and—owing to bureaucratic bungling—operated relatively freely and prosperously for almost another year. The Davies later maintained that they never received the temporary injunction, and Judge Hendricks blamed Sheriff Wade and the county attorney—both of whom were preoccupied with running reelection campaigns in 1950—for losing interest in the case.[41] Ogden police knew perfectly well that business at the Rose Rooms was booming; they dropped by for occasional vice checks but left the Davies untouched.

During a sergeant's visit in December 1949, Rosetta showed off a fairly sophisticated electronic eavesdropping system that allowed her to monitor her ladies. In each bedroom, a microphone hung in a corner near the ceiling, connected to speakers in Rosetta's private living room and kitchen. She knew if the women pleased the men, if the men became abusive, and if the women were chiseling on her by withholding portions of customers' fees.[42]

During one visit, Deputy Sheriff Raymond Jones asked Rosetta how she recruited her working women. "I didn't," she answered. "They come to me." The Davies, reported City Attorney Paul Thatcher, "brought their girls in from Nevada and San Francisco, particularly the latter where Mrs. Davie worked as a prostitute for some time and is said to have connections. One informer [an airport employee] said Mrs. Davie had regularly met planes from San Francisco at the Ogden airport [transporting] girls whom she took to the Rose Rooms."[43]

The sheriff's department hinted at possible reasons for the Davies' impunity. Sheriff Wade acknowledged "indications" of payoffs for police protection by "certain unlawful establishments" and promised to investigate.[44] Much later, Deputy Raymond Jones revealed that William Davie was a valuable informant. "He knew all the crooks in Utah, and in the country, and those who may have come to Ogden to cool off until the heat was off," recalled Jones. "He helped us track down crooks, especially those with Montana connections."[45]

Rosetta was also an informant. She told police in January 1949 that Eddie Doherty "had two girls working the bars and cafés for customers." The police rounded up these two women, one of whom was Doherty's common-law wife, Frances Neff, and "put them on an eastbound bus, informing them never to come back."[46]

The Davies earned sixteen thousand dollars in 1949—mostly from the Rose Rooms and the Key Club—as a

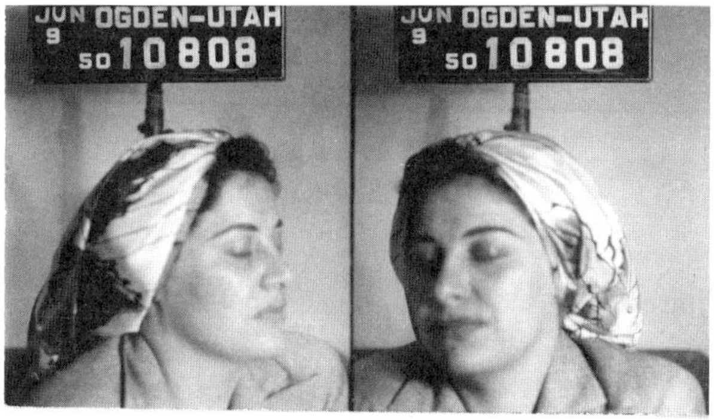

Mary Apollo a.k.a. Rose Chavez, one of four women arrested for vagrancy and soliciting at the Benevolent Hand Club. As Rose Chavez, she had been arrested for lewd and lascivious conduct at the La Siesta Hotel at 225½ 25th Street on January 19, 1949. *Photo courtesy of Kelli Garside McFarland.*

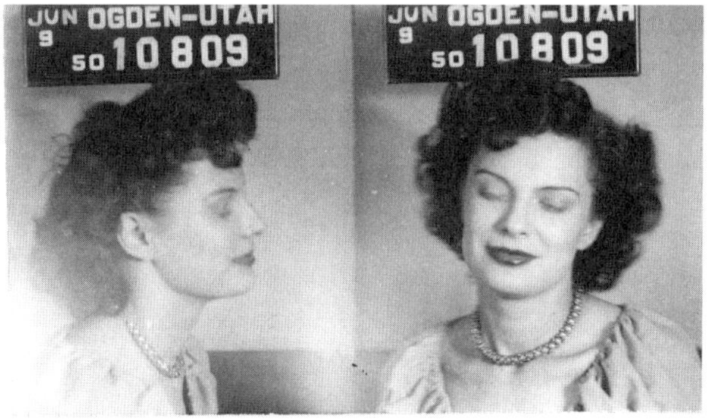

Virginia Lamson of the Benevolent Hand Club. Under the alias Candice Richards, she solicited Police Chief Maurice Schooff when he came to the Rose Rooms looking for William Davie on July 2, 1949. *Photo courtesy of Kelli Garside McFarland.*

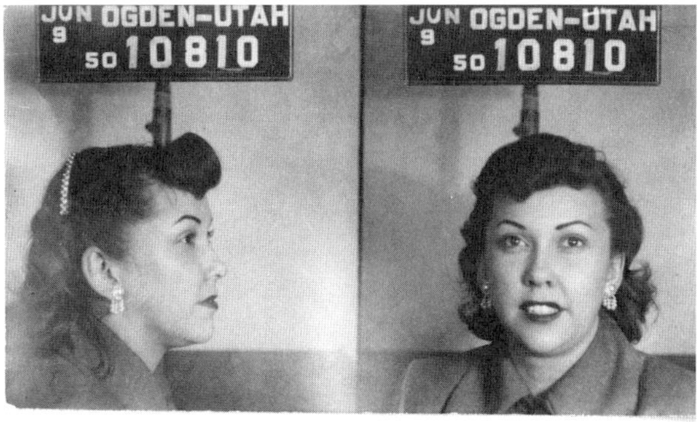

Betty Baker of the Benevolent Hand Club. *Photo courtesy of Kelli Garside McFarland.*

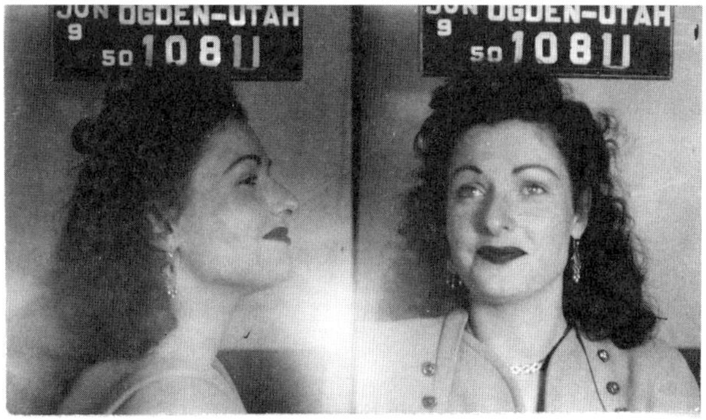

Marlene O'Day of the Benevolent Hand Club. *Photo courtesy of Kelli Garside McFarland.*

later tax-evasion case revealed.[47] Flush with cash, they expanded into Davis County, leasing a barn on a remote stretch of Burke Lane (675 North) west of Farmington from Ogden dairyman Ezra Moroni Peterson. They renovated and lavishly decorated the barn and christened it the Benevolent Hand Club.[48]

Maurice Richards—the Davies' lawyer until he became Weber County attorney—said the Benevolent Hand was "the most luxurious cathouse you ever saw in your life," equipped with a lounge area and bar and six bedrooms, each with a private bathroom. It had its own power-generating plant. Davis High School students riding the bus from Centerville to Kaysville snickered as they passed signs on the main highway pointing the way to the club that depicted a man's and woman's hand entwined.[49] Richards said it was impossible during those heady days to hail a taxi in Ogden or Salt Lake for ordinary business because the cabs were chauffeuring gentlemen to the Farmington compound.[50]

Jeanette Lewis a.k.a. Sarah Roe. When arrested for prostitution at the Rose Rooms on July 23, 1950, she was a brunette. *Photo courtesy of Kelli Garside McFarland.*

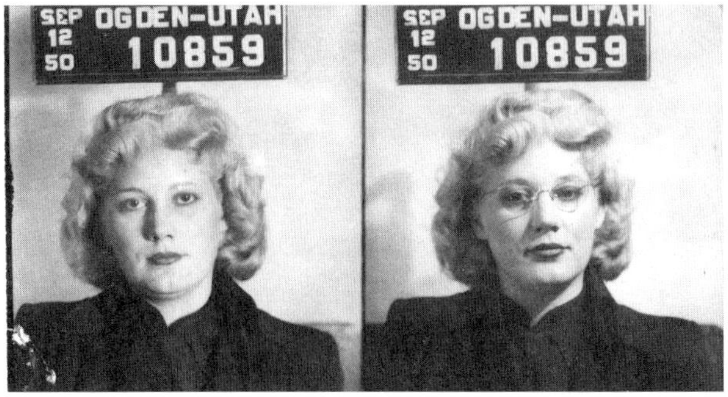

Jeanette Lewis after becoming a blonde. She was acquitted when Juan Mandonado could not identify her. *Photo courtesy of Kelli Garside McFarland.*

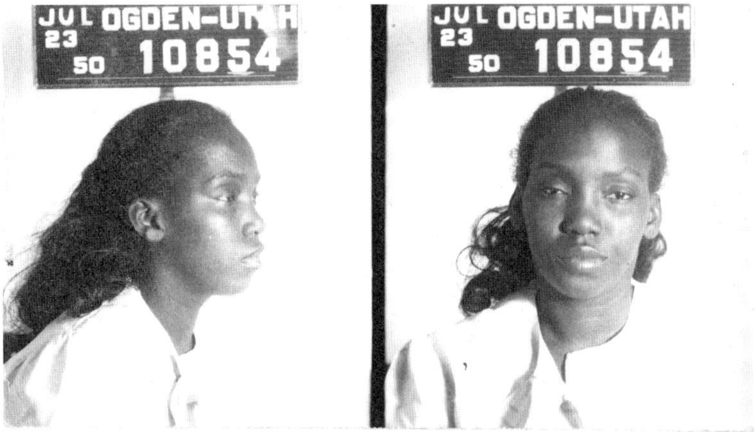

Addie Davis a.k.a. Elizabeth Mike was the Rose Rooms doorkeeper. Davis was arrested in the Benevolent Hand Club raid for selling illegal liquor but was not photographed. This mug shot followed her arrest in the Rose Rooms on July 23, 1950, on charges of keeping, managing, and caring for a house of ill fame. *Photo courtesy of Kelli Garside McFarland.*

But luck would not be a lady to Rosetta and William Davie in 1950 when authorities staged three game-changing raids against them. The first came on April 29, when Ogden police visited the Key Club at 200½ 25th Street,[51] a luxuriously furnished gambling resort that William ran with his partners, the Estrada brothers: Johnny, Frank, and David. William hired a professional gambler, "Frisco" Lee, to run the card games and a local thug, Tommy Moore, as the bouncer.

Since the previous summer, the Key Club had attracted poker players and craps shooters from Weber County and Hill Field, but it was also a haunt of prostitutes and pimps, who drank and gambled together. David Estrada was convicted in February 1950 of carnal knowledge of a minor girl at the Key Club; his testimony during his trial established that—in violation of the club's state charter—its gambling and liquor sales were clearly for profit. Thus enlightened, city and state officials became keen to close it.[52]

Four policemen stole into the Key Club on the heels of two customers who were buzzed in after ringing a bell. Eight more officers came in quietly after the first four. Detective Arlyn "Lynn" Garside, who was developing a special interest in the Davies, entered the main gambling room and watched a twenty-one game for a few minutes before he was recognized. The police seized gambling equipment, ripped out the buzzer system, and arrested William Davie, the other managers, and forty customers.[53] In a conversation with Garside in front of the Key Club later that month, Davie said he wished he "had something" on Garside and would not hesitate to use it to pay the detective back for the trouble he had caused.[54]

The next raid—on the Benevolent Hand Club—came late at night on June 9 when three Davis County deputy sheriffs disguised as ranchers ambled into the gilded barn, bought hard liquor, and flirted with women who offered sexual favors for a price. Crouched outside were five other deputies who soon followed on the rancher impersonators' heels and put a damper on the evening by arresting Rosetta and William Davie, four prostitutes, and a bartender. Eight male customers were questioned and released. A search of Rosetta's purse yielded $483 in cash, a bulging address book, and a .22-caliber pistol. Deputies padlocked the premises before leaving.[55]

Investigators found that the Benevolent Hand Club's incorporation papers had been filed with the Davis County clerk just two days before the raid. The club's stated purposes were "to encourage and foster high ideals among members for justice and patriotism" and "to promote the principles and objectives of the democratic form of government." The club's officers were listed as ArZella Perrie (yet another of Rosetta's pseudonyms), chairman; Birdena Nance, vice chairman; Donna Mathewson (their mother), treasurer; Grant Sprunt (an Ogden cab driver, Iwo Jima veteran, burglar, and Birdie's then-boyfriend), secretary; and Elizabeth Mike (a.k.a. Addie Davis, maid and doorkeeper at the Rose Rooms), director.[56]

The third raid, on the Rose Rooms, came after weeks of surveillance by Ogden police. In the early morning of July 23, Detective Garside and another officer arrived at the Rose Rooms and arrested Rosetta and her loyal housekeeper, Addie Davis; Jeanette Lewis, a prostitute; two military men, who were turned over to their superiors at Hill Field; and Tommy Moore, former bouncer at the Key Club, now charged with procuring.[57] William Davie—whose whereabouts that morning were unclear—was charged with lodging in a house of prostitution.[58] The Rose Rooms may have ceased to operate as a brothel at this time because no subsequent raid was reported in the media.

Club Zebra operated on the second floor of the center buildings, 227 25th Street, in 1951; the space's previous tenant was the La Siesta Hotel. The photo was taken in 1933. *Photo courtesy of Special Collections, Stewart Library, Weber State University.*

With the heat on, the Davies' usual composure began to fray. Detective Garside's notes on this raid say that Rosetta warned him she would find a way to embarrass him if it was the last thing she did. When he returned to the Rose Rooms two weeks later to serve additional warrants, William Davie told him, "I don't like this. This is making me mad, and that ain't good." Later that evening Davie called Police Chief Schooff to say he was ready to put a "G-note," or thousand-dollar bill, on Garside, which meant he intended to have the detective framed, or even bumped off.

Within the next few days, Garside's wife received several telephone calls reporting the detective had been observed with other girls. One call came from a woman who was eager to tell all about herself and the detective. Mrs. Garside also spotted an unfamiliar man and woman trying to peer into the windows of her house. "Those two people," Garside wrote, "is [*sic*] believed to be Grant Sprunt and Birdena (sister of Rosetta Davie)."[59]

The three attention-getting raids were followed by three high-profile trials. First was the Benevolent Hand Club case in Farmington. Among fifteen witnesses, the principals were the three deputies who had posed as ranchers. After two days of testimony, the jury found Rosetta and William Davie guilty of operating a house of ill fame.[60]

Ogden, unlike Davis County, prosecuted Rosetta and William separately on Rose Room charges. Rosetta's Ogden trial began less than a week after her Benevolent Hand Club conviction. Witnesses included a radio repairman, who described the Rose Rooms' microphone eavesdropping system; a cab driver, who said a maid (Addie Davis) gave him a commission of one dollar on each five-dollar fee; and Utah Power and Light's John L. Shorten, who testified that electricity at 205 25th Street was billed to Rosetta Davie. Customers who testified to sexual transactions with prostitutes included military men and rodeo impresarios; Lester Muir, a World War II veteran from Davis County; and, surprisingly, Juan Mandonado of Rock Springs, Wyoming, who had misidentified the Rose Rooms' Jeanette Lewis in an earlier trial but now been coached into reliability.[61]

Rosetta's longtime attorney for morals infractions, John F. Wahlquist, had been called to serve in the army's Judge Advocate General's Corps for the duration of the Korean War and withdrew before the Ogden trial.[62] Her new Salt Lake City lawyers presented no witnesses and introduced no exhibits; they merely argued that the Rose Rooms was not a house of prostitution. After three days in court, Rosetta was convicted but remained free on bail of twenty-five hundred dollars.[63]

One day after Rosetta's Ogden verdict, she and William were back in court in Farmington, where Judge Hendricks sentenced both to 360 days in jail. After they announced their intention to appeal, Hendricks upped their bail from one thousand to five thousand dollars apiece. Both spent the night in the Davis County jail. Rosetta told the press her bed was too hard. "I am used to more luxury," she confessed. By morning the Davies had raised the expensive bail and were released.[64]

In a surprise development, Judge Hendricks reopened the Benevolent Hand case one week later, not for further proceedings against the Davies but to gather new evidence on statements by Weber County Chief Deputy Sheriff Jack Card. The judge grilled Card relentlessly over the statements: an alleged threat by William Davie to shoot Davis County Sheriff Hess "when this is all over" because Davie had paid Hess to run for the office, and a suggestion that Hendricks himself was taking protection money from 25th Street. Card emphatically denied making the statements. His boss, Sheriff Wade, accused Hendricks of personal animosity toward the sheriff's department.[65]

Although their most sensational trials were behind them, the Davies' troubles were just beginning. William's guilty plea in February 1951 to operating the Rose Rooms as a house of ill fame reminded Judge Hendricks of his temporary injunction of October 4, 1949. From William's admission of guilt and Rosetta's Ogden conviction, it was now obvious that they had flouted the injunction.[66] Hendricks fined them five hundred dollars each for contempt of court. Because the Davies could not immediately pay, Hendricks ordered their new Lincoln convertible seized and auctioned, but prior liens against the car prevented its sale. Then Hendricks ordered their refrigerator, freezer, and gas stove seized.[67] Rosetta's scramble to secure the cash was successful, however, and the car and appliances were returned.[68]

Even with multiple jail sentences and thousands of dollars in bail, fines, and legal fees threatening them, the Davies could not resist opening a new venture, a speakeasy dubbed Club Zebra, one door east of 25th Street's Star Noodle Parlor.[69] Club Zebra's festive clientele danced enthusiastically to live organ music and imbibed gin and whiskey, but the fun could not last. It was one of many charter clubs that Mayor Rulon White lamented had "broken out like a rash" in Ogden since a Salt Lake City judge ruled that the locker system—where private clubs labeled and stored members' liquor on-site—was legal in Utah.[70] Utah Representative George Frost of Ogden called the locker system in Ogden "a contemptible disguise to cover up what amounts to sale of liquor by the drink."[71]

Not surprisingly, city hall's displeasure prompted the largest post-Prohibition raid in Utah history on March 31, 1951—a "knockout blow," according to Mayor White. Along with three other charter clubs on 25th Street that were selling illegal liquor, Club Zebra was shut down, and its furnishings and equipment were seized. Ogden police found William Davie himself behind the swanky club's bar, dapper in a double-breasted suit. Rosetta stood at the foot of the stairs, glowering, as all Club Zebra's employees, including her sister, Birdie, were arrested.

Donna Mathewson, mother of Rosetta Davie, was an author and member of the Utah Writers League. *Photo from Comet Press Books in the author's collection.*

As police busied themselves labeling the club's bottle supply, customers danced, oblivious to the commotion.[72]

Club Zebra proved to be the Davies' last stand. William's trial on the year-old Key Club gambling charges—the third and last trial stemming from the 1950 raids—finally began on May 15, 1951, providing sensational testimony on crooked card games, drunken patrons, and brawls.[73] Convicted and sentenced to five years in state prison, William was locked up in the Weber County jail as soon as the judge's gavel fell.[74] Rosetta visited him daily, bringing baskets of gourmet food from nearby Washington Market, where she had taken a job.[75] But her devotion came to a halt on June 14, 1951, when she surrendered to deputies to begin her one-year Benevolent Hand Club sentence. She served her time in Weber County's jail since Davis County had no facility for female prisoners.[76]

The Davies' incarceration prompted a municipal farce that summer because it aggravated a chronic feud between Judge Hendricks and Weber County Sheriff Mac Wade. Hendricks was indignant to learn that an outside source was supplying William Davie with special meals, freshly laundered sporting clothes, and shined shoes and that his cell was on the ground floor, right next to Wade's office. During a hearing on the Club Zebra charges—with Rosetta and William in attendance—Hendricks ordered William moved to the ninth floor with the other prisoners and shouted—for emphasis—"Right now!" But within two days, Wade had William returned to the ground floor. A visibly enraged Hendricks arrived at the jail and told William he would get no credit for time served as long as he was downstairs.[77]

After three months of Sheriff Wade's "valet service," Hendricks told William his time to appeal his Key Club conviction had run out and gave deputies thirty minutes to clear his cell and get him on the road to state prison. They brought Rosetta down from the ninth floor to say good-bye.[78] Aside from joint court appearances, Rosetta and William did not see each other again until 1954, after she had served all her sentences and could visit him in prison. He was not present in court when she pleaded guilty to the Club Zebra nuisance charges three days later.[79]

The Junior Chamber of Commerce's (Jaycees) annual Roosters' Roast that fall revealed how much the Davies' perceived lavish lifestyle dominated cocktail conversation in Ogden. Among other skits lampooning local politicos, thespian Jaycees portrayed an obsequious Sheriff Wade opening beer bottles and running errands for William Davie, who had appropriated Wade's office as his personal jail cell. While Wade bustled about at William's command, he took a phone call from Judge Hendricks, who was desperately seeking the key endorsement of William Davie for membership in the Weber Club.[80]

Seven months after Rosetta was locked up, the State of Utah Board of Pardons refused to commute any of her sentences, even though Sheriff Wade and her attorney vouched for her as a "very model" prisoner.[81] For good behavior, her Benevolent Hand and Rose Rooms sentences were reduced, and she worked for the sheriff's department processing criminal records, taking breaks for fresh air in the municipal gardens while clad in a light orange prison jumpsuit.[82] However, she spent portions of 1952 in St. Benedict's Hospital following orders from the county physician and getting treatment for ulcers and other unidentified medical conditions.[83]

In December 1952, Rosetta and William Davie were tried and convicted in federal court for income-tax evasion.[84] Two months later—after she completed her two shortened sentences in the Weber County jail—Rosetta left immediately for the women's federal penitentiary in West Virginia to serve her one-year tax-evasion sentence.[85]

During Rosetta's absence, her mother, Donna Mathewson, who now lived in the defunct Rose Rooms, wrote a letter to the *Ogden Standard-Examiner* chiding her fellow Ogdenites for poor attendance at the weekly free organ recitals at the local Mormon Tabernacle.[86]

Soon after Rosetta's return from West Virginia, she reclaimed her former prominence in Ogden's headlines when a federal narcotics agent and Detective Garside arrested her and three friends from 25th Street as their car approached the mouth of Weber Canyon. A grand-jury indictment charged them with buying dilaudid tablets, an industrial-strength painkiller, from a doctor in Evanston, Wyoming, for "other than a legitimate medical purpose."[87] Rosetta's sister, Birdie, was also in considerable trouble, accused of performing an illegal abortion on a divorcée, Mrs. Evva Bruce, and held up to public scorn on the front page of the *Ogden Standard-Examiner*.[88] Both sisters sought the help of Ogden attorney L. G. Bingham.

In both cases, Bingham's strategy was to portray Detective Garside as having a personal agenda against the women. During Birdie's trial, Garside denied under Bingham's cross-examination that he had said he intended "to clean out that family." But the detective had earlier acknowledged investigating Rosetta's 1950 Rose Rooms case. "Who is Rosetta Davie?" asked Bingham. Garside replied he could "best describe" Rosetta "as the sister of the defendant."[89] "I wanted to make sure," Bingham recalled much later, "that the jury knew Garside knew Rosetta, that he was dedicated to getting Rosetta through her sister."[90] Birdie was acquitted.

Bingham also got Rosetta acquitted of the narcotics charge. "I kept trying," he says,

> to find what probable cause Garside had. He'd had no warrant. He gave illegal "silver platter" evidence to the feds, and they could use it if it was not obtained by a fed. Silver platter evidence hadn't yet been overruled. Garside had a number of those cases. The judge called the jury back in and told them to acquit Rosetta. I can't really say she was framed, but I was suspicious.[91]

On Rosetta's initial consultation with Bingham, he told her to call him L. G. "She replied, 'You can call me Rosetta, and I'll call you Mr. Bingham. I'm hiring you as my lawyer, not as my friend.' And she didn't say it rudely," the attorney remembers. "Once my wife met her in my reception room and they talked for half an hour. My wife thought she was wonderful. Another time I traveled to Las Vegas to represent Rosetta. My wife was jealous of some of my other clients, but never of Rosetta."[92]

With William still in state prison and facing another year in the Leavenworth, Kansas, federal prison for tax evasion, Rosetta found herself with time on her hands. She typed the manuscript for *Down Mexico Way,* her mother's 1956 book on travels south of the border, published by Comet Press in New York.[93] When William finally did get out of jail, he and Rosetta felt their talents were only wasted in Ogden. In 1958 they were arrested in Reno, Nevada, for burglarizing a private residence.[94] The following year William was apprehended in Texas for an armed robbery committed in Las Vegas.[95] So Rosetta typed a second manuscript for her mother, *Bananas Have No Bones* (1960), a sequel to the earlier Mexico travelogue.[96]

Maurice Richards recalled that the Davies eventually settled down in Las Vegas, where Rosetta managed a casino and William became a gardener at a major hotel.[97] In 1976 a Pocatello, Idaho, newspaper carried a notice of William's divorce from Rosetta.[98] She died in 1980 in Mexico, and he died two years later in the San Francisco Bay area.[99]

Despite Rosetta's reputation for glamour and high living, running the Rose Rooms was no bed of roses. From 1948, when she first hung out her shingle, to 1955, her last major entanglement with the law in Ogden, Rosetta spent more time in courtrooms or jail than she did as a free woman. Her fame equaled Belle London's of half a century before, and she was an equally smart manager. But a much-expanded criminal code and changes in society's expectations of law enforcement made it impossible for her career to have the longevity or political clout that London's did. Twenty-fifth Street had seen the last of its red-hot madams.

The Rose Rooms' home, 205 25th Street, remained in Giuseppina Prantil's hands until she died in 1982 at ninety-four; it then passed to her son and daughter.[100] Since 1977—when a Utah State Historic Sites survey listed the street's historic buildings—205 25th Street has been called the C. C. Keller Building after a nineteenth-century tenant.[101] Bruce Edwards, its owner in the first decade of the twenty-first century, received an award in 2005 from the Utah Heritage Foundation for restoring it.[102]

Without Rosetta Davie to keep it in the public eye, the Keller Building's high visibility ebbed. During the 1950s, its first-floor tenant was El Borracho, a bar patronized by Latinos. El Borracho's reputation as unruly and dangerous contributed to the perception that 25th Street must be cleaned up. This was Ogden's policy toward the street throughout the next quarter century.

CHAPTER EIGHT

OGDEN SHRUGGED

Such disorderly combats with evil produce no permanent good...a city is usually in worse condition after it has been "cleaned up" than it was before....The Puritans who finance such enterprises get their thrills, not out of any possible obliteration of vice, but out of the galloping pursuit of the vicious.

—H. L. Mencken, *A Book of Prefaces*

One of Ogden's most tenacious legends is that 25th Street was cleaned up in the 1950s. Tradition attributes the cleanup to Mac Wade, Weber County sheriff; Jack Card, Wade's chief deputy; Rulon White, mayor of Ogden; and Maurice Richards, county attorney.

The cleanup's cast of characters coalesced in the postwar years. Wade, a farmer, deputy game warden, and chair of the Weber Wildlife Federation's law-enforcement committee, was elected sheriff in 1946.[1] As a longtime local baseball-team manager, he knew Jack Card, an Ogden pitcher who had played for the St. Louis Cardinals, and recruited him as a deputy.[2] He promoted Card to chief deputy three years later.[3] Rulon White was elected mayor of Ogden in November 1949.[4] Maurice Richards, a young lawyer specializing in criminal defense, won the race for Weber County attorney in November 1950.

Wade's first year as sheriff was quiet. He later said he needed to learn the ropes, train his deputies, and find out who the local criminals were. In 1948, however, he sprang into action, announcing a program of systematic raids on Ogden's gambling joints and warning that he would not stop until he had driven their operators out of town. The sheriff's large flatbed truck could be spotted backed up to illegal operations' doors as deputies carted out expensive and heavy dice and blackjack tables and other equipment. He claimed an influx of big-time gambling men from Montana, Idaho, and Wyoming had invaded Ogden in the wake of Harman Peery's mayoral victory in November 1947: "That's why no arrests were made before,"[5] he said.

Rulon White, a former speaker of the Utah House of Representatives, succeeded Harman Peery as mayor with an agenda highly focused on crime. Just days after being sworn in, White dispatched Police Chief Maurice Schooff to warn brothels and gambling joints that they must close. Schooff reported that some proprietors "felt the move was inevitable under the new city

Sheriff Mac Wade (center) and deputies Blaine Farr (left) and Ray Gibson (right) inspect a 12-gauge shotgun and other items recovered from a Plain City robbery, March 1954. *Photo courtesy of Special Collections, Stewart Library, Weber State University.*

administration." As the Korean War escalated late in 1950, the army warned it would crack down on any prostitution near Ogden's military installations. "We feel," responded Mayor White, "that our ten months of effort to close down houses of prostitution, gambling joints and other commercial vice operations in Ogden [have] been thorough." Venereal disease statistics from the Utah State Board of Health seemed to validate Mayor White's claim; Ogden's case total for 1950 had dropped sharply from the previous three years.[6]

The proliferation of private clubs in Ogden during 1950 particularly rankled Mayor White. Fifteen or more of these clubs were selling illegal liquor and shielding themselves from police surveillance through their state charters. One proprietor boldly sent membership cards to Mayor White and Chief Schooff.[7] White finally persuaded Utah's liquor commission to investigate and issue search-and-seizure warrants, enabling the March 31, 1951, raid that brought down William Davie's Club Zebra and others on 25th Street. Utah's secretary of state agreed not to rubber-stamp charter applications but to hold hearings in Ogden before granting any more.[8]

Ogden's alignment of crime-busting public officials was complete once Maurice Richards was sworn in as county attorney on January 1, 1951. "Twenty-fifth Street was as dissolute and dangerous as any three-block street in America," said Richards, recalling his impression of the city in 1949 when he returned from Yale Law School.

> After trying a whole lot of criminal cases I came to feel that our police department—a lot of its people—was corrupt. When I became county attorney, I told Mayor White I was going to clean up the city. He just gave me carte blanche. Mac Wade was a great sheriff, and Jack Card was fearless. Jack usually fronted every raid, would crash down the door, sell everything in the joint, bundle the prostitutes out of town.[9]

Of all these reformers, it is Mac Wade whose legend has endured. By the time Wade was turned out of office in the election of 1954, most of 25th Street's higher-profile criminals had fled. Eight months elapsed before the new sheriff, LeRoy Hadley, could ferret out his first gambling den, and that was in Ogden Canyon, not in town.[10]

Wade's impressive arrest and closed-case statistics created effective campaign literature, but some citizens may have wondered if the street was better off in its new vice-free guise. And once cleaned up, would it stay that way? Had Wade's anticrime crusade conformed to notions of fairness? Moreover, Ogden's railroad-passenger business—the lifeblood of 25th Street—was beginning its long slide into oblivion. Would the loss of this economic cornerstone have brought about the same reduction in illegal gambling, liquor sales, and prostitution as time went on?

Historians have focused on Wade's activities as sheriff but not as politician. While some admired the sheriff's February 1948 blitzkrieg against gambling operations, Mayor Harman Peery saw it as politics: an inscrutable encroachment on the Ogden Police Department's turf. "Why did he wait to make the raids until I took office [less than two months before]?" Peery objected. "It was common knowledge on the street that gambling operations were going on last year." A Weber County commissioner later told Wade, "I have never run across a smoother politician than you are. You play them from the time you get up in the morning until you go to bed at night."[11]

Some in Ogden's African American community believed Wade's dealings with them were politically motivated and designed to make certain they knew their place. The city's black population, historically clustered near 25th Street, numbered about three hundred until the manpower needs of local military installations during World War II brought the total up to twenty-five hundred.[12] Wartime accommodations for blacks in Ogden were "either absent or inadequate," noted the Office of Community War Services. "The community has never had any experience with any large Negro group [and] has therefore never learned how to deal with Negroes, and in consequence is not fully cognizant of or sympathetic with the plight of these people. Now, a reasonable method of handling the problem must be found." Inadequate housing, scarce recreational facilities, lack of child care, poor transportation to schools, and a dearth of restaurants willing to serve them were the principal challenges confronting Ogden's African Americans during the war.[13]

In June 1943, Leon King's proposed transfer of a beer license from the Davis Hotel, an African American hostelry on Wall Avenue, to his planned Little Harlem Café at 245 25th Street provoked the fury of a town "not fully cognizant or sympathetic" toward its burgeoning black population. Angry protests at Ogden City Commission hearings on the transfer came from the Salvation Army and Labor Temple; the Little Harlem's nearby neighbors on the 200 block; police officers; clergy; and business owners, all envisioning unpleasant encounters for their constituencies and customers. Mayor Peery and Ogden's provost marshal argued that African Americans should have a place of amusement and denying the transfer was blatant discrimination, but they could not sway the vote. The transfer was denied.[14]

Leon King eventually opened the Shadowland nightclub at 165 25th Street, one block west of his unrealized Little Harlem Café. During World War II, the 100 block of 25th Street (between Wall and Lincoln avenues) was segregated by use, with blacks gathering on the south side and whites on the north. The Porters and Waiters Club, Ogden's premiere African-American institution, was located here at 127 25th. A state-chartered and railroad-subsidized club since 1906,[15] Porters and Waiters lodged off-duty Pullman porters and railroad stewards in quarters highly convenient to Union Station. It had an in-house restaurant and tavern. In keeping with the block's segregated status, Porters and Waiters denied

Churchgoers in front of the Porters and Waiters Club. *Photo courtesy of Union Station Archives.*

access to whites during the war, sending them across the street to The Club, owned by the Pappas brothers. The Club reciprocated, directing any blacks who wandered into its establishment to Porters and Waiters.[16]

The street's rigid segregation relaxed somewhat after Annabelle Weakley, manager of Porters and Waiters since her 1947 marriage to proprietor Billy Weakley, and saxophonist Joe McQueen began presenting live jazz music in the club's basement lounge and welcoming all customers. "Annabelle's only condition on my use of the club," remembers McQueen, "was that it had to be open to all. We made Porters and Waiters so popular that we could hardly hold all the people who came, and we made musicians' pay go up every place in Ogden." The community agreed. "Annabelle Weakley was a real social pioneer and did more for racial harmony than anyone else in Ogden's history," recalls Ogdenite Tom Owens, a young jazz fan in the late 1950s.[17]

The expanded African American population impelled the Ogden Police Department and Weber County Sheriff's Department to hire their first black peace officers. In 1945 Marshall N. White began working with the Ogden City Health Department on venereal-disease cases but soon joined the regular police force after he was credited with breaking up an interracial brawl on 25th Street.[18] Walter Epps, formerly a redcap at Union Station, became a deputy sheriff around 1947. Initially both men did their jobs in street clothes. During an Ogden City Commission meeting, Mayor Peery moved that they be required to wear regular uniforms, but Sheriff Wade said uniforms would announce their presence in the community and hinder their work.[19]

The shaky relationship between African Americans' and the Sheriff's Department was not necessarily improved by a liaison of the same race. "Walter Epps was a deputy sheriff," noted Annabelle Weakley, cryptically adding, "but [he was] trying to be a friend at the same time." In October 1948, the Beau Brummell Key Klub, a social venue for African Americans at 2522 Wall Avenue, sought a restraining order to bar Sheriff Wade and Deputy Epps from entering its establishment and interrupting private parties.[20]

The nadir of the uneasy relationship came on April 13, 1954, when the Sheriff's Department, brandishing search warrants, burst into Porters and Waiters to intercept gambling games and illegal liquor sales. This was no ordinary raid. Sheriff Wade personally headed the phalanx of deputies with County Attorney Maurice Richards, reporters, and press photographers in tow. Although Porters and Waiters had rigged a flashing-light alarm system to alert backroom gamblers about police

Annabelle and Billy Weakley. *Photo courtesy of Union Station Archives.*

proximity, the raiding party moved too swiftly for it to be tripped. The lawmen seized a poker table, chips, cards, cash, and a mechanical ticker that kept track of poker pots.[21]

Half a century after the great raid of 1954, Annabelle Weakley recalled it for Ogden filmmaker Issac Goeckeritz: "Sheriff Wade decided he was going to get me off of 25th Street. They said I was running a gambling house. There was gambling in Porters and Waiters before I was born; how was I going to stop them? This was political. I was a Democrat; Mac Wade was a Republican." Major Neil Farley, provost marshal at Hill Field, shared Weakley's opinion. He told a visiting social worker that the Porters and Waiters raid was "politics" and had created an "explosive" racial situation.[22] Wade said "several months of investigation by special undercover agents" had led to the raid.[23] It might have occurred sooner, but 1954 was an election year for both Wade and Richards. As with his sudden gambling raids of February 1948, timing was everything.

"Listen," Weakley continued,

> white people have a problem with black people and money. I could've been a very wealthy person on 25th Street if not for Mac Wade. All of it was about money. Once [deputy] Jack Card asked me if I'd loan Rosetta Davie five thousand dollars for some trouble she was in. I didn't have it. That's one reason Wade gave me hell. We weren't paying the sheriffs money. That's why we got raided. I promised him one thing: he would never be sheriff no more. He promised me I'd be broke on 25th Street, and we both kept our promises. I got broke, and he never was sheriff no more.[24]

When the city prosecuted Weakley for illegal liquor sales and gambling, the old feud between Sheriff Wade and Judge Hendricks began to fester again. Wade sought to have Hendricks disqualified from hearing any case involving the Porters and Waiters Club. He said Weakley was leasing the La France Hotel, an annex to Porters and Waiters, from Hendricks, who owned it.[25] An alternate judge ultimately heard the case, where Weakley's lawyer, John Snow, noted that Wade had never raided the Weber Club or Ogden Golf and Country Club even though they openly sold liquor. "This [Porters and Waiters] is the only place Negroes can go," Snow

Judge John A. Hendricks. *Photo courtesy of Karen Hendricks Belnap.*

Annabelle Weakley, ready to ride in a Pioneer Day parade. In the background are Union Station's GO BY TRAIN sign and the east side of the Earle Hotel. *Photo courtesy of Union Station Archives.*

argued. The jury found Weakley innocent on the gambling charges. She pleaded guilty to the other charge—selling illegal liquor.[26] Four weeks earlier, Sheriff Wade had lost his reelection bid to newcomer LeRoy Hadley.[27]

Weakley acknowledged that other establishments on her block—such as The Club, owned by the Pappas brothers—had also been raided. "But you see, they didn't dog Pappas," she said. "They dogged me." Wade had good reason to tread gently where the Pappases were concerned. The brothers were not only tavern owners but prominent bondsmen in Ogden. Because Wade refused to pay a bill for attorney's fees from his bonding company, neither that company nor any other would bond his second term. The Weber County Commission set a deadline for him to secure his bond, or it would declare the office of sheriff vacated. At the eleventh hour, Wade came in with the Pappases' personal bond of ten thousand dollars.[28]

Sheriff Wade's aggressive raids, chronic feuding with Judge Hendricks, and siblinglike rivalry with the Ogden Police Department made for riveting news but distracted the public from the broader context of economic and infrastructural changes that were occurring in Ogden.[29] Of nationwide significance was the "accelerating transportation revolution" stemming from air travel and interstate-highway construction and their shakeup of the railroad industry.[30] At the local level, aging buildings and physical facilities discouraged robust business conditions on 25th Street.

Union Pacific Railroad President Arthur Stoddard had prophetically noted some of the changes affecting railroads in his April 1949 speech at the Ben Lomond Hotel when he had said that taxes and wages were increasing three to four times faster than passenger and freight rates. In the 1950s, net railway operating losses from passenger traffic were averaging $645 million per year. Simultaneously the actual portion of the national rail network utilized by passenger trains was dropping

Annabelle Weakley *(standing at right)* presides at a Porters and Waiters social. *Photo courtesy of Union Station Archives.*

A view of the Big 4 Furniture Company at 241 25th Street in 1933. Today the one-story building is the Needlepoint Joint. The vacant building on its left—247 25th Street—was number two on the fire chief's 1937 public-enemy list of fire hazards and derisively called the "canned-heat palace" because of its homeless inhabitants. *Photo courtesy of Special Collections, Stewart Library, Weber State University.*

by roughly five thousand miles per year.[31] To counter the notion that airlines were putting them out of business, railroads launched aggressive advertising campaigns, appealing to travelers' ideas about comfort, amusement, and value.

As a major hub, Ogden dodged much of the economic harm from railroad attrition felt elsewhere in the United States in the 1950s. However, by 1960 the writing was on the wall. In August the Union Pacific Railroad laid off twelve hundred workers systemwide in anticipation of continuing freight and passenger-traffic declines. One month later, the same company consolidated its flagship streamliners—City of Los Angeles and City of San Francisco—into one line linking Chicago and Ogden, cutting the ranks of passenger crews. Bids by both the Southern Pacific and Atchison, Topeka and Santa Fe railroads to merge with the Western Pacific, which operated the competitive Oakland, California, to Salt Lake City route, caused considerable consternation in Ogden, where unions lamented that "we will lose jobs no matter what."[32]

One effect of diminishing railroad ridership that 25th Street did feel during the 1950s was a significant drop in its hotel business. The former Healy Hotel, called the Earle since 1946, was so underutilized that the Army Advisory Committee of Ogden established a center there to accommodate the ballooning numbers of servicemen during the Korean War. Whether stationed in Ogden or passing through by train, servicemen could relax and socialize with preapproved junior hostesses. If they needed to stay over, rooms cost them only one dollar per night.[33]

While declining railroad prosperity was not immediately apparent to ordinary Ogdenites, the deterioration of 25th Street's buildings was. Most had been constructed before 1900 and were showing their age.[34] The last wave of new construction on the street had occurred

By 1952 the Big 4 Furniture Company had given way to the Rex Café. Only the first floor of the canned-heat palace to its left, signed Salvation Army, remained. Now demolished, its lot serves as Roosters Brewing Company and Restaurant's outdoor patio. *Photo courtesy of Special Collections, Stewart Library, Weber State University.*

To the immediate east of the canned-heat palace (with "Big 4" in its window) was the Reliable Furniture Company, occupying two buildings. Fans of Roosters Brewing Company and Restaurant will scarcely recognize this 1933 view of its two-story building (behind the man in overalls crossing the street). *Photo courtesy of Special Collections, Stewart Library, Weber State University.*

in 1910–1911.[35] Only one building, the Art Moderne bus depot on the southwest corner at Grant Avenue, erected in 1940, was even remotely new.[36]

Several fires in the 1930s—both accidental and deliberate—had taken their toll on façades and structural soundness. The upper two stories of the three-story National Hotel at 242 25th Street burned on September 16, 1935, after a fire combusted in its dance hall, killing two guests.[37] An arsonist set aflame its neighbor three lots to the west, the abandoned New Central Hotel, in December 1936; five more kerosene-fueled fires were started there before the city could tear it down, and the arsonist was never caught.[38] In September 1937, an arsonist also burned the remains of the National, whose top two stories had been razed, leading investigators to suspect someone with "an obsession to force removal of all unsightly buildings on the street."[39] These conflagrations prompted the fire chief to draw up a public-enemy list of serious fire hazards that needed to be repaired, demolished, or cleaned up; six were on 25th Street.[40]

During the Depression, the street's economy had weathered its share of rough patches. From 1935 to 1937—when Utah's liquor commission had restricted Ogden to a paltry thirteen draft-beer licenses—landlords on the street found they could not rent their buildings. The Maule estate, a major property owner, complained of losing $250 per month. "If [Utah] would even permit the sale of beer, we would be in pretty good shape," said William W. Maule. Speaking for an informal group of 25th Street property owners, Maule said they planned to refuse to pay property tax until the law was changed.[41]

Property values on the street fell between the world wars; in 1943 *Ogden Standard-Examiner* editor Darrell Greenwell attributed the drop to the street's risqué reputation. "The persons who make the most money on the street no longer live there," Greenwell wrote. "They have moved their families elsewhere. It's a good place for them to make lots of money but not a good place for their own children."[42]

However, the enormous volume of business engendered by World War II temporarily stemmed 25th Street's decline. After the war, prosperity and cultural changes introduced a relatively upscale clientele to the street. During the brief period when charter clubs flourished, middle-class couples danced and imbibed in plush venues. Concurrently Rosetta Davie and her ladies lent an aura of glamour to the street. They shopped by appointment at the L. R. Samuels apparel store at 2467 Washington Boulevard, where they were welcomed through the front door and given a good parking spot. "The ladies in Samuels used to love to see Rosetta come in because she bought expensive clothes," recalled Helen Booth of 25th Street's Eagle Clothing Co.[43]

The postwar tension between gentrification and deterioration was candidly revealed in a 1950 advertisement of available space at Eddie Doherty's old Calico Cat tavern. "There's nothing wrong with 25th Street that the elimination of undesirable elements and businesses could not cure," declared the landlord optimistically. "Legitimate business does not need to find high-rent Washington Boulevard locations. Twenty-Fifth Street could again be the main business center if good business would crowd out the bad."[44]

Sheriff Wade's raids occurred just as 25th Street seemed to be holding its own, and were, in effect, a coup de grâce that chased away middle-class entrepreneurs and customers. Those who remained were an assortment of impoverished drifters and drug- and alcohol-addicted unfortunates. The street's cultural arbiters now became the Salvation Army at 253 25th and the state liquor stores at 101 and 269 25th.

Ogden's policy on drunks aggravated the situation. While neighboring cities such as Pocatello and Salt

Fans of today's La Ferrovia Restaurant at 234 25th Street may be surprised to see the building's 1933 appearance, when its west half was the Economy Clothing Store, and the east half was vacant. The building to its west is long gone. *Photo courtesy of Special Collections, Stewart Library, Weber State University.*

The vanished building at 228 25th Street housed the Lincoln Café in 1952. *Photo courtesy of Special Collections, Stewart Library, Weber State University.*

Lake City "floated" their drunks—suspended their jail sentences if the offenders left town within twenty-four hours—Ogden sent its drunks to jail for five days. After the incarceration, "we still have them on our hands," noted Police Chief Maurice Schooff. "This has a tendency to clear the drunks out of surrounding communities and into Ogden."[45]

Sightseeing and slumming—popular pastimes on the street since the advent of state Prohibition in 1917—became a craze in the mid-1950s. Teenagers and college kids who are now septuagenarians liked to park and watch the drunks. They remember inebriated men and women staggering out of bars, collapsing, and resisting their equally plastered companions' fumbling efforts to pry them off the sidewalk. "I watched a guy struggle to pull a rather chubby lady back up," remembers former Ogden City councilwoman Dorrene Jeske, "but her dress was the only thing coming up. I was horrified when I realized I was looking at her bare bottom."

Dorothy Scott Harvey recalls ogling the street as a child from inside a parked car while her father haunted the pawn shops. "Men would hit the women, and some of the women would hit back," she says. "All of this was fueled by drink. Those women landed lots of good punches, and the sound effects were scintillating to me. There was lots of loud cursing and complaining. Sometimes my sister and I couldn't stop giggling and laughing."[46]

The question of whether cleaned-up streets stay that way in the long run may be answered by an unintended consequence of Wade's raid on Porters and Waiters. Annabelle Weakley was so disillusioned that she no longer wanted to manage the club. To replace herself, she hired Lyle Kurisaki, a mover and shaker in the Utah Japanese American Citizens League and manager of the Colored Club of Ogden. Kurisaki's background in army intelligence and as an agent for the federal Office of Price Stabilization in Utah gave no hint to Weakley or anyone else that he would become arguably the most corrupt individual on 25th Street in the late 1950s.[47]

Lyle Kurisaki.
Photo courtesy of Union Station Archives.

"The reason I quit being a federal agent [in Utah] was the graft and corruption I saw. It was even worse at the state level," Kurisaki recollected in the 1970s after several stints in California prisons. He pointed to his arrival in Ogden as the beginning of his criminal career. "I always had fronts, businesses that kept police from harassing me too much," he admitted.[48] During his five years at Porters and Waiters, he was arrested frequently for gambling offenses or aggravated altercations while his more serious crimes, such as fencing stolen property or planning robberies of luxury items, flew under the radar. He also insinuated himself into Ogden's upper echelons by loaning his Lincoln Continental to officials at Weber College, the state industrial

A rare (and dark) view of the three-story Denver Hotel at 161–169 25th Street on the far left. Built before 1880 as the Chamberlain Hotel, the structure was demolished in 1960. This photograph shows the 100 block when it had no vacant lots. *Photo courtesy of Special Collections, Stewart Library, Weber State University.*

school, and Detective Lynn Garside of the Ogden Police Department.[49]

However, the city knew all was not right with Kurisaki. After Police Chief Maurice Schooff ordered Porters and Waiters closed in January 1960 following a shooting, he allowed it to reopen on condition that Kurisaki resign and never darken its door again, even though Kurisaki had nothing to do with the shooting. Officials also forced him out as proprietor of Pancho's Tavern on the northeast corner of Lincoln Avenue and 25th Street.[50]

Pancho's figured prominently in Eddie Doherty's ill-fated return to Ogden. After Doherty's parole in 1956 from federal prison, Sheriff Hadley, Police Chief Schooff, and a parole officer agreed that he could work as a purchasing agent for Pancho's. His boss, Helen Oki Estrada, shot him in the leg during an early morning quarrel (in self-defense, she claimed), but the parole officer remained unconcerned. What triggered the seemingly inevitable revocation of Doherty's parole was his banal crime of selling bottled beer to minors. He was whisked back to

The Montana Hotel at 160 25th Street was built by David Maule in the early 1900s. After fires in 1967 and 1971, its second story was torn down. Present-day occupants of its surviving ground-level space are Shin-Sei Sushi Bar, Art House Cinema 502, and the Historic Place bar. *Photo courtesy of Special Collections, Stewart Library, Weber State University.*

federal prison.[51] Although he had been Ogden's most notorious criminal in the late 1940s, Doherty was now only a shadow of his former self and no competition for Lyle Kurisaki.

In 1962 L. G. Bingham represented Doherty on a burglary charge. "A young woman talked Eddie into going along with her and a safecracker to this market in North Ogden," relates Bingham.

> Eddie was drunk and passed out in the car. KSL-TV was there with cameras and a spotlight, ready and waiting. It was entrapment. But Eddie was convicted; the problem was that as a felon, he had to disclose details about his priors if asked on the witness stand. He asked me to come to a parole hearing. The parole board guy was a Salt Lake bank president with an Irish name. Eddie cracked, "We Irish are either cops or crooks, and I've never worn a badge." The guy laughed, then gave Eddie only a year.[52]

Originally the Van Ness Hotel (and later the Virginia), the Pacific Hotel burned in 1969 and sat vacant for three decades. The building was demolished in 1997. *Photo used by permission of the Utah State Historical Society.*

Dwindling patronage from railroad customers doomed two of the street's grandest old hotels. The Broom, formerly Ogden's premiere public space, was sold to Commercial Security Bank for a new headquarters on the northwestern corner of 25th Street and Washington Boulevard. Demolition began at a public ceremony on July 8, 1958, with three special guests: Governor George D. Clyde and two great-great-grandsons of builder John Broom, who were granted the honor of heaving bricks through the front windows. A crowd of five thousand watched the mayhem and then filed through the lobby and suites for one last glimpse at the renowned opulence.[53] Although considered seedy in its final years, the Broom's structural soundness amazed the

The sun-lit six-story federal building is visible in the 300 block of 25th Street in the center of this post-1965 photo. On the right, the aggregation of vacant lots in the 100 block awaits more promising times. *Photo courtesy of Union Station Archives.*

wrecking crews, who called it the best-built hulk they had ever torn down.[54]

The Healy/Earle Hotel reached its end in November 1967 with no apparent commercial interest in its forlorn lot across from Union Station. Its once-beautiful marble lobby, onyx and marble grand staircase, and cut-glass chandeliers had earned admiration for Ogden, but the place had become ramshackle. Earlier that year Ogden had refused to renew the Earle's business license because it had not complied with an order to install an automatic fire alarm-system.[55]

As buildings were razed randomly, the street became pockmarked with trash-strewn vacant lots. The south side of the 100 block was almost completely denuded. Its Denver Hotel (161–169 25th Street) was torn down in September 1960, and—like dominoes—the block's other buildings from east to west fell to the bulldozer.[56] The last to go was the abandoned Porters and Waiters Club in 1973. For the next four decades, only numbers 101–115 remained, and more than once the city issued demolition orders on some of those, fortunately never executed.[57]

Fires were no less a menace on 25th Street in the era of railroad decline; the Labor Temple burned in February 1961, followed by the vacant Weber Hotel (formerly Belle London's Fashion Rooms) less than a year later after transients camping inside lit fires to keep warm. On the north side of the 100 block, the old Montana Hotel incurred a blaze fatal to two tenants in October 1967, believed by investigators to be arson. Its neighbor to the west, the Pacific Hotel (formerly Fred J. Kiesel's Van Ness Hotel) suffered a fire fatal to one guest in June 1969. The Pacific's manager, Helen Oki Estrada, had to alert the fire department from a neighboring restaurant because the hotel phone was out of order.[58]

In the late 1950s, a new player—the federal government—shook up the dynamics of 25th Street as never before. The saga began when the *Ogden Standard-Examiner* revealed how cramped for space Ogden's old federal building at 24th Street and Grant Avenue had become. Within the 1909 structure, the Post Office was restricted to the same space it had had for twenty years, even though its business had quintupled. The Social Security Administration, Bureau of Reclamation, Farmers Home Administration, Soil Conservation Service, Agricultural Stabilization and Conservation Service, and Selective Service had all moved out and rented quarters elsewhere. The Internal Revenue Service and Civil Service Commission remained in the building but needed more room. The U.S. District Court, which occupied half of one floor, had adequate space but had not used it during the previous two years.[59]

The newspaper article reached the desk of Utah Senator Wallace F. Bennett. Within one month, the U.S. General Services Administration (GSA) began a comprehensive investigation of Ogden's federal office-space requirements. Although the GSA concluded a new federal building was "very much needed," it took nearly four years for Congress to authorize funds to build it.[60] During the earliest stages of planning, 25th Street appeared close to losing its single choicest stretch of historic architecture located on the north side of the 200 block.

In anticipation of its new federal building, Ogden hired Ebasco Services Inc., an engineering firm in San Francisco, to write a development plan for its central business district. The plan that emerged encouraged the U.S. government to buy and develop the entire block bounded by 25th and 24th streets and Lincoln and Grant avenues (block 24). This recommendation was endorsed unanimously by the Ogden City Council, Chamber of Commerce, Weber County Commission, and the key player, Senator Bennett.[61]

Luckily the government was not moved by those endorsements because it did not need block 24's ten acres. It announced the federal building would occupy just four and one-half acres on 25th Street between Grant and Kiesel avenues.[62] The government's frugality saved the buildings treasured today on block 24's north side—from the Frazzini Brothers Saloon at 200 to the Creston Hotel at 290, with gems like the former Davenport Saloon, London Ice Cream Parlor, and the Porter Block in between.

But the reprieve granted to block 24 doomed the half block to its immediate east. To have its federal building, Ogden had to sacrifice a splendid row of nineteenth-century structures that had once housed Maggie Kirk's place, the Little King Saloon, and the White Elephant gambling palace, among many other picturesque establishments. Congress approved the federal building's construction costs in 1962.[63] Demolition of the historic buildings on the site was postponed several times, but the wrecker's ball finally began swinging in July 1963.

Andrew Wahlquist, assistant news director at KCPX-TV in 1963, realized the new federal building meant the extinction of much of Ogden's colorful history. An Ogden native, Wahlquist decided to write and produce a television documentary on the doomed half block before it was too late. "They were about to tear down several buildings," he recalls. "So we went through them filming the history. We broke down walls on the upper floors and found gambling rooms with cards and chips still on the dust-covered tables." The documentary, called "Scrapbook of a Grand Old Lady: Ogden's 25th Street," won a Utah Broadcasters Association award.[64]

In its own way, the federal building did more to clean up 25th Street than years of raids and arrests. In lieu of endless cat-and-mouse games played out by vice squads and lawbreakers, the federal building created an ultimate solution by obliterating the venues where vice occurred. But one consequence of destroying a portion of 25th Street to save it is the difficulty present-day Ogdenites have in understanding the nineteenth-century economic forces that made their city rich and desirable.[65]

The last word belongs to Ogden's politicians, who realized that a vice-free 25th Street would deprive them of their most potent weapon against incumbents. Political diatribes against disgraceful conditions on the street have continued unabated from the time of Sheriff Wade's cleanup to the present day. The perception of 25th Street as public shame has always depended on whether a person is in or out of office.

When County Attorney Maurice Richards ran for the Utah Senate in 1962, his campaign touted his success in cleaning up 25th Street a decade earlier.[66] But while Richards was out on the hustings, defrocked Ogden Police Chief Nephi Golden Jensen—running for Mac Wade's old job as county sheriff—was stump-speaking to civic and church groups, deploring the sinful and lawless state of affairs that he said persisted down on 25th Street.[67]

Neither man won his race.

CHAPTER NINE

OGDEN RENAISSANCE

One of the most cynical clichés in architecture is that poverty is good for preservation. The poor don't bulldoze historic neighborhoods to make way for fancy new high-rises.

—Architecture critic Nicolai Ouroussoff, *New York Times*, November 14, 2008

During World War II, 25th Street's neon-studded vibrancy had given it the ambience of New York's Times Square. But its subsequent decrepitude evoked a much less luminous Gotham neighborhood: the Bowery. In the 1960s and '70s, Ogden's bourgeoisie shunned the street almost completely. The public's neglect may actually have been a blessing in disguise, however. Had 25th Street been desirable, its remaining historic structures might have been demolished to make way for new, ersatz modern ones. The buildings still flanking the street survived by hiding in plain sight. However, the city's patience was not infinite. "Back when the street was derelict, abandoned, and dangerous," noted city planner Greg Montgomery, "early plans talked about tearing it all down."[1]

The street's salvation began with a fortuitous left turn by the right person. In 1975 Allen Roberts, a young architectural historian at the Utah State Historical Society, was commuting to Ogden for meetings to establish the Eccles Avenue Historic District. "Driving north on Washington Boulevard," Roberts recalls, "something on the left caught my eye. I had never seen 25th Street before. I made a quick detour onto it." Roberts's keen eye immediately registered unique decorative touches of tin, plaster, and carved wood. By the time he reached Wall Avenue, he had counted forty intact old buildings, many from the Victorian period. Roberts—sufficiently passionate about architecture to claim he would practice for free if he had to—says, "Anyone who knows me well knows I get excited about such discoveries."[2]

One year earlier, renowned preservationist Dana Crawford, savior of Denver's Larimer Square, had been the featured speaker at the annual Utah Heritage Foundation meeting. Crawford praised Utah's "great acceptance of the idea of preservation" and said that renovating historic buildings allows "a more personal feeling" to pervade downtown areas. Back in 1965—after Denver's urban-renewal authority had already bulldozed five of Larimer Street's historic blocks—Crawford bought the

A boy on the 100 block of 25th Street in the 1920s. There is an excellent view of the Greiner Hotel's original façade on the left. Today a tile and stucco façade covers the front of its successor, the Roosevelt Hotel. *Photo used by permission of the Utah State Historical Society.*

The 100 block of 25th Street shortly before 1913, when trolley poles in its center were removed. *Photo courtesy of Union Station Archives.*

single remaining intact block, comprising eighteen old buildings. She persuaded restaurants and retail stores to rent space and managed the block as if it was a small specialty center.[3]

Crawford's address inspired Allen Roberts, and he traveled to Denver to check out Larimer Square. Seeing it gave Roberts a vision of what could be accomplished on 25th Street. No shrinking violet, he called the Ogden City Council and asked to be put on its agenda. The plan he presented in mid-November 1975 proposed restoring the street to its pre–World War I appearance. To jump-start the process, Roberts suggested placing the street on state and national registers as an historic district, enacting a moratorium on demolition, and moving the state liquor store to a different location. Eventually, Roberts said, there should be design guidelines, sources of financial incentives for renovation, and improvements to the street itself, such as benches, sculptures, landscaping, and expanded parking. Mayor Stephen Dirks and the council agreed enthusiastically with Roberts's proposals and ordered a task force to study feasibility.[4]

Unknown to Roberts or city officials, their notion of a pre–World War I appearance for 25th Street was ironic because in 1913 Ogdenites had been decidedly unhappy with the way the street looked. It "has put visitors in a panic and has driven more than one resident out of town," noted the *Ogden Examiner.* "It is a shame and a disgrace." Chief among the 1913 eyesores was the crumbling asphalt. Business owners on the street had refused to pay a special assessment to repave, making Ogden seem "a backwoods town to strangers." In addition, unsightly billboards had proliferated, prompting the city's newspapers and women's clubs to demand their removal.[5]

A 25th Street Improvement Association formed to help the street give a better impression to travelers arriving at Union Station. Although the Healy Hotel across Wall Avenue from the station sparkled after a top-to-bottom renovation, the Murphy Block directly opposite on 25th had never been painted since its 1889 construction, and many other façades were considered plain.

Boosters wanted the Murphy Block and other lackluster façades to have the same cherry hue as the Healy Hotel and to add touches of blue so the street could adopt red, white, and blue as its theme and change its name to American Way.[6] The intended redecoration coincided with the removal of worm-eaten trolley poles from the center of the street and installation of beautiful arc lights along the sidewalks. The new illumination approach was dubbed Ogden's Great White Way and planned to allow the city "to take upon herself rather metropolitan airs."[7]

Similar discontent cropped up in 1934. "It is getting to be almost a disgrace to say you live on 25th Street," complained Roy Steele, a business owner. Announcing a plan to remove objectionable features and dispel prejudice, Steele and his cohorts said that changing the street's name was the best initial step and circulated petitions advocating Roosevelt Avenue, Park Avenue, or Broadway. However, no sooner had Steele launched his campaign than an opposing camp materialized, so that pro-change petitions moving along one side of the street were challenged by anti-change ones on the other. The final score was fifty-two for change and fifty-five for the status quo. Putting the matter to rest, Mayor Harman Peery announced the receipt of two

The Congress building in 1952, when the Harlem Club Hotel was located in it. *Photo courtesy of Special Collections, Stewart Library, Weber State University.*

petitions from the residential east end of the street vigorously protesting a change.[8]

The critical issue in 1975, to be sure, was neither reputation nor aesthetics but actual survival. Allen Roberts not only goaded city officials into a plan of action but became personally invested in the outcome. He immediately purchased two historic buildings: the Congress at 115 25th Street for forty-three hundred dollars and the adjacent Senate for twelve thousand. His first crisis occurred within days after he acquired the Congress. The chief city inspector ordered Roberts to secure the building within three weeks or it would be demolished. The inspector said he agreed with the restoration concept, but it was his duty to prevent threats to public safety.

Roberts appealed to the Ogden City Council. The council, in turn, consulted local architect and preservationist Ronald Hales, who assured it that the benefits of a restored 25th Street were "an economic sleeping giant." Roberts won a six-month reprieve to file a plan to return the Congress to its "early twentieth-century condition."[9]

The Congress building as it looked when Allen Roberts bought it in 1975. *Photo used by permission of the Utah State Historical Society.*

The Senate building at 111 25th Street in the mid-1970s. *Photo used by permission of the Utah State Historical Society.*

Restoration of the Congress building was a two-decade labor of love for Roberts. He kept the original doors, windows, and transoms, but the roof, walls, and floors required a structural engineer's intervention. Remnants of the building's past as a bordello abounded. "I discovered that rooms on the west side of the third floor were painted with pornographic scenes," Roberts remembers.

> One mural was a gigantic champagne glass with a nude woman floating in it. Others were somewhat more graphic. The style impressed me as being from the thirties or forties. I don't recall if the murals had been done on canvas affixed to the walls or directly on the plaster. The plaster work was good, but deteriorating fast. It may eventually have just fallen off.[10]

Another building that benefitted from Roberts's scrutiny was the Porter Block, famous today as the City Club with its world-class collection of Beatles memorabilia. Built in 1900 by James L. Porter, a Nevada hotelier new to Ogden, the building had a Mesker Brothers façade.[11] From the late 1800s to the early 1900s, the Mesker Brothers Iron Works of St. Louis, makers of prefabricated building façades of cast iron and galvanized steel, distributed half a million catalogs per year. A two-story sheet-metal façade cost between two and three hundred dollars, one-fifth the price of cast iron or terra-cotta. Façades were shipped by rail and assembled on-site in just a day or two. Small-town builders could

This 1952 partial view of the Grill Tavern, the then-occupant of the Porter Block, shows the "totally inappropriate" black tile covering its ground-floor façade. *Photo courtesy of Special Collections, Stewart Library, Weber State University.*

act as their own architects, ordering the façades they wanted at a good price.[12]

By the time Charles Edwards, a local dentist who was Allen Roberts's uncle, bought the Porter Block in the mid-1970s, its street-level façade had been covered with "totally inappropriate" glossy black tile in the style of a midcentury bar. Thanks to an old photo, Roberts recognized the original façade for what it was. "I have been to every city and town in Utah," says Roberts, "and I know most of Utah's historic buildings. There happened to be a similar, intact Mesker Brothers façade in Panguitch."

Edwards and Roberts drove to Panguitch and persuaded the owner to let them make castings of his storefront. Here Edwards's years as a dentist came in handy. "We put Vaseline on the cast-iron elements, then built wood frames around them and poured fast-drying dental plaster into the openings, against the iron pilasters and ornament," Roberts explains.

> When they dried, we took away the frames and took the plaster molds to an aluminum foundry, where we had exact replicas made of the pieces of the Panguitch façade. Back in Ogden, we removed the Porter Block's black tiles and attached the metal pilasters and other ornamentation to the front façade and painted them, restoring the storefront to its 1900 appearance.[13]

In supporting Allen Roberts's suggestions for restoring 25th Street, Ogden's mayor and council may have been swayed by currents of historic preservation beginning to inspire the rest of the country. The unpopular demolition of New York City's Pennsylvania Station in 1963 galvanized many cities into reversing policies favoring destruction of significant buildings. The formidable New York City Landmarks Preservation Commission, created in 1965, saved Grand Central Station by giving it landmark status in 1967.[14]

A preservationist consciousness began to suffuse Ogden, too, in 1967, following the obsolescence of rail postal cars and consequent collapse of passenger service. Perceptive Ogdenites realized that their Union Station's existence was in jeopardy. The city had independently explored options for a convention center, and early in 1968, the *Ogden Standard-Examiner* suggested Union Station might be the solution. At the same time, the approach of the Golden Spike centennial on May 10, 1969, led city officials to propose a railroad museum that would be housed at the station.[15]

The railroads agreed to provide space in the station for museum displays.[16] A nonprofit agency, the Golden Spike Empire, was incorporated to operate the station as a museum/convention center. But following the centennial, the railroads' cooperative spirit seemed to ebb in tandem with the tourists. Overtures from Ogden were met with silence. Finally—in response to a late-1971 letter from city and county officials—the Ogden Union Railway & Depot Company replied that transferring title to the station was "not compatible with the long term plans for utilization of the property."[17]

Right away *Standard-Examiner* editor Murray Moler telephoned R. D. Spence, head of the Ogden Union Railway & Depot Company, who was a personal friend. Moler informed Spence of the uproar following the recent demolition of a Mormon tabernacle in Coalville, Utah, despite its historic landmark status, and said Ogdenites would be outraged if Union Station suffered the same fate. "I can assure you we won't do *that,*" replied Spence. "We simply need more time to make up our minds. Ogden will be the first to know if we find we don't need Union Station." Soon after this exchange, Utah Senator Wallace F. Bennett, who had already finagled the federal building for Ogden, went to bat again and contacted the Department of Interior, asking for assistance in turning the station into a museum.[18]

A task force comprising officials from Ogden, Weber County, and the railroads formed to oversee Union Station's future operation and resolve on-site issues of personnel space and jointly owned equipment. Negotiations lasted nearly four years.[19] As the two-hundredth birthday of the United States approached, the Utah American Revolution Bicentennial Commission awarded Ogden a $150,000 grant to convert Union Station to a museum. The city hired Stephen Baird of Salt Lake City as chief architect, with Ronald Hales of Ogden as consultant and Weber State College's history department as collective project historian. The city also created an advisory board chaired by Murray Moler. Mayor Dirks announced the station conversion as Ogden's official bicentennial project.[20]

The Ogden City Council approved formal documents transferring Union Station to Ogden City on February 5, 1976. However, Governor Rampton vetoed an anticipated appropriation of $425,000 by the Utah Legislature for the station, saying that the 1976 aggregation of special projects exceeded budget allowance. Although the city pushed ahead with plans, major construction work at the station could not start without sufficient funds in place. The American Revolution Bicentennial sailed past.[21]

Architects Baird and Hales presented their master development plan in October 1976. Phase one would replace the station's roof and clean the façade. The state bicentennial commission's earlier grant would allow roofing to begin immediately. Next would come rehabilitating and consolidating the railroads' remaining office space at the south end of the station, plus modernizing the electrical wiring and other utilities. Phases three and four would create museum spaces and renovate the lobby as a multipurpose civic center.[22]

By this time, a fortunate new development had eased the sting of Governor Rampton's veto. Val A. Browning, chairman of the Browning Arms Company, agreed to donate to the station his incomparable collection of sporting and military firearms, most of them invented by his father, John Moses Browning. The railroad museum would now be paired with the John M. Browning Firearms Museum.[23]

Weber County legislators who sought state funding for Union Station had better luck in 1977. A new governor, Scott Matheson, had been a Union

Union Station soon after its 1978 restoration. *Photo courtesy of Union Station Archives.*

Pacific Railroad attorney and key figure in negotiating the station's transfer to Ogden. Matheson signed a bill authorizing $600,000. With major funding assured, the advisory board organized the Union Station Development Corporation and named Elizabeth "Teddy" Griffith, a member of the city planning commission, Utah Heritage Foundation, and state bicentennial commission, as executive director. One of Griffith's first acts was to hire Consortium West Inc. of Salt Lake City to design the museums.[24] She also secured a federal grant of $650,000, most of which was earmarked for a new heating system, installation of elevators, and remodeling of the post office into a multipurpose activities center.[25]

The corporation ambitiously announced Union Station's grand reopening for the next Golden Spike anniversary on May 10, 1978. However, the restoration work could not be finished in time, and the event was rescheduled for the fall. The ensuing Golden Spike Empire Week, held in mid-October 1978, came off so well that it justified the wait. Each day of the week featured the dedication of a different public space—the various new museums and galleries—inside the revamped station. Interspersed with the dedications were performances of *The Music Man* and *Pippin* by Weber State College and a lecture by native Weber County historian Fawn McKay Brodie.

Culminating Golden Spike Empire Week was the nostalgic arrival of the Union Pacific's last-remaining steam locomotive, Engine No. 8444. Reserved for special occasions as Union Pacific's goodwill ambassador, the train left Salt Lake City transporting Governor Matheson, Union Pacific President John Kenefick, and many other dignitaries. Inside Union Station's beautified lobby, Matheson hammered a replica of the Golden Spike into a railroad tie. Murray Moler received the Utah Travel Council's Friend of Utah award for his years of work in securing Union Station's survival for future generations. Moler summed up community sentiments by calling Union Station "an anchor for the pride of Ogden." Congressman Gunn McKay added, "Ogden is the crossroads of the West. Sorry, Salt Lake."[26]

Two of the most exciting enhancements at Union Station were fifty-by-twelve-foot murals portraying construction crews of the Union Pacific and Central Pacific railroads for the lobby's north and south walls. Thanks to a $100,000 grant from the National Academy of Design, the station commissioned Edward Laning, an outstanding American muralist, noted especially for installations at the New York Public Library and Ellis Island. In 1980 Laning—by this time an elderly man—traveled to Ogden to supervise installation of his majestic work. "We crossed our fingers every time he climbed up the scaffolding," remembers Teddy Griffith. These were Laning's final completed murals.[27]

While planning Union Station's future as a community resource, city officials knew a thriving 25th Street would enhance the chances of achieving that goal. Five months after Allen Roberts's seminal appearance before the Ogden City Council, Ogden allocated twenty-nine thousand dollars to study the street's rejuvenation. In awarding the funds to Baird and Hales—the architects already working on Union Station—the city asked them to show ways the station could revitalize the street and vice versa.[28]

Scheduled for the fall of 1976, the study's release was delayed for a full year by "disagreements over technical work."[29] When it finally appeared, the study recommended a two-million-dollar investment in street work, lighting, and utility improvements. It called for four "reasonable concepts for development on the street": a farmer's market, residential condominium project, transportation center complex, and motel/convention center.[30] Today's Ogdenites will recognize that all four projects have become reality, even if the latter two did not end up on 25th Street.

Coinciding with the study's publication, Allen Roberts completed a nineteen-page application for the Utah State Historical Society, nominating the proposed Lower 25th Street Historic District for inclusion in the National Register of Historic Places. The application was an exhaustive inventory of forty-two buildings, including Union Station, giving their history, educated guesses about when they were constructed, individual descriptions of architectural style and materials, and a list of owners. A portfolio of handsome photographs accompanied the nomination, documenting what Mayor Dirks called "the most complete contiguous selection of turn-of-the-century commercial architecture in the state of Utah."[31] The National Register granted the designation the following year.[32]

In this 1952 photograph, the London Ice Cream Parlor is on the right, and the Davenport Saloon is on the left. *Photo courtesy of Special Collections, Stewart Library, Weber State University.*

The first property on the street to be rehabilitated was another building Allen Roberts had bought, the London Ice Cream Parlor at 254 25th Street. "I made a deal with the city's redevelopment agency [RDA]," says Roberts. "In exchange for a low-interest loan from the RDA, I agreed to renovate it, then rent it to the city at a low rate for five years. As the architect, I did the drawings. For the RDA, it was a demonstration project. It was brave of them." City planner Greg Montgomery says his department moved into the London Ice Cream Parlor to set an example: "We wanted to show what could be done."[33]

Unfortunately, the first contractor on the London Ice Cream Parlor did sloppy work, breaking into the sewage line in the basement, hanging doors upside down, and failing to use structural bolts in support beams. During the first winter after the city planning department moved in, the London's roof caved in from snow. The renovation had also uprooted a homeless man, Robert Leatherman, who had been squatting in a six-foot-wide space underneath the staircase. Leatherman relocated to a hotel room on the west end of 25th Street's 200 block. One frigid night he crumpled newspapers in his sink and lighted them with a match to get warm. The fire spread to the rest of the hotel, killing four tenants and harming several others.[34]

Allen Roberts's protracted work on the Congress building got a welcome boost from Spring Productions, an independent movie company shooting *Wait until Spring, Bandini* at various Utah locations in March 1989. "They were looking for a 1920s, Edward Hopper-like building for exterior shots, and they had seen the Congress and thought it was perfect for one of their sequences," Roberts says. "I proposed that if they would agree to fund the restoration, we'd call it even. That's partly how I got the façade done." Although Faye Dunaway starred in the film, she apparently had no scenes in Ogden. But noted actor Joe Mantegna played Bandini, the title character, and filmed a scene in front of the Congress where he was offered a job that would introduce him to Dunaway. Producers had anticipated an abundance of snow during the March shooting, but after a seventy-degree heat wave, crews had to truck in snow from the canyons and scatter it along the sidewalk.[35]

By the time the *Bandini* company filmed the Congress building's wonderful façade, restoration on 25th Street was gaining momentum. Eric and Terry Zenger, enthralled with the sense of place they felt on 25th Street, purchased 272 (formerly the Palace Billiard Hall) and established a Great Harvest bakery there. Nightlife on the street was reborn in 1991 thanks to William Parker and Heidi Harwood, who opened the City Club in the Porter Block. "We had excellent credit and a sound financial plan," Parker explains, "and yet no one wanted to finance us. No one wanted to deliver to 25th Street, even for cash payment. No one wanted to insure us. It took a bunch of great, daring employees to become guinea pigs." Luckily—once City Club opened—"people thought it was the place to be," says Harwood. "We were lucky to be on the second floor, where it was less likely that people would wander in who weren't supposed to be there. We also had plenty of parking in back and a secure entrance."[36]

Both Great Harvest and the City Club benefited considerably from locating in buildings already renovated and retrofitted by Margaret Hunter, one of 25th Street's most intrepid rescuers. "I just like old things, old buildings," Hunter explains. "I have an indulgent husband, I guess. I knew 25th Street needed help and thought of it as my community project." Hunter had earlier restored Ogden's historic Don Maguire home and the Shupe-Williams Candy Company building just south of Union Station (destroyed by fire in March 2006). In the mid-1980s, she owned the five contiguous properties on 25th Street from the Porter Block to the James O. Stephens Building (262 through 274). During renovations she found barrels cemented into the rock foundation wall between 272 and 274 that she assumed had helped someone conceal liquor during Prohibition.[37]

Twenty-Fifth Street got its first new building in more than half a century when Mark Altice built his twelve-thousand-square-foot Altice Corner on the site of the Healy Hotel across from Union Station. Altice says he "wasn't thrilled" with the neighborhood when he bought the property and his family was "100 percent against" the project. Today he feels the street's respectability has improved immensely since 1997, due in part to the businesses in Altice Corner. During excavation Altice was surprised to find the Healy Hotel's north foundation wall, which was assumed no longer to exist. "We also found beautiful porcelain tiles in concrete from the Healy, and liked [them] so much that we had replica tiles made and incorporated them into the building."[38]

In 2000 Congress gave 25th Street a major boost when it created the Crossroads of the West National Historic District, authorizing up to five million dollars in matching funds for restoring buildings and interpreting historic resources in an eight-block area contiguous to Union Station. The federal largesse resulted from a fortunate convergence of northern Utah Congressman James Hansen's clout as chair of the National Parks and Public Lands Subcommittee and Ogden's role as host for competitions in the upcoming 2002 Winter Olympics. Testifying before Hansen's subcommittee, Mayor Glenn Mecham asserted that if Ogden could successfully restore its railroad history, the city would be a "captivating place for millions of visitors."[39]

The street's largest public-works project—Union Square condominiums and commercial properties—was completed in 2003, in one fell swoop making the 100 block's south side more attractive than ever. Plugging the block's remaining holes in quick succession were Ogden Blue printing and supply company and the Time Square building with its four-story clock tower. Each of these three projects sports a façade that pays tribute to the surrounding historic architecture without imitating it. In making the 100 block whole at long last, these buildings reestablished the sense of flow between the 200 block and Union Station.

Nearby downtown restorations and additions lending synergy to 25th Street include Peery's Egyptian Theater, the Eccles Conference Center, and Lindquist Field, all completed in 1997; the Ogden Municipal Building in 2000; Colonial Court Apartments in 2000 and 2009; the Ogden Transit Center in 2002; the IRS Twin Rivers Complex, including the Boyle Furniture warehouse and Scowcroft building, in 2002–2004; the new IRS building at 24th Street and Lincoln Avenue in 2012; and The Junction recreational complex on Washington Boulevard between 22nd and 24th streets (a multiphased project still in progress).

Regrettably, the rising tides buoying Union Station and 25th Street seemed to stop short of the magnificent Ben Lomond Hotel. With occupancy flatlining at 6 percent in 1977, the hotel had become a casualty of the trend toward the informality of drive-in lodging and away from the grandeur of large hotels. The Woodbury Corporation—the Ben Lomond's owner since 1965—donated it as an unrestricted gift to Weber County in exchange for the county's assumption of an eighty-thousand-dollar mortgage.[40] County agencies and local state-tax-commission employees soon moved in. The transition to a government office building was lamented as the end of an era when notable Ogdenites had made it their genteel home. *Ogden Standard-Examiner* publisher Abe Glasmann; defense attorney Arthur Woolley; Maisie (Mrs. Marriner) Eccles; Coca-Cola magnate Ben Day; and Mr. and Mrs. Horace Walker, parents of actor Robert Walker, had all lived there. Famous guests had included Norma Shearer, Clark Gable, Gary Cooper, and Senators John F. Kennedy and Harry S. Truman. Meredith Willson, composer of *The Music Man,* had once startled a coffee-shop waitress with a very generous tip.[41]

The county sold the building to Daniel Cook's DCA Development Corporation in the spring of 1983. "The county actually took my lower bid because they supported saving the Ben Lomond Hotel as an historic property," explains Cook. "The other bidder would have torn it down." Cook formed a limited partnership with a large group of investors in individual units in the building called Ben Lomond Suites, Ltd.; it took nearly two years to renovate and earthquake-proof the building. In January 1985, the Ben Lomond resumed its life as a hotel, operating as a franchise under the Radisson flag for fourteen years. "The problem in 1999," explains former general manager Jim Budge, "was that Radisson wanted the owners to shell out a lot of money to bring it up to radically new standards. They said no."[42]

Reverting to the name Ben Lomond Suites, Ltd., the hotel was filled to capacity during the 2002 Winter Olympics, lodging Secret Service agents, Japanese tourists, and Greek dignitaries. Sadly, however, the Olympics were merely a temporary blip in a malaise pervading the entire hospitality industry since the 2001 New York World Trade Center attacks. Dismal business forced the Ben Lomond to close indefinitely in November 2002.[43]

The Ben Lomond's hibernation persisted for sixteen months until it was reopened by 2510 Washington LLC, owned by Dan Tabish and Jeff Van Dyke. With a vision of "keeping people living in Ogden," Tabish and Van Dyke began converting rooms on the upper six floors to condominiums while running the lower floors as a hotel. The condominiums did not sell well, and a scarcity of guests led the partners to seek affiliation with a nationally known hotel chain. Tabish and Van Dyke announced sale of the Ben Lomond in January 2008 to UIG Resorts of Las Vegas, which promised extensive remodeling and a hip restaurant. That acquisition, however, was never completed, and 2510 Washington LLC lost the hotel in a July 2009 foreclosure sale.[44]

The new and current owner, Ben Lomond Suites LLC, attracted considerable publicity with immediate efforts to reclaim some of the venerable institution's former cachet. Six-hundred-pound chandeliers dating back to 1927 were taken down, rewired, and cleaned, crystal by crystal. Floors were shined, rooms renovated, and new bed linens and flat-screen televisions introduced. Public scrutiny was invited by including the hotel in historic property tours by the Weber County Heritage Foundation. Promotion of elegant public events such as First Friday Afternoon Tea emphasized the Ben Lomond's status as a high-class, but accessible, venue to please both local citizens and visitors. Support of the hotel's amenities seems to have caught on among Ogdenites who want the city to maintain its distinction of having the only early-twentieth-century grand hotel still operating in Utah.[45]

The unsolicited popularity of the Ben Lomond Hotel as a destination for Halloween-season "ghost tours" prompts a look into 25th Street folklore. Ghost aficionados believe that many of 25th Street's buildings are haunted, and many northern Utahns are convinced that a network of tunnels underlies the street from the Ben Lomond Hotel to Union Station. The tunnels are imagined to have facilitated escapes from police raids, especially during Prohibition, or opium-smoking sessions among brotherhoods of Chinese immigrants who wished to remain undetected. "People believe there are tunnels, and no matter what you say, they still believe there are," observes city planner Greg Montgomery. "During the reconstruction of 25th Street in the late 1970s, we dug up and replaced all the utilities and the sidewalks. There were no tunnels full-length of the street."[46]

What most old buildings along the street did have were basements and storage spaces underneath the sidewalks. Portions of walls were removed to allow passage from one underground warehouse to another. "If you stood underground and saw connecting passageways, your perception would be that there were tunnels," explains Montgomery. George Pappas Jr., owner of seven buildings from The Gift House to the Lighthouse Lounge on the north side of the 100 block, showed a visitor the basements underneath his properties, all of which connect. "No other owner on 25th Street has as many contiguous buildings as I do," Pappas notes. "My basements connect, but there aren't any tunnels."[47]

Brewski's, a club in the middle of the 200 block, is the remnant of the three-story European Hotel built in 1891. In its day, the hotel was noted for its "airy, commodious basement," divided into compartments for the convenience of business tenants on the ground floor. The basement's role in a colorful 1917 grand-jury investigation may be one of several possible smoking guns that fostered rumors of mysterious subterranean passageways. On March 24, 1917, hotel proprietor Denny Smyth was indicted for evading liquor laws. According to the indictment, Smyth made arrangements at the beginning of 1915 to lease a basement storeroom and help unnamed lessees sell liquor "without having procured a license to do so." Smyth installed a lock on the storeroom door connected to an electric button at the hotel desk so the clerk could admit "fitting" persons into the clandestine liquor store.[48]

In the second decade of the twenty-first century, new businesses on the street should reinforce the public's growing conviction that it is a hip destination. Jared Allen, a young entrepreneur who has owned the C. C. Keller Building since August 2011, built a roof-deck bar—Alleged—giving Ogden a distinctly modern dining option while respecting the building's history. The name "Alleged" pays homage—supported by strategically named drink selections—to Rosetta Davie, Sheriff Mac Wade, and other personalities who long ago acquired prominence in the pantheon of mythic 25th Street figures.

Through charm and skillfully drawn architectural and business plans, Allen and his team surmounted two obstacles to the realization of Alleged. The 200 block already had the maximum number of bars—two—allowed by municipal ordinance. But thanks to an entrance door around the corner on a bar-free block, Alleged sails under a Lincoln Avenue flag. Also the Ogden Landmarks Commission had to approve the addition of a deck to an historic building, and Ogden's building guidelines and line-of-sight rules, which required fifteen-foot setbacks from roof edges bordering a street, would have confined Alleged within a small space. Allen persuaded the city to change the guidelines to require only a five-foot setback.[49]

The ultimate white knight on 25th Street may emerge from an old, familiar, and friendly wellspring: rail travel. Since April 2008, the Utah Transit Authority's FrontRunner commuter trains have carried riders between Ogden and Salt Lake City.[50] While the majority of FrontRunner customers are Weber and Davis County residents who work or attend school in Salt Lake, others ride north to Ogden's downtown IRS buildings, Mormon Temple, Lindquist Field, or Weber State University (with a bus transfer). The train's potential to bring workers, students, sports fans, and tourists to Ogden has scarcely begun to be tapped. Howard M. Blackson III, a San Diego urban designer, called FrontRunner the most promising way to revive Ogden's downtown through its ability to attract new permanent residents, shoppers, and commuters.[51]

During its first year of operation, the FrontRunner drew predictable criticism about lower-than-predicted ridership and revenue and carrying commuters "from where they don't live to where they don't work."[52] However, by enabling transit-oriented development in the communities they serve, public-transportation systems do much more than move riders from point to point.

It took Arlington County, Virginia, three decades to develop its three-mile Rosslyn/Ballston corridor along the Orange Line train operated by the Washington Metropolitan Area Transit Authority (WMATA). The county proactively chose to build a community around public transportation, instead of relying on outdated park-and-ride models that kept transit along major highways and away from commercial thoroughfares. Nowadays one-third of Arlington County's tax revenue comes from what had been a dying corridor. WMATA now negotiates with federal agencies to locate their headquarters at "underutilized" rail stations, thereby bringing thousands of workers to their jobs, keeping them off crowded streets, and reducing costs of road maintenance. WMATA has marshaled its clout behind transit-oriented development, announcing its intention to encourage mixed-use facilities at stations.[53]

Utah shows signs of taking the same path. In Salt Lake County, Sandy has a thirty-year master plan for high-density housing near transit hubs. City planners envision villages with condominiums, offices, retail stores, and plenty of green space, parks, and trails. The planners have found that young adults want to maximize quality time and minimize yard work and commuting. Living near their jobs and amenities in mixed-use environments allows this kind of lifestyle. Sandy's plan is coordinated with the Wasatch Front Regional Council's (WFRC) thirty-year study, *Wasatch Choices 2040*.[54]

The same WFRC study calls for a streetcar similar to Salt Lake City's TRAX between the Ogden Transit Center and Weber State University, a goal the university has included in its ten-year master plan. With its eye on the improvements TRAX enabled at the University of Utah—conversion of former parking lots to classroom buildings or green space—Weber has called the proposed Ogden streetcar "a really critical project for us." Foot traffic on 25th Street could benefit immeasurably from hundreds of students strolling over from the Ogden Transit Center at Wall Avenue and 23rd Street, their transfer point between the FrontRunner and a streetcar.[55]

If we peer even further into the future than the birth of an Ogden streetcar system, the day will come when the city must think about replacing the current federal building. Ogden may do well to furnish space far away from 25th Street. While federal employees have certainly patronized the street's businesses, the current building has never been compatible with the special historical characteristics the city is now avid to promote. When it was built, it destroyed part of the street to save it. While some argued in 1963 that this de-facto cleanup of the street was for the best—indeed, Ogden was then floundering in uncharted waters as its railroad commerce slipped away—in the twenty-first century, the building continues to destroy the street spiritually.

Modern security requirements dictate that ordinary citizens cannot venture too close to the federal building. Both its architecture and menacing aura disrupt flow between Ogden's prime street corner at 25th Street and Washington Boulevard and the two charming blocks of 25th Street to the west. Surely city planners who have labored mightily to resurrect the street would prefer to have a Union Square–style development in the 300 block to unify the corridor from Union Station to the Ben Lomond Hotel. Ideally, these three blocks should be harmonious, charismatic, and uninterrupted.

Nowadays 25th Street often buzzes with levels of activity reminiscent of its heydays, thanks to adroitly planned public events. As envisioned in the 1977 master plan, civic parades now form there as they did a century ago, while street festivals showcase plein-air painting, classic cars, motorcycles, rock and blues music, and summer and winter athletic competitions. Film festival aficionados spill onto the street after screenings at Peery's Egyptian Theater. In the summer months, locals and out-of-towners swarm the farmer's market vendors on Saturdays, while on every first-Friday evening—both in warm and cold months—art lovers meander from gallery to gallery. Weber State University has boarded the bandwagon, steering its students toward business plans and history projects.

Yet most of the time, 25th Street remains far too quiet. The progress of the past four decades is exemplary, but ongoing infusions of elbow grease and ingenuity are as necessary now as in 1977. The street has yet to live down its skid-row reputation among many of Ogden's citizens. Many women are still not confident they will feel safe; even those who live on 25th Street come and go through their secure back entrances, seldom stepping out on the street and contributing to the activity that the general public needs to perceive.

Denver's Larimer Square helped Ogden to envision a revitalized 25th Street in 1977, and it may still be a worthy example. The brain behind Larimer Square, Dana Crawford, advised, "You have to celebrate your downtown to get people there who haven't been there in twenty years. They're not going to come because they are patriotic. They'll come if there is something fabulous to do and see." Although Larimer Square was a certifiable success soon after its transformation began in 1965, it continually reinvents itself to withstand competition from rival entertainment districts. Thousands of persons now live nearby in mixed-use buildings, and Larimer Square has phased out restaurants aimed at tourists, replacing them with higher-end options that appeal to locals.[56]

In 1998 architectural students investigating Ogden's industrial and commercial areas concluded that without the railroad and 25th Street, the city's economy could only have remained "localized and stagnant." The marketplace of 25th Street "allowed the construction of the Egyptian Theater and large homes on the east bench."[57] Thanks to the historical treasures along 25th Street secured for the future by committed city officials and citizens, Ogdenites can comprehend how the rest of their city became important. They learn about their unique identity and discover an anchor for their pride.

APPENDIX A

Mayor Harman Peery's Memorandum, "Additional Police Officers," from Minutes of the Regular Meeting of the Board of Commissioners of Ogden City, Utah, October 14, 1943 (series 09731, box 227850, p. 574, Utah State Archives, Division of Archives and Records Service, Salt Lake City).

As has been customary in many previous elections, the Police Department has been in for considerable panning and criticism coming principally from disgruntled politicians, the press, radio, etc.

As you no doubt know, Ogden is unfortunate in the fact that our fair City only has one public newspaper and one local broadcasting station owned principally by the same interests. They try in every conceivable manner, through ugly editorials, etc., to sway public opinion in the electing of public officials who are friendly to their selfish interests. I, personally, think it is high time that our populace resent and protest such tactics. No doubt they, the owners, are very much displeased that they cannot control the actions of our respective Mayor and Commissioners elected to public office.

One of the principal attacks through their editorials has been centered on the operation of "Amusement Devices" in operation at a great many of our business houses. As Mayor of Ogden, I don't recall one single complaint coming before our City Commission Meetings relative to the operation of such devices in our community. The "Amusement Devices" are duly licensed by Ogden City at the rate of $50.00 per year for each and every machine. The total received by our Ogden City Treasurer for this year up to date, amounts to a grand total of $7,250.00. In addition to the City license fees, our U.S. Federal Government licenses them at a rate of $100.00 per year for each and every machine. Our merchants are not compelled to rent or take on percentage, machines from operators. If a merchant is desirous of using "Amusement Devices" in his place of business and cares to, he can purchase such machines outright such as he does with his own cash register or other equipment owned by him.

The "Amusement Devices" license fees are most helpful in a financial way in meeting increased costs in the operation of our city, helpful to our own U.S. Government in helping meet increased costs in the operation of the war, helpful to the merchant in carrying on his business, and gives added enjoyment to a great many of our citizens.

It appears most strange to me that the owners and writers of our local paper would turn reformers for a few weeks prior to yearly elections.

If I am not mistaken, the writer of a great many of the editorials in such paper, Mr. Darrell Greenwell, has always appeared to me as a most "human person" and without a reform attitude. As I recall, Darrell's own father, a splendid gentleman who liked his sports, baseball, and, if I am not mistaken, was a great admirer of "Cock-Fights" which in conformity with our laws are not permitted in Utah.

I would like to quote the words of one of our would-be Commissioners, Harold L. Welch, who quotes on the back of one of his many political cards the following: "O Lord, Give me the strength to keep my big mouth shut when I don't know what the hell I'm talking about." Harold, I think it would be well for both you and Darrell to carefully study and carry out the above saying as printed on the back of your own political cards.

As for automobile traffic fatalities, I find that the total to date for this year amounts to a total of eight persons killed and also shows a total of eight persons killed for the year 1942. If I am not mistaken, these figures are prior to war times. However, we all want to do all in our power to prevent accidents of any nature whatsoever, and, I again want to caution the many automobile drivers, as well as our own traffic officers, to use every preventive in preventing accidents. Let's all observe the 35-mile speed limit set by our own Federal Government.

Our budget appropriations for the year 1943 will not allow the employing of additional officers at this time, but, as I have stated before, I would recommend at our budget meetings to be held next month that moneys be appropriated at that time for the employing of several extra men and women for our Police Department.

I would also recommend that our Civil Service officials be advised of such action; that it is our desire to increase the personnel just as soon as money is available to pay their salaries.

Yours for Victory,
[signed] Harman Peery, Mayor.

APPENDIX B

"Report on Activities of This Date by Lt. D. B. Ballantyne, Detective Ray Clawson, and Detective Arlyn Garside," January 7, 1950 (Arlyn Garside Papers, MS400, Special Collections, Stewart Library, Weber State University, Ogden).

While going down 25th Street [Ogden Police Detectives Clawson and Garside] saw the sheriff's Packard with [Deputy Jack] Card and [Deputy Blaine] Farr in it stop in front of the Beehive Tavern [200 25th Street]. They sat in the car for awhile then got out and went in the Beehive and talked to Frank Estrada. We patrolled the streets for about thirty minutes and the [sheriff's Packard] was still there so we parked our car and watched for [Deputies] Card and Farr to come out of the Beehive as we wanted to go through the Pan-American Club [a.k.a. the Key Club, one floor above the Beehive at 200½ 25th Street]. We waited for about thirty minutes then Garside got on the phone and called Lt. Ballantyne and informed him of the activities of the two deputies. Lt. Ballantyne came down and went in the Beehive. [Clawson] let Garside out and he joined the lieutenant in the Beehive. Clawson drove around in the car and waited for the two deputies to come out.

Lt. Ballantyne walked partway through the Beehive and never saw Card or Farr. He asked Frank Estrada if he would take him up into the Pan-American Club. Frank told him that he never had a key for the place. Clawson and Garside had seen a man go up into the Pan-American Club two different times just before Ballantyne and Garside went in the Beehive. This same man was setting on a stool near where Ballantyne was standing when Frank Estrada told Ballantyne that there was no key to let him in upstairs. In a little while David Estrada drove up in a car and Lt. Ballantyne asked him if he had a key for upstairs. David said no, that Bill (William Davie] had them. Ballantyne and Garside walked east to the Pioneer Tavern [214 25th Street] and then came back. Frank then came and said that they had a key, all this time Bill Davie was not to be seen. Garside and Ballantyne went upstairs with David and Frank Estrada. David showed us around, turning on all the lights. We went to the north end of the hall and he showed us the bathroom. In the west wall of this room was a door that went into another room. We asked him if he would open that door for us. He said that he didn't have a key for that one door but that it was only the sleeping quarters for his brother Johnny. (We have been told by those that are better acquainted with the upstairs that that room is also the living quarters of David Estrada.) While in the hall, we noticed that there is an outside door that goes out on a stairway that will take you to the rear of the Beehive Tavern. Against this door was stacked several cases of empty Coke bottles and on the floor was a white cloth that they had put there to keep the draft out.

Ballantyne and Garside went downstairs and stood on the corner directly in front of the Beehive. We looked all around to see if we could see anything of the two deputies. They were not in sight. We walked across the street and sat in [our] Mercury car. Our first thoughts were for Garside to go over to the service station that is on the southwest corner of 25th and Lincoln and watch and see just where they (the deputies) would come from. This idea was given up. While we were setting in the car Bill Davie came over and asked us if we would like to see their [the Pan-American Club's] charter. We looked at it and he told us if we would like to see the charter members to come upstairs with him and he would show us their names. We went up and looked over the names, some of which is, Johnny Grant, Dick Smith, Kenny Tribe, Francis Neff, Art Davies [Labor Temple manager], Ernie Wilson, Jay London, Johnny Estrada, David Estrada, Helen Oki Estrada, Frank Estrada, Eddie Doherty, Peter Cooper (a known pimp) and many others some of which are known criminals.

At this time Ballantyne and Garside went to the rear of the hallway again...the door had been opened since the time that we were up there before. Garside told Bill Davie, "Bill, it looks like when the boys [deputies] went out they didn't get the cloth back against the door and there is a draft coming in now." Bill said, "I guess I had better fix it." Ballantyne, Garside, and Bill [Davie] then left the [Pan-American] club rooms and went back down to the car. As we got in the car we noticed for the first time in the hour and half that we were around there, the deputies.

It is our belief that the two deputies were in the rear room of this club and for some unknown reason, did not want us to see them in a place that has a wild reputation and behind closed doors. There was a report to us this day that the same deputies had said they were going to get Chief [Maurice Schoofff] out as chief of police and about the same time there was another report that Bill Davie was out to get the chief. From the actions of these two deputies and the way Bill Davie, Frank Estrada, David Estrada, and the general actions of those around this place this day, it is our opinion that Weber County deputies along with the help of criminal characters will stop at nothing to cause embarrassments and disgrace to the chief and the police department.

APPENDIX C

Judge John A. Hendricks's admonition to Sheriff Mac Wade following a hearing on seized contraband in Second District Court, December 18, 1950 (transcribed and published in the *Ogden Standard-Examiner*, December 18, 1950).

Now, Mr. Sheriff, I want to tell you something, seeing you wanted to try this in the newspaper.

I have never said anything about the way you have conducted your office, publicly. Now, I'm going to tell you this: Things that you can expect to do in 1951.

First: The lawyers have bitterly complained about the service of civil papers, the first time in the history of twenty-five years that I've known of the constable serving a lot of civil papers, that your office is supposed to serve because lawyers say that they can't get service out of your office.

Now, one prominent attorney told your deputy, just prior to election, why certain members of your political party, lawyers, would not support you. He gave him definite statements as to times and places and papers, so I'm sure your deputy will tell you about it if he hasn't already. That, you've got to correct.

You were informed by the county attorney that—seeing you published that—that you had no legal right to an excess budget. Apparently you don't think much of the county attorney's advice because you went ahead and bought a shiny new black car before the first of the year that might just as well have been purchased after the first of the year. Now I'll advise you that you take [your lawyer] Mr. [John] Snow down, before he leaves, and have him read that budget law to you, because it's only going to mean embarrassment to you if you attempt to do, in the years to come, what you did in the past year.

Second: You've had nobody in charge of your office to whom complaints could be made since [former Chief Deputy] Mr. Olson left, no one there now that directs your office. You've got some good men, fine men down there, but there is no direction in your office, you are not there all the time, and there's nobody in charge when you are not. That you must correct, or should correct.

As to [Chief Deputy Jack] Card: You said I challenged him because of his statement. I made no statement about him. I merely asked him about a conversation he had. He denied even having the conversation, but I'll tell you now, upon investigation since then, that Mr. Card is totally unfit for a criminal deputy. I'll call your attention to recent cases. When two girls were involved with seven men, when they came up in this court, investigation by the parole department found out that there was no investigation carried on in any sensible and reasonable manner. Certain parties were involved and were never found out by Mr. Card.

In advising the county attorney, Mr. Card made a nine-line report that had no information of value to the prosecution. When it got to the probation office, he had even lost that, and the probation office said there were two more involved.

Another thing that shows Mr. Card is totally unfit is the fact in this very [Rosetta and William] Davie case, you and Mr. Card knew that they were under an injunction and neither one of you found out any of the facts in this nor in the companion cases in the court as to whether they were in business. Apparently it was open so all officers could find out.

Now, another thing you have done unwisely, I think. You appeared as character witness for [Eddie] Doherty. The district court thought so much of your testimony that he put [Doherty] in for fifteen years.

Now, your failure to cooperate with the city is eminently demonstrated by the fact that the mayor [White] and the chief of police [Schooff] filed opposition to the issuing of a charter for certain people for a club down on Twenty-Fifth Street, and yet you've written, advising, urging the issuing of that charter.

The taxpayers of Ogden City are the majority of the taxpayers of Weber County. Now, you should either show cooperation with the other law enforcement agency or you should keep out of the matters entirely...

...you paid [a reward] out of a special fund. I went to the county commissioners and said, "Does the sheriff have a special fund?" They informed me yes, you could draw up to four hundred dollars a month. I said, "Does he report to you who he pays it to?" They said, "Absolutely," so I paid no further attention to it. The other day I thought I would be interested in finding out just how much you paid out of that special fund to this juvenile and the other fellow. I called on the county auditor and found out an amazing thing. Since, beginning March 5, 1948, from then on until August 15 of this year, 1950, you have spent about three thousand dollars to which you have absolutely furnished no information as to who you paid it to or for what. The county commissioners and the auditor have allowed you to spend from $25.00 up to as high as $366.00 without a single explanation as to who you paid it to or for what.

Apparently the most charitable thing I can say is that the auditor and the county commissioners were afraid of you. You can't spend any more money like that. I and the taxpayers will see to that. Regardless of the county commissioners or auditor, you will have to account for the money you spend...

You have used prisoners to work on your farm. Whether it's true, as some people say, all your work has been done on your farm by prisoners is immaterial. Whether it's all or any part, you've absolutely no right to take a prisoner out to your own farm, especially have you no right to take them out on county time and county expense and charge the county expense for meals while they are working out there.

It may be that in this coming period when manpower will be restricted, that prisoners should be used, but there is a proper way for you to secure that authority to use them. Most certainly there is no way that you can secure them for doing your own farm work.

Now these are a few things that I'm telling you publicly so that you can go out and do as you want. My advice is that you hereafter secure proper authority for the things you do.

There will be no further disposition on the part of the people to allow you to run free and wild on the theory that you don't know anything about the job you are in. You've had four years' experience now. That's all.

APPENDIX D

Sheriff Mac Wade's prepared statement in response to Judge Hendricks, published in the *Ogden Standard-Examiner*, December 20, 1950.

Because of doubt placed in the minds of some people by the statements made by Judge John A. Hendricks and due to so many people calling and insisting that I publicly answer the allegations made in the paper, I feel that I should make the following statement.

My use of an investigation and revolving fund was questioned. Law enforcement officers all over the world have an investigation fund and as long as it is kept within reason they need not give any public accounting. My fund has at all times been within reason. What the judge failed to mention was that also from this same fund is paid the expenses of out of the county travel for officers. Matron service, for example, for females committed to the state hospital and American Fork training school, and minor office and car incidentals. Never has one cent of this fund been paid a prisoner.

The judge also said that my chief deputy was incompetent and unfit for criminal investigation. It is easy to make accusations, but the record speaks for itself. In the past two years Deputy Card has made more than twenty felony arrests. Without exception, everyone pleaded guilty in the lower and district courts. This has saved the taxpayers thousands of dollars in jury fees and prosecution cost[s]. Not once has the district attorney had to prepare or to expend funds in prosecuting these cases. Is this incompetent and inefficient investigation, or a waste of my small investigation funds?

As for cooperation with other law enforcement officers, we will cooperate with any officer that we feel can be trusted.

As for working prisoners on my farm. With prison labor, an old potato cellar was repaired for storing onions, potatoes and vegetables for the use of the jail. The last flood that washed out the highline canal, the county Pole Patch road came from the mountain down through my farm. A group of citizens appearing before the county commissioners asked for help in eliminating this hazard. At the suggestion of the county commissioners, prisoner labor was used.

Relative to the twelve watches. They are part of an $85,000 jewelry store robbery in Butte [Montana]. We have endeavored many times through both the county and district attorney to get prosecution on these items which were found in Eddie Doherty's safe in Lucky's Tavern. At the present time we are working with a special investigator furnished by the insurance company from San Francisco. The watches have never at any time been outside the sheriff's office.

OGDEN
RANSFER
OPEN
CONTINUOUS
5 10

NOTES

Acknowledgments

1. Richard F. Selcer, *Hell's Half Acre: The Life and Legend of a Red Light District* (Fort Worth: Texas Christian University Press, 1991), x.
2. No evidence of Kate Flint's residing or operating in Ogden has ever been produced. Jeffrey Nichols relates her essential history in Corinne and Salt Lake City in *Prostitution, Polygamy, and Power: Salt Lake City, 1847–1918* (Urbana: University of Illinois Press, 2002), 27–28, 42–43. The rumor of her purchasing Brigham Young's carriage began in the *Salt Lake Tribune* on November 2, 1876, but was meant as a joke; the same issue of the paper identified the actual buyer, J. A. Fitzgerald. Bernard DeVoto embellished the Flint story—also intending it as a joke—in "Ogden: The Underwriters of Salvation," in *The Taming of the Frontier*, ed. Duncan Aikman (New York: Minton, Balch, 1925), 48–49. Fanny Dawson was never tried for any murder and was merely guilty of operating a boarding house without a license. *Ogden Standard*, January 21, 1916. Dawson was held as a state's witness under a thousand-dollar bond in a prosecution stemming from the mysterious death of one of her boarders. *Salt Lake Tribune*, January 26, 1916. The man accused of murdering the boarder was acquitted, however. *Salt Lake Telegram*, April 23, 1916.
3. In claiming Capone's sub-rosa presence during Prohibition, Ogden must get in line with other cities professing the same distinction, including Aguilar and Glenwood Springs, Colorado, and Johnson City, Tennessee.
4. F. Ross Peterson and Robert Parson, *Ogden City: Its Governmental Legacy: A Sesquicentennial History* (Ogden, UT: Chapelle Ltd., 2001), 216.

Chapter 1, Ogden Envy

1. Janice P. Dawson, "Frederick Vining Fisher: Methodist Apologist for Mormonism," *Utah Historical Quarterly* 55 (1987): 367; *Ogden Standard-Examiner,* September 2, 1937; Dorrene Jeske, e-mail

to the author, June 2, 2008; Tom Owens, e-mail to the author, May 14, 2010.

2. "Through Nevada's Desert," *New York Times,* March 20, 1881.
3. Union Pacific engine no. 117 was "the first locomotive to enter Ogden," while no. 119, following behind, soon gained fame as the Union Pacific engine at the Golden Spike ceremony at Promontory Summit on May 10, 1869. See Gerald M. Best, "Rendezvous at Promontory: The 'Jupiter' and No. 119," *Utah Historical Quarterly* 37 (1969): 74.
4. Ogdenite Joseph Hall wrote the most detailed account of the March 8, 1869, celebration for the *Deseret News* (weekly ed.), "Railway Celebration at Ogden," March 17, 1869. See also Work Projects Administration for the State of Utah, *Utah: A Guide to the State* (New York: Hastings House, 1941), 205; *Ogden Standard-Examiner,* December 31, 1925; June 14, 1939; January 11, 1940. The celebration's total cost to the city was $66.45. Ogden City Council, Minute Book A, April 27, 1869, p. 12, typescript, Utah Historical Records Survey, Ogden City Recorder's Office.
5. Howard R. Lamar, *The Far Southwest, 1846–1912: A Territorial History* (New Haven: Yale University Press, 1966), 371.
6. Hall, "Railway Celebration," *Deseret News* (weekly ed.), March 17, 1869.
7. LDS "Journal History," May 29, 1868, and letter of George Reynolds to George F. Biggs, June 4, 1868, both cited in Leonard J. Arrington, "The Transcontinental Railroad and Mormon Economic Policy," *Pacific Historical Review* 20 (1951): 149.
8. *Deseret News* (weekly ed.), March 3, 1869.
9. The early arrests were reported in Francis A. Brown, "Ogden City Police Record," 1859–1869, MSS 57, box 165, folder 5, Work Projects Administration typescript, Utah State Historical Society, Salt Lake City.
10. Edward W. Tullidge, "Ogden City," *Western Galaxy* 1 (1888): 434; Alma W. Hansen, "A Historical Study of the Influence of the Railroad upon Ogden, Utah, 1868–1875" (master's thesis, Brigham Young University, 1953), 5–6.
11. *New York Times,* January 4, 1869 (written on December 24, 1868).
12. See also *Ogden Junction,* April 30, 1873 ("The pay car of the Union Pacific is anxiously expected"); October 25, 1873 ("The pay car of the Union Pacific will leave Omaha next Monday, and may be expected here Thursday or Friday succeeding"). By 1880 the railroads employed about 225 men in Ogden with monthly payroll disbursements between sixteen thousand and twenty thousand dollars. *Salt Lake Tribune,* February 17, 1880.
13. *Salt Lake Herald-Republican,* December 23, 1909.
14. "Across the Continent: The Frank Leslie Excursion to the Pacific," *Frank Leslie's Illustrated Newspaper,* December 15, 1877, 242. For a description of a similar frenetic scene at Ogden's depot, see "Through Nevada's Desert," *New York Times*, March 20, 1881.
15. William G. Marshall, *Through America* (London: Sampson Low, Marston, Searle and Rivington, 1881), 238–39. The four rail lines at the time were the Union Pacific, Central Pacific (later Southern Pacific), Utah Central, and Utah and Northern Railway.
16. O. A. Kennedy, "Old Timer Avers Ogden Hasn't Changed So Much in Half Century," *Ogden Standard-Examiner,* July 18, 1943. Kennedy is recounting a conversation he heard roughly half a century earlier between the sheriff and the marshal, whom he did not name. When 25th Street's saucy

Novelty Theater closed, the *Salt Lake Tribune* of June 9, 1891, said the street would "seriously" feel the loss of the Novelty's fifteen-hundred-dollar weekly payroll: "This money was to the benefit of 25th St. merchants especially."

17. Richard E. Kotter, "An Examination of Mormon and Non-Mormon Influences in Ogden City Politics, 1847–1896" (master's thesis, Utah State University, 1967) 109; Edward L. Lyman, *Political Deliverance: The Mormon Quest for Utah Statehood* (Urbana: University of Illinois Press, 1986), 112. Kotter and Lyman merely assume a relaxation of law enforcement, failing to cite statistics or actual amendments to vice ordinances by the Liberal city council. On the contrary, the council more than doubled the police force. Ogden City Council, Minute Book H, September 13, 1889, p. 294; May 16, 1890, p. 562, Ogden City Recorder's Office. It also voted down petitions to permit saloons to stay open past midnight. Minute Book H, August 8, 1890, p. 662; August 29, 1890, p. 688. See also *Salt Lake Tribune,* August 9, 30, 1890.
18. The laws were the Edmunds Act, *U.S. Statutes at Large* 22 (1882): 30–32; and the Edmunds-Tucker Act, *U.S. Statutes at Large* 24 (1887): 635–41.
19. Jean Bickmore White, "The Right to Be Different: Ogden and Weber County Politics, 1850–1924," *Utah Historical Quarterly* 47 (1979): 259.
20. *Deseret News* (weekly ed.), March 9, 1889.
21. *Aspen (CO) Daily Times,* February 12, 1890; *Deseret News* (weekly ed.), March 1, 1890. Judge Franklin D. Richards wrote in his journal that Ogden's city government was "turned fraudulently over to our enemies." White, "Right to Be Different," 263.
22. Lyman, *Political Deliverance,* 111. As his authority, Lyman cited Kotter, "Examination of Mormon and Non-Mormon Influences," 100–110, but Kotter downplayed allegations of fraud: "The Liberal majority of votes was too astoundingly large [on the average, pluralities of four hundred] for the Mormons to claim that the election was obtained through fraud and fraud alone."
23. *Annual Report of the Utah Commission, 1889,* 51st Cong., 1st sess., 1889, H. Doc. 1, pt. 5, 176–77.
24. *Daily Alta California,* February 12, 1889; *Sacramento Daily Record-Union,* February 12, 1889; *Los Angeles Herald,* February 12, 1889; *Pueblo (CO) Chieftain,* February 12, 1889.
25. *Ogden Standard,* February 14, 1889.
26. Ogden City Council, Minute Book H, March 1, 1889, p. 29; *Ogden Standard,* March 6, 1889; *Salt Lake Tribune,* March 5, 13, 16, 1889. A later city council granted a petition from the Ogden Chamber of Commerce asking that Tabernacle Square be restored to the Mormon Church. *Ogden Standard,* December 21, 1893. In the interim, Tabernacle Square was host to circuses and the Order of Monte Cristo during the Mardi Gras celebration in 1890. Minute Book H, June 28, 1889, p. 190; May 29, 1890, p. 576.
27. *Annual Report of the Utah Commission, 1889,* 187; *Ogden Standard,* August 6, 21, 1889; *Salt Lake Tribune,* August 21, 22, 1889. In creating the new precinct boundaries, the county court refused to use the Liberal city council's new street names of Washington Avenue and 24th Street. Judge Preshaw sued to restore the original Ogden precinct and his position in it but lost. *Ogden Standard,* December 4, 1889; *Preshaw v. Dee,* 6 Utah 360, 23 P. 763 (1890) [Utah Supreme Court].
28. *Deseret News* (weekly ed.), May 25, 1889; *Salt Lake Herald,* August 17, 1889.
29. Pil [pseud], "Liberalism Is Wealth," *Salt Lake Tribune,* December 5, 1889.

30. *Deseret News* (weekly ed.), May 25, 1889; *Ogden Standard,* August 16, 17, 1889; *Salt Lake Herald,* August 20, 28, 1889.

31. *Salt Lake Herald,* August 22, 24, 1889; *Ogden Standard,* August 22, 1889.

32. O. A. Kennedy recalled, "Soon after the Liberal party carried the [February 1889] election, plans were made to start a Liberal daily paper in opposition to the *Standard,* which was the organ of the People's party." The *Daily Commercial's* articles of incorporation were filed on March 18, 1889, and its first issue appeared about May 1, 1889. See Kennedy, "The Story of the Ogden Daily Commercial," *Ogden Standard-Examiner,* November 21, 1920.

33. *Ogden Daily Commercial,* August 23, 1889 (cited in *Ogden Standard* (semiweekly ed.), September 7, 1889); *Utah Daily Union,* August 23, 1889 (cited in *Ogden Standard,* September 6, 1889).

34. At least three of the Republicans who signed were Mormon: Sidney Stevens, carriage dealer; George W. Driver, druggist; and Amos Bonesteel Corey, contractor. Parsons was tried for numerous crimes while he was U.S. marshal, including permitting gambling in a building he owned and lewd conduct toward female prisoners. He was acquitted, however. The *Salt Lake Tribune's* Washington, D. C., bureau reported that the U.S. attorney general's office, "while exonerating Parsons from criminal derelictions and malfeasances in office, thinks he is not the caliber of material for a marshal." *Salt Lake Tribune,* January 25, 1892.

35. All correspondence between the Weber County Republican Committee and U.S. Marshal Parsons is reprinted in the *Ogden Standard* (semiweekly ed.), September 4, 1889.

36. *Ogden Herald,* March 22, 31; April 6, 1887. The boom coincided with Frank J. Cannon's March 1887 debut as editor of the *Ogden Herald* and was the dominant theme of his time at the paper. Cannon had "taken the initiative in pursuing a well-deliberated plan to ventilate Ogden's natural facilities.... We've got the location. We have the best railroad facilities. Our businessmen have the necessary grit and enterprise." Ibid., March 31, 1887.

37. *Annual Report of the Utah Commission, 1889,* 179; *Report of the Governor of Utah,* 51st Cong., 2nd sess., 1890, H. Doc. 1, pt. 5, 642. Perhaps owing to boom-era psychology and hopes of surpassing Salt Lake City, Ogden felt it was drastically undercounted in 1890. A special census committee urged a recount. Ogden City Council, Minute Book H, July 11, 1890, pp. 628–29. However, Ogden's 1900 population figure of 16,313 makes the 1890 tally appear relatively accurate.

38. The new arrivals were first mentioned in connection with Ogden as follows: London in the *Ogden Standard,* May 16, 1889; Desmond in the *Ogden Standard,* May 22, 1889; Patton in the *Salt Lake Herald,* April 20, 1889; Harvey in the *Salt Lake Herald,* June 26, 1889; and Reed in the *Ogden Standard,* September 1, 1889. Bigelow's and Smyth's obituaries said they arrived in 1889. *Salt Lake Tribune,* March 20, 1923; *Ogden Standard-Examiner,* January 3, 1922. Kennedy recalled his date of arrival in "Gun Scene 'Cooked Up?' Scribe Still Wonders These 50 Years After," *Ogden Standard-Examiner,* July 28, 1939.

39. *Ogden Standard,* May 7, 1893.

40. Ibid., May 20, 1893; *Ogden Standard-Examiner,* March 6, 1922. The Stephens brothers were also part owners of 25th Street's White Elephant gambling house. *Ogden Standard,* April 8, 1909.

41. Mormon ordinances were performed by proxy for Rosetta Davie under her legal name of Ada ArZella Beveridge in the Ogden LDS Temple in 2005. Her

childhood baptism date of May 28, 1927, and other data are available at http://www.familysearch.org

42. *Salt Lake Tribune,* September 1, 1889. Elsewhere in the same issue, a reporter gloated that "the *Tribune* is still on deck in Ogden."

43. Tullidge, "Ogden City," 440.

44. *New York Times,* August 31, 1868. Richard Francaviglia traces Young's long-held confidence that the railroad would run through Salt Lake City in *Over the Range: A History of the Promontory Summit Route of the Pacific Railroad* (Logan: Utah State University Press, 2008), 38–76.

45. *Joint Resolution for the Protection of the Interests of the United States in the Union Pacific Railroad Company, the Central Pacific Railroad Company, and for other Purposes, U.S. Statutes at Large* 16 (1869): 56.

46. *Ogden Standard,* October 18, 1901; January 29, February 1, 1902.

47. Ibid., January 30, 1902.

48. Ibid., March 17, 1902.

49. See Richard F. Selcer, *Legendary Watering Holes: The Saloons That Made Texas Famous* (College Station: Texas A&M University Press, 2004), 230–31; Selcer, *Hell's Half Acre: The Life and Legend of a Red Light District* (Fort Worth: Texas Christian University Press, 1991), x–xv, 150–60; John Costello, *Virtue under Fire: How World War II Changed Our Social and Sexual Attitudes* (Boston: Little, Brown, 1986), 210–18; and Karen Anderson, *Wartime Women: Sex Roles, Family Relations, and the Status of Women during World War II* (Westport: Greenwood Press, 1981), 102–11.

50. Bernard DeVoto, "Utah," *American Mercury* 7 (1926): 319–20.

51. John McCormick and John R. Sillito, *A History of Utah Radicalism: Startling, Socialistic, and Decidedly Revolutionary* (Logan: Utah State University Press, 2011), 17.

52. *Ogden Standard,* September 27, 1909; *Ogden Evening Standard,* October 19, 1911.

53. *New York Times,* May 30, 1903; *Ogden Examiner,* September 14, 1912; *Salt Lake Tribune,* September 14, 1912. Early automobile enthusiast Denny Smyth was noted for driving on 25th Street with his pet parrot "perched on the radiator cap, screeching warnings to pedestrian targets." Frank Tinker, "Old 25th Street Gets New Look," *Salt Lake Tribune,* September 15, 1963.

54. *Ogden Standard,* September 23, 1919.

55. *New York Times,* April 24, 25, 1906; *San Francisco Call,* April 24, 1906.

56. Charles Winick and Paul M. Kinsie, *The Lively Commerce: Prostitution in the United States* (Chicago: Quadrangle Books, 1971), 198. This statement reinforces the *Salt Lake Tribune*'s observation on April 7, 1890, that "the [Ogden] hotels were crowded with commercial men, who always make Ogden their Sunday lay-over point."

57. The August 25, 1941, issue of *Time* magazine printed a letter from Girard T. Bryant at Ogden's Porters and Waiters Club objecting to terms *Time* had used to refer to African Americans: "Damn! It's getting so I can't read an article about the race without being insulted." Bryant, a Kansas City educator and railroad worker, was on a month's vacation "courtesy of Union Pacific."

58. Michael Wutz, "Riffing about a Century of Jazz: A Conversation with Joe McQueen at 88," *Weber: The Contemporary West* 24 (2007): 21–24.

59. Ibid.; Joe McQueen, conversation with the author, September 21, 2011.

60. Wutz, "Riffing about a Century," 21–24. Jack McVea and his group played at the Dixieland Club, later the New Cotton Club, in North Salt Lake. *Salt Lake Tribune,* December 25, 1948; December 17, 1949. On March 5, 1947, McVea held court at

Ogden's Glen Brothers Music, signing his biggest hit record, "Open the Door, Richard." *Ogden Standard-Examiner,* March 4, 1947.

61. Sally Denton and Roger Morris, *The Money and the Power: The Making of Las Vegas and Its Hold on America, 1947–2000* (New York: Alfred A. Knopf, 2001) 159–63; *Ogden Standard-Examiner,* May 22, 1927; February 19, 1950; *Nevada State Journal,* May 3, 1970.
62. Interview with Robert Peery King, May 26, 2009. When Mayor Peery called for legalized gambling and liquor by the drink, he cited Las Vegas as proof that such measures did not lead to social ills: "When I was in Las Vegas I failed to see any signs of drunkenness like we have in Utah every night and the gutters and back lots weren't littered with bottles." *Ogden Standard-Examiner,* February 7, 1948.
63. Ibid., October 16, November 3, 1933.

Chapter 2, Ogden Hosts

1. The exception was Main Street (Washington Boulevard), which was 132 feet wide. The 1851 platting followed earlier visits by Brigham Young on September 3, 1849, and in August 1850, during which he established Ogden's location and city limits. See [Dale L. Morgan], *A History of Ogden* (Ogden, UT: Ogden City Commission, 1940), 21–25; *Deseret News,* August 31, September 7, 1850; Edward W. Tullidge, "Ogden City," *Western Galaxy* 1 (1888): 431–33; Leo Haefeli, "A Stroll through Ogden," *Tullidge's Quarterly Magazine* 1 (1881): 475; O. A. Kennedy, "Ogden Once a Walled City," *Ogden Standard-Examiner,* June 19, 1921; Brenda C. Scheer, "The Mormon Grid: Zion in the Desert," (paper presented at the International Center on Urban Form, Trani, Italy, 2003), available online at http://content.lib.utah.edu/utils/getfile/collection/uspace/id/3215/filename/2052.pdf (accessed March 17, 2013).
2. [Morgan], *A History of Ogden,* 36; Joseph Hall, "Railway Celebration at Ogden," *Deseret News* (weekly ed.), March 17, 1869.
3. Ogden City Council, Minute Book B, December 12, 1870, p. 104, typescript, Utah Historical Records Survey, Ogden City Recorder's Office.
4. *Ogden Standard-Examiner,* July 24, 1923; *Ogden Standard,* April 17, 1902.
5. Originally built as a meeting house for Mormon "seventies," members of the higher priesthood charged with missionary work, Seventies Hall near the southwest corner of 5th and Young was subsequently used as a city hall and firemen's hall. *Deseret News,* October 8, 1862; *Ogden Herald,* August 21, 1884; Richard W. Sadler and Richard C. Roberts, *Weber County's History* (Ogden, UT: Weber County Commission, 2000), 261. Later it functioned as a Salvation Army barracks, National Guard armory from 1897 to 1903, and—remodeled and enlarged—the Lyceum Theater until it was torn down on July 18, 1910. The Maule estate replaced it with a new Lyceum Theater, which still stands at 269 25th Street. *Salt Lake Herald,* June 6, 1897; *Ogden Standard,* June 27, 1897; November 10, 1903; July 18, 1910.
6. W. R. Thomas, "On the Wing, an Editorial Letter," *Denver Rocky Mountain News,* May 3, 1869; *Deseret News* (weekly ed.), May 26, 1869. In the earliest weeks of transcontinental service, Taylor's Mills was, in fact, called "Ogden Station," as noted by the *Deseret News*'s correspondent.
7. Thomas, "On the Wing," *Denver Rocky Mountain News,* May 3, 1869.
8. *U.S. Statutes at Large* 16 (1869): 56.
9. *New York Times,* June 16, 1869; *Deseret News* (weekly ed.), March 31, 1869.

10. *Ogden Junction,* January 1, 1870.
11. Milton R. Hunter, *Beneath Ben Lomond's Peak* (Salt Lake City: Deseret News Press, 1944), 424. In December 1874, Mayor Lorin Farr assigned surveyor James H. Martineau to plan the location of Ogden's anticipated "grand depot." Richard Francaviglia, *Over the Range: A History of the Promontory Summit Route of the Pacific Railroad* (Logan: Utah State University Press, 2008), 167. However, no such edifice materialized until 1889.
12. *Deseret News* (weekly ed.), December 22, 1869.
13. Ibid.
14. In Ogden's earliest years, Bishop Chauncey West had a monopoly on liquor vending: "We were informed that Bishop West did keep the first saloon in Ogden, and sold the poorest whisky to be had." *Salt Lake Tribune,* January 24, 1885. From 1850 to 1863, the city council issued thirty-six permits, mostly temporary, for the manufacture or sale of alcohol. Alma W. Hansen, "A Historical Study of the Influence of the Railroad upon Ogden, Utah, 1868–1875," (master's thesis, Brigham Young University, 1953), 6. Six times during the period 1859–1869, minutes from the Ogden Police Department reflect abhorrence for persons selling liquor without a license, more than for any other crime. See Francis A. Brown, "Ogden City Police Record," 1859–1869, October 13, 1860; July 26, 1862; August 10, 1862; January 9, 1863; May 17, 1863; June 29, 1866, MSS 57, box 165, folder 5, Work Projects Administration typescript, Utah State Historical Society, Salt Lake City.
15. Salt Lake City licenses "are left to the discrimination of the City Council....Thus, a Gentile pays one figure, and a Mormon pays another." *New York Times,* October 3, 1871. See also *Daily Corinne Reporter,* November 11, 1871; *Salt Lake Tribune,* October 14, 1876.
16. *Denver Rocky Mountain News,* January 10, 1870.
17. *Deseret News* (weekly ed.), December 22, 1869. On December 7, 1869, petitions from J. M. Harriss and the partnership of Adolph Landt and F. Fullride to sell liquor at the depot were denied. Ogden City Council, Minute Book B, December 7, 1869, pp. 27–28.
18. Ogden City Council, Minute Book B, December 12, 1870, p. 103.
19. *Deseret News* (weekly ed.), November 12, 1873; *Corinne Daily Reporter,* November 11, 1873.
20. *Ogden Examiner,* October 5, 1912. The Pulaski House, seldom spelled the same way twice, is mentioned in the *Ogden Junction,* June 17, July 7, 1873; *Deseret News* (weekly ed.), November 12, 1873; and *Corinne Daily Reporter,* November 11, 1873. Pulaski may have been the original lessee's name; however, his identity and history in Ogden are elusive. U.S. Bureau of the Census, ninth census (1870), Weber County, p. 58, line 14, has an S. Plonsky twelve lines below Fred J. Kiesel; both were merchants and immigrants from the German Empire. Ogden native Aaron McIntyre recalled a boyhood playmate in the early 1870s, Moses Polunski (possibly the son of a Pulaski?), with whom he watched the trains at the depot every morning. See "Son Reviews Service of Pioneer Physician," *Ogden Standard-Examiner,* August 24, 1934.
21. *New York Times,* July 6, 1871.
22. Erb's Civil War experiences are described in his obituaries. *Salt Lake Tribune,* December 9, 1895; *Salt Lake Herald,* December 11, 1895. He was in Ogden by December 19, 1870, when he petitioned the city council "to sell liquor by the bottle at the railroad eating house." The license was granted but later restricted to sales to passengers only. Ogden City Council, Minute Book B, December 19, 1870; January 9, 1871, pp. 104, 107.

23. U.S. Bureau of the Census, ninth census (1870), Adams County, Illinois, p. 79, shows Erb (line 24); his first wife, Elizabeth Chapman (line 25); and William Chapman (line 19) in the same large household in Quincy. Dr. Nellis was business partner to Ogden merchant William Driver and the first master of the Weber Masonic Lodge between its December 27, 1873, dispensation and November 12, 1874, charter. *Salt Lake Tribune,* January 17, 1897. Nellis left Ogden around 1874 and eventually settled in San Francisco.
24. *Corinne Daily Reporter,* June 24, 1872; *Salt Lake Tribune,* December 9, 1872.
25. *Corinne Daily Reporter,* June 24, 1872.
26. *Daily Alta California,* July 19, 1872. The Chicago Bakery was adjacent to the Pulaski House on the south. Justice of the Peace Thomas D. Dee recalled that the Junction House's "passenger portion" was destroyed by fire and rebuilt. *Pacific Railway Commission,* 50th Cong., 1st sess., 1887, S. Doc. 51, vol. 3, 2225–226.
27. *Corinne Daily Reporter,* February 4, 6, 1873.
28. As Walker House proprietor, Major Erb hosted numerous celebrities of his era. After Irish dramatist Oscar Wilde stayed at Walker House during his lecture tour of the U.S., public curiosity was so great that Erb had to post a sign saying, "Oscar Wilde has left the city." See *Salt Lake Tribune,* April 13, 1882. Despite his fame in Salt Lake City, Erb was buried at Mountain View Cemetery (now Aultorest Memorial Park) in Ogden.
29. Sadler and Roberts, *Weber County's History,* 127.
30. Hunter, *Beneath Ben Lomond's Peak,* 107. No records detailing Burch's involvement with his hotel were located, but the Ogden police held meetings at a Birch House during the winter of 1860–1861; see Brown, "Ogden City Police Record," 1859–1869, December 8, 29, 1860; January 21, 30, 1861.
31. Ogden native Aaron McIntyre recalled Herrick's proprietorship in "Son Reviews Service," *Ogden Standard-Examiner,* August 24, 1934; and Simon Bamberger said it was the Lester House when he reached Ogden in 1869. Eileen H. Stone, *Homeland in the West: Utah Jews Remember* (Salt Lake City: University of Utah Press, 2001), 92. *Ogden Junction,* January 1, May 28, 1870.
32. *Ogden Junction,* April 27, 1870. Bamberger's business partners were Briner Cohen and then A. C. Hobart in Ogden and Augustus Podlech in Salt Lake City.
33. *Ogden Standard-Examiner,* June 29, 1975, based on recollections of Ogden pioneer Lamoni Grix.
34. Orson F. Whitney, *History of Utah,* vol. 2, *Biographical* (Salt Lake City: G. Q. Cannon & Sons, 1904), 163, gives a life sketch of William Nicol Fife, the Ogden city marshal. See also Jack Goodman, "Jews in Zion," in *The Peoples of Utah,* ed. Helen Z. Papanikolas (Salt Lake City: Utah State Historical Society, 1976), 209.
35. *Wisconsin State Journal,* August 1, 1870; *St. Joseph (MI) Herald,* August 6, 1870; Stone, *Homeland in the West,* 92.
36. Stone, *Homeland in the West,* 93.
37. In August 1871, two young men driving a livery wagon failed to notice a Utah Central train that was backing up to its freight warehouse and collided with it, killing one of their horses and injuring the other. See *Ogden Junction,* August 19, 1871. A grand jury "severely blamed the railroad companies for their imperfect safeguards against accidents and loss of life at the depot," noted the *Ogden Standard* of September 5, 1888.
38. Ogden City Council, Minute Book C, November 25, 1872, p. 14; November 10, 1873, p. 137. (Scally's Arcade Hotel of 1872 should not be confused with the Arcade Hotel of the early 1900s in what is today called the Congress building at 115 25th Street; see

Ogden Standard, February 5, December 28, 1901.) Early boarding houses on 5th Street were run by Lindeloff and Son (see *Ogden Junction,* October 31, 1874) and Geoff Moore (see *Deseret News* [weekly ed.], February 24, 1875, reporting Utah Governor Axtell's stay at Moore's).

39. *Ogden Junction,* June 21, 1873; *Deseret News* (weekly ed.), December 10, 1873; *Ogden Herald,* April 10, 1882; July 18, 1883. Poole got a license to run the Traveler's Rest boarding house (street and location unspecified) on December 19, 1870; it may have later become the Globe Hotel. See Ogden City Council, Minute Book B, December 19, 1870, p. 104. The Globe was later run as the Anthon House (see *Ogden Junction,* January 11, 1879); and the Occidental (see *Ogden Herald,* November 12, 1883).
40. On January 20, 1873, George Loomis and C. L. Creek were granted a license to operate an unnamed bar at the depot. Ogden City Council, Minute Book C, January 20, 1873, p. 34. The *Ogden Junction* of March 6, 1873, mentioned the "Junction Hotel, kept by Mr. George W. Loomis." On July 10, 1873, it reported, "The Junction Hotel is being remodeled and extensive additions erected." On October 29, 1873, the paper observed, "We hope Mr. Loomis will soon be in a condition to erect another building or two like the Junction Hotel, which, under the direction of Chapman & Scally, the lessees, has an established reputation as a first class house."
41. *Ogden Junction,* October 8, 1873. The *Corinne Daily Reporter* also praised Chapman and Scally on September 22, 1873, as did the *Deseret News* (weekly ed.), April 8, 1874. There is no reference to it after *Deseret News* (weekly ed.), August 25, 1875.
42. *Corinne Daily Reporter,* November 11, 19, 1873.
43. Ibid., November 11, 1873.
44. "War and Desolation, An Ordinary Hen's Egg with a Strange Inscription," *Daily Nevada State Journal,* May 13, 1874.
45. *Salt Lake Tribune,* June 9, July 7, 1877.
46. Ibid., June 9, 1877. Dissolution of the partnership forced Keeney out of the Keeney House in 1879; bankruptcy forced Zeigler out in 1880. See *Ogden Junction,* September 23, 1879; December 4, 1880. Mills H. Beardsley resumed control, retaining the Keeney House name and running it simultaneously with his Union Depot Hotel. *Ogden Junction,* June 5, 1880; *Ogden Herald,* July 11, 1881. The locals now referred to the Union Depot Hotel informally as the Beardsley House. Beardsley left Ogden in 1887, but his son, Willis, revived the name Beardsley House in 1892, opening an upscale, but short-lived, hotel in the Murphy Block, 103–5 5th Street. *Ogden Standard,* July 8, 1892. It was Ogden's third Beardsley House.
47. Hunter lists the Keeney and Beardsley Houses as separate entities in *Beneath Ben Lomond's Peak,* 107, as does Sadler and Roberts in *Weber County's History,* 100.
48. *Salt Lake Tribune,* December 4, 1871. The proprietors between Bamberger and Shakespeare were the partnership of Eudey and Williams. Ibid.; *Ogden Junction,* June 21, 1873.
49. These biographical details come from Shakespeare's obituary in the *Ogden Standard,* November 15, 1891; and Edward L. Sloan, *Gazetteer of Utah and Salt Lake City Directory* (Salt Lake City: Herald Publishing Company, 1874), 108, 111. Prior to 1875, Shakespeare ran one of Ogden's depot hotels, possibly Chapman and Scally's Junction Hotel. See *Salt Lake Herald,* November 15, 1891.
50. *Salt Lake Tribune,* September 9, 1875.
51. Ibid., January 16, 1873.
52. *Lashus v. Chamberlain*, 24 P. 188 (1890) [Utah Supreme Court]. George Lashus's role at the

driving of the Golden Spike on May 10, 1869, is ambiguous. Most recent literature identifies the engineer of the Central Pacific's Jupiter engine as George Booth; see Michael W. Johnson, "Rendezvous at Promontory: A New Look at the Golden Spike Ceremony," *Utah Historical Quarterly* 72 (2004): 64; Francaviglia, *Over the Range*, 137–38; National Park Service, "Golden Spike: A Moment in Time," Golden Spike National Historic Site brochure, available online at http://www.nps.gov/gosp/historyculture/upload/Russell.pdf (accessed October 31, 2011). However, Lashus was widely publicized at Ogden's Golden Jubilee celebration on May 10, 1919, as the original Jupiter engineer fifty years earlier. See "Camera Story of Golden Spike Fête at Utah," *Southern Pacific Bulletin* 8 (June 1919): 5; *Ogden Standard-Examiner,* May 9, 1919; and "Daughter of Engineer Who Piloted 'Jupiter' Recounts History of Road Building," *Ogden Standard-Examiner,* April 23, 1939. Lashus's obituary in the *New York Times* of February 23, 1938, makes the connection. The 1969 convention of the Brotherhood of Locomotive Engineers invited Harvey Lashus to represent his grandfather, "the engineer at the throttle of...Jupiter"; see *Ogden Standard-Examiner,* May 14, 1969. These associations of Lashus with the Jupiter were apparently never challenged. Perhaps the reality resides in the account that Lashus gave to Noble Warrum, Charles W. Morse, and W. Brown Ewing, the compilers of *Utah Since Statehood,* vol. 2, *Historical and Biographical* (Chicago/Salt Lake City: S. J. Clarke Publishing Co., 1919), 374: "[Lashus] was present when the last spike was driven....He was then an engineer on the Central Pacific and with engine No. 95 pulled the train westward that carried many noted visitors....He also brought the first Central Pacific passenger train into Ogden, composed of cars built of California redwood at Sacramento shops."

53. *Ogden Junction,* November 20, 1880.
54. In his last letter to posterity, Broom declared, "The theological God I have no use for, but I adore the infinite, all-pervading spirit of love and wisdom, goodness and truth that is everywhere manifest in nature." He did not endorse or mention any organized Utah spiritualist movement such as the Godbeites. See *Ogden Standard,* July 8, 1893.
55. "David S. Tracy Recalls Pioneer Day Adventures," *Ogden Standard-Examiner,* August 28, 1934; July 8, 1956; April 3, 1958.
56. *Ogden Standard-Examiner,* July 8, 1956; April 3, 1958. John C. Brown said his grandfather Broom's trade to Browning also included sorghum and hay.
57. "Utah News," *Millennial Star* 33 (1871): 175; Leo Haefeli and Frank J. Cannon, *Directory of Ogden City and Weber County* (Ogden, UT: Ogden Herald Publishing Co., 1883), 114; "The Broom Hotel," *Ogden Herald,* December 30, 1882; *Ogden Standard-Examiner,* July 8, 1956.
58. *Ogden Standard,* June 30, 1893.
59. Haefeli and Cannon, *Directory of Ogden City,* 115–16; *Ogden Herald,* February 19, 1884; *Salt Lake Tribune,* January 1, 1885; *Ogden Standard-Examiner,* July 8, 1956; August 31, 1958.
60. Shakespeare "lost a large sum on an Ogden political election," and his creditors took his assets. *Ogden Standard-Examiner,* July 8, 1956.
61. *Ogden Herald,* December 10, 1883; March 18, August 13, 1885; April 14, 1887; *Ogden Standard,* August 10, 1890; January 15, 1891.
62. *Salt Lake Herald,* July 11, 1890.
63. *Ogden Standard,* July 18, 1890; *Salt Lake Tribune,* August 8, 1890.
64. *Salt Lake Tribune,* January 13, 22, 1884; *Ogden Herald,* March 17, 1884; *Weekly Reno Gazette,*

March 27, 1884; O. A. Kennedy, "Depot Was Scene of Exciting Life Fifty Years Ago," *Ogden Standard-Examiner,* February 14, 1932.

65. French Pete's actual name was not preserved, but the Franco-American Hotel, a successor to Chauncey West's Ogden House at 4th and Main streets, was operated by Charles Bernard, "better known in Utah as French Charley," who proudly advertised his "first-class restaurant" in the *Salt Lake Tribune,* October 20, 1875.

66. Bernard DeVoto, "Ogden: The Underwriters of Salvation," in *The Taming of the Frontier,* ed. Duncan Aikman (New York: Minton, Balch, 1925) 45–47. DeVoto, born in 1897, was too young to have known the Chapman House. His source for this and his entire understanding of Ogden's nineteenth-century history was his father, Florian B. "Frank" DeVoto, a former deputy Weber County recorder.

67. "Utah News," *Weekly Nevada State Journal,* August 23, 1884. Lambert Molinelli had run a hotel in Eureka, Nevada.

68. *Ogden Standard,* October 15, 1902. William Chapman's brother, Sam, ran the Chapman House from 1893 until his own death in 1901.

69. *Ogden Evening Standard,* August 1, 1911; *Ogden Examiner,* October 5, 1912.

70. Richard Roberts, "Railroad Depots in Ogden: Microcosms of a Community," *Utah Historical Quarterly* 53 (1985): 77–80; *Pacific Railway Commission,* 2209 (testimony of David H. Peery); *Ogden Herald,* September 29, October 2, 1886. Eli Glover Sheldon's 1875 map of Ogden does not show the numbered streets extending west of Wall Street, but by the time of the 1884 Sanborn map, the numbered streets all reached the depot grounds.

71. Kiesel first proposed a combined "magnificent" hotel and opera house complex in the *Ogden Standard,* March 12, 1889. He also said he would build his own hotel at 24th and Wall streets, a promise he kept but not until 1912 with the Hotel Brigham. *Ogden Standard* (semiweekly ed.), September 25, 1889; *Ogden Examiner,* October 5, 1912. The Broom Hotel was turning away several guests per night. *Salt Lake Tribune,* August 16, 1888.

72. *Ogden Standard,* March 12, 1889.

73. Ibid., September 6, 1889; *Ogden Daily Commercial,* January 2, 1890, reprinted in *Ogden Standard-Examiner,* June 3, 1927. At this same time, Corey Brothers, a local construction firm, made numerous feints toward erecting a hotel at 25th and Wall streets across from the new Union Station. They expected a bonus subscription of ten thousand dollars, but the Chamber of Commerce made its award to Reed. The Coreys' scheme "was dropped after it was discovered that the moneyed men of Ogden were unwilling to aid the enterprise with anything more substantial than wind." *Salt Lake Herald,* July 16, 1889. A bird's-eye-view etching of downtown Ogden on the front page of the *Standard* of June 21, 1891 (and again on August 21, 1892) included an impressive five-story hotel on the Corey lot as if they had built it. However, the lot remained empty until the Healy Hotel went up in 1901.

74. Kiesel's city council changed the north/south streets' names to U.S. presidents and renumbered the east/west streets, designations that remain today. Ogden City Council, Minute Book H, April 5, 1889, p. 82. See also the *Salt Lake Tribune,* June 5, 1890: "In a probate case which came up recently before [Ogden's] Judge Cross, the fact was developed that the resolution of the City Council changing the names of [Ogden's] streets has never been recorded with the City Recorder, so that the old names are the legal names according to the record." Demolition of the old White House

(most recently operated as the Junction City Hotel) began in December 1886. See the *Ogden Herald,* December 18, 1886; February 10, 1887; and the *Salt Lake Tribune,* March 2, August 16, 1888.

75. *Salt Lake Herald,* December 19, 1889; June 19, July 9, 1890; *Salt Lake Tribune,* July 18, 1890. Several terminated stonecutters were itinerants who had come to Ogden for the Mardi Gras celebration; see chapter 3.
76. *Ogden Standard,* January 25, 1891; *Ogden Daily Commercial,* April 19, 1891.
77. *Ogden Standard,* July 4, 1891.
78. On the Reed's grand-opening day, the Broom announced it would be repapered and painted and "put in first class shape." *Salt Lake Tribune,* July 4, 1891.
79. *Ogden Daily Commercial,* January 2, 1890; *Ogden Standard,* January 3, 1892.
80. *Ogden Standard,* May 9, 1893.
81. Ibid., June 11, 1893.
82. Ibid., January 3, August 27, 1892; July 13, 1893; March 16, 1894. Reed died on March 15, 1894, in Stockton, California.
83. *Salt Lake Tribune,* March 20, 1923; *Ogden Standard-Examiner,* March 22, 1923.
84. *Salt Lake Tribune,* April 20, 1892.
85. Ronald W. Walker, "The Panic of 1893," in *Utah History Encyclopedia,* available online at http://www.uen.org/utah_history_encyclopedia/p/PANIC_1893_Financial.html (accessed March 17, 2013).
86. O. A. Kennedy, "Stovepipe Hats, Real Estate Talk Marked Ogden of Fifty Years Ago, Newsman Recalls" *Ogden Standard-Examiner,* July 9, 1939.
87. *Ogden Standard-Examiner,* March 6, 1922.
88. Leo Haefeli, "A Stroll through Ogden," 479–80.
89. *Ogden Standard,* November 28, 1893; November 21, 1899. Before its paving in 1893, 25th Street had been graveled in 1887; see *Salt Lake Democrat,* March 2, 1887. Trees lining the street were cut down in 1891, "which improves the appearance of the thoroughfare very much." See *Salt Lake Herald,* November 17, 1891.
90. *Ogden Standard,* May 8, 1892.
91. Ibid., April 3, 1899; September 23, 1890. In the *Salt Lake Tribune* of December 5, 1901, David H. Peery Jr., who sold Healy the lot, commented, "As everyone knows, a good part of Ogden property is absolutely valueless; it can't be sold at any price."
92. *Ogden Standard,* October 25, 1900.
93. Ibid., July 8, December 21, 1901. Despite its original grandeur, the Healy underwent a gut renovation just twelve years later. The project added an annex with thirty new rooms and a modernized lobby finished in Siena marble and Mexican onyx. See the *Ogden Examiner,* March 30, 1913; *Salt Lake Tribune,* June 12, 1913.
94. *Salt Lake Herald,* February 2, March 1, 1901. The murder case was John Benbrook shooting Burton Morris over the affections of Morris's fiancée, Leda Stromberg. *Salt Lake Tribune,* July 18, 1899.
95. *Ogden Standard,* June 6, 1906. The Boston Realty Company built the hotel in 1891. Ibid., November 9, 1890; July 24, 1891; December 20, 1902. Even before the 1906 renovations, the owner's grandiosity was apparent from his name displayed—D. A. SMYTH—in large block letters atop the European's roof. Smyth's family home, a mansion at 635 25th Street, has been restored as the law offices of Gridley, Ward & Van Dyke.
96. *Ogden Standard,* January 3, 1892.

Chapter 3, Ogden Hostesses

1. *Salt Lake Tribune,* January 18, 1880; *Deseret News* (weekly ed.), January 21, 1880. Exactly where the Morton-McMillan gun battle occurred is

uncertain. The *Ogden Junction* of June 12, 1880, said it was "in a house of ill repute in this city." The *Ogden Standard* of December 11, 1897, said McMillan was killed "in the back of Jim Dee's saloon [on Main Street]." Morton himself was severely wounded; doctors initially feared he would lose a leg, but he recovered. *Salt Lake Tribune,* June 9, 1880. Five months after Sam McMillan's death, Clara Allen was sentenced to 107 days in jail for keeping a house of ill fame. *Ogden Junction,* June 12, 1880. Incarcerated again the following year, Clara was freed after a stranger paid her fine and announced he would escort her to Blackfoot, Idaho. "Good riddance," said the *Ogden Herald* of July 13, 1881.

2. *Ogden Standard,* December 8, 1897.
3. Ibid., Dec. 11, 1897.
4. *Salt Lake Tribune,* February 27, 1880.
5. Leo Haefeli and Frank J. Cannon, *Directory of Ogden City and Weber County* (Ogden, UT: Ogden Herald Publishing Co., 1883), 63; *Ogden Standard,* July 4, 1908. Further elaboration came in the *Ogden Herald* of August 21, 1884, which said *Rustler* editor King was the "gentleman upon whom the husband of a giddy blonde was instrumental in applying tar and feathers."
6. *Ogden Junction,* May 29, 1880.
7. *Ogden Herald,* July 20, 1882.
8. Ibid., October 23, 1882.
9. *Ogden Standard,* June 11, 26, Dec. 18, 1892.
10. Ibid., December 17, 1897; January 15, February 24, March 17, 1898; *Salt Lake Herald,* March 6, 1898.
11. *Salt Lake Tribune,* April 19, 1898; *Ogden Standard,* April 19, 1898; *Salt Lake Herald,* April 19, 1898.
12. R. L. Polk's 1899 edition of the *Ogden City Directory* (Ogden, UT: R. Polk and Company, 1899) lists Kirk still at 304 25th Street. U.S. Bureau of the Census, twelfth census (1900), Weber County, p. 124, line 4, shows her on the 300 block of 24th Street. Polk's 1907 *Ogden City Directory* lists her at 256½ 25th Street.
13. *Ogden Standard,* April 23, 1890; *Ogden Herald,* October 2, 1887.
14. Historian Jeffrey Nichols unearthed London's origins from her daughter, Ethel Topham's, California death certificate and census records; see *Prostitution, Polygamy and Power: Salt Lake City, 1847–1918* (Urbana: University of Illinois Press, 2002), 77. In a divorce petition, London asked "for the restoring of her maiden name, Dora Bella Hughes." *Ogden Standard,* March 11, 1902. A Belle London had operated the Fashion rooming house at 2005 Market Street in Denver; see Forbes Parkhill, *Wildest of the West* (New York: Holt, 1951), 15. Ogden's Belle London also ran a Fashion rooming house at 268½ 25th Street. Noted Salt Lake City illustrator John Held Jr. wrote that London had her business cards engraved in Denver; see *The Most of John Held, Jr.* (Brattleboro: Stephen Greene Press, 1972), 100. The *Salt Lake Herald,* in its "News of Ogden" column of August 11, 1889, noted, "'Sports' who have been driven out of Denver and other tough towns have rendezvoused here [Ogden] and the police know them all."
15. *Ogden Standard,* May 16, 1889.
16. *Salt Lake Tribune,* November 8, 1889; *Ogden Standard,* March 4, 1898. The *Ogden Standard* of November 9, 1889, said one bordello was "on the [river] bottoms," and the other was "on the bench toward the mountains." London's establishment must have been the one on the bottoms because the other madam, Elsie St. Omar, kept a "big square house on the hill" on 26th Street, *Salt Lake Tribune,* May 25, 1890. In a later advertisement for hired help, London said she was located near the Ogden Cracker Factory on Washington Avenue just

north of the Ogden River bridge. *Ogden Standard,* October 25, 1892. Elsie St. Omar soon gained renown as a Salt Lake City madam (see Nichols, *Prostitution, Polygamy, and Power,* 66, 89, 101), and London may have assumed control of the 26th Street house because Polk's 1890–1891 *Ogden City Directory* lists her on the "south side of 26th St. between Adams and Jefferson." The 1889 raid was one of many Ogden forays by Salt Lake City federal marshals that began the previous August. See chapter 1, note 30.

17. *Ogden Standard,* May 20, 1893. Polk's 1892–1893 *Ogden City Directory* lists London on "Stephens Alley, 4 W[est] of Grant," probably the passageway's unofficial name before Electric Alley came into vogue.
18. In London's parlor house, there were "star electric device[s]" in the ceilings. See *Ogden Standard,* August 4, 1910. Later, when Salt Lake officials persuaded London to build and manage a regulated prostitution district, the Stockade, in that city, the site's plans showed a street running through the compound called Electric Street. *Salt Lake Herald,* August 20, 1908.
19. "Fire Insurance Map of Ogden, 1906" (New York: Sanborn-Perris Map Co., 1906), sheet 42, shows Electric Alley's layout. It labels the prostitutes' cubicles as F.B. or female boarding. The *Ogden Standard,* August 4, 1910, had this description: "The alley seemed to be very quiet. Here and there stood a group of Jap[anese], a group of Greeks and in most of the places the doors and windows were open and sitting in modest positions were seen girls of all shapes and sizes. Some were fat and some were thin." The prostitute cubicles were still standing in 1955, rented out as small apartments by their owner, a Stephens family descendant. *Ogden Standard-Examiner,* January 8, 1955.
20. Classified advertisements of masquerade balls at No. 10 Electric Alley were published in the *Ogden Standard,* June 28, October 25, 1894; November 27, 1895; and December 21, 1897.
21. *Salt Lake Herald,* January 4, 1894; *Salt Lake Tribune,* August 14, 1896; *Ogden Standard,* January 3, 1895; December 20, 1901; May 10, 1905.
22. *Ogden Standard,* March 4, 1898; March 11, 1902.
23. Ibid., December 1, 3, 1900. U.S. Bureau of the Census, twelfth census (1900), Weber County, p. 145, line 16, lists Guy Dufloth, boarder at No. 2 Electric Alley, age twenty-five, Pennsylvanian, occupation: housework. Line 12 on the same page lists Leona Jioniei, head of household at No. 5 Electric Alley, age twenty-six, French, occupation: lodging house. Joseph Hall, decades earlier, had authored the *Deseret News*'s account of the March 8, 1869, arrival of the first locomotives in Ogden ("Railway Celebration at Ogden," March 17, 1869).
24. *Ogden Standard,* February 6, 1895; *Salt Lake Tribune,* February 7, 1895.
25. *Deseret News* (weekly ed.), November 16, 1889.
26. *Ogden Standard,* August 21, 1895.
27. Ibid., August 20, 1895; *Salt Lake Herald,* February 13, 1896.
28. *Ogden Standard,* December 13, 14, 1895.
29. Ibid., April 25, 1897; *Salt Lake Tribune,* April 25, 26, 1897.
30. *Ogden Standard,* May 8, 1905.
31. The *American Journal of Industry* described the Mint in an 1897 brochure, cited in the *Ogden Standard-Examiner,* December 22, 1965.
32. *Ogden Standard,* January 26, 1899. The only advertisement found for the Mint appeared in the *Ogden Standard* on December 21, 1901.
33. *Salt Lake Tribune,* September 26, 1899.
34. *Ogden Standard,* March 30, 1898.

35. Ibid., March 30, 1898; September 25, November 6, December 14, 1899; November 19, 1906; *Salt Lake Tribune,* September 26, 1899; May 17, 1904; *Salt Lake Herald,* November 19, 1906.
36. *Salt Lake Tribune,* July 1, 1890. The Ogden River Resort was the first building on the west side of Washington Avenue just across the Ogden River bridge.
37. Robert K. DeArment, *Deadly Dozen: Twelve Forgotten Gunfighters of the Old West* (Norman: University of Oklahoma Press, 2003), 33–34; *Ogden Standard,* July 20, 1889. O. A. Kennedy wrote about Desmond's wild career in Ogden but mistakenly called him Bat Beaumonde. Kennedy, "The Story of the Ogden Daily Commercial," *Ogden Standard-Examiner,* November 21, 1920. A life sketch of Desmond appears in *History of the Arkansas Valley, Colorado* (Chicago: O. L. Baskin & Co., 1881), 793–94.
38. *Ogden Standard,* March 6, June 25, 1890; *Salt Lake Tribune,* July 1, 1890; *Pueblo (CO) Chieftain,* March 2, 1890. Desmond had been shot and wounded in Pueblo during a drunken quarrel just before he moved to Ogden. *Aspen (CO) Daily Chronicle,* December 18, 1888.
39. *Ogden Standard,* November 19, 1903; January 25, 28, 1904.
40. Ibid., February 8, May 11, 1890. Gambling debts forced Hutchins to close the Little King in March 1891 and triggered his suicide the following month. *Ogden Standard,* April 17, 1891. The author's grandfather wrote, "It leaked out that [Hutchins] had gambled and lost all his possessions…[his sister] always said if [Hutchins] didn't quit going to town so often he would come to some bad end." Henry E. Holley, "Personal History," 1949, p. 7, typescript, Special Collections, Stewart Library, Weber State University, Ogden, UT.
41. George H. Tribe "established a first class wholesale and retail wine and liquor establishment….It is [now] the next oldest mercantile concern in Ogden, having been run successfully since 1869." *Ogden Herald,* January 1, 1886. Dee was the first husband of Ann Eliza Webb Dee Young Denning, later famous as Brigham Young's nineteenth wife and father of her sons, James E. and Leonard L. Dee. *Ogden Standard,* June 8, 1897. See also *Ogden Herald,* May 3, 1886.
42. "Chubb" Browning was installed as the Fischer Beer Hall's manager in April 1885 but fired a year later after "running behind some $1,550." *Ogden Herald,* April 7, 1885; *Salt Lake Herald,* June 24, 1886.
43. Allen Stout, nephew to prominent Mormon lawyer and legislator Hosea Stout, also had a dance hall just north of the Ogden River. *Salt Lake Democrat,* March 23, 1887. His saloon was on 5th Street. *Ogden Junction,* September 18, 1876.
44. David Farley was the son of polygamist Winthrop Farley and Lydia Pons Farley. This list of Ogden's Mormon saloon owners is not exhaustive by any means.
45. David Nasaw, *Going Out: The Rise and Fall of Public Amusements* (New York: Basic Books, 1993), 13–14. See also Richard F. Selcer, *Legendary Watering Holes: The Saloons That Made Texas Famous* (College Station: Texas A&M University Press, 2004), 15–16.
46. *Ogden Standard,* March 26, 1889; *Salt Lake Tribune,* July 18, August 11, 1889. The Novelty opened for business on April 1, 1889, under proprietor Frank Monroe and manager Pat Foy. Then Foy opened the rival Lyceum Theater on May 20, 1889. *Salt Lake Tribune,* May 17, 1889. The address of Foy's Lyceum is unknown; it may not have been on 25th Street. It should not be confused with the two later Lyceum Theaters at 269 25th Street (1903–1910 and 1910–present).

47. Jeremy Agnew, *Entertainment in the Old West: Theater, Music, Circuses, Medicine Shows, Prizefighting, and Other Popular Amusements* (Jefferson, NC: McFarland & Co., 2011) 92–93. By the time the Oatley sisters, Polly and Lottie, were performing in Alaska and the Yukon at the dawn of the twentieth century, they had appeared in "all the lower states." Ibid. If they are the same Polly and Lottie Oatley—ages seventeen and fifteen—mentioned in the *Salt Lake Tribune* of February 28, 1893, for sending handiwork to the Chicago World's Fair, they were extremely young while at Ogden's Novelty Theater in 1889. As itinerants their origins are hard to pinpoint. On August 18, 1888, the *Salt Lake Herald* announced the arrival from Denver of "Mrs. Oatley and three sisters." The *Portland Oregonian* of November 22, 1888, noted "the remarkable dancing of the three Oatley sisters." Eventually one sister left the act.
48. O. A. Kennedy, "Gun Scene 'Cooked Up?' Scribe Still Wonders These 50 Years After," *Ogden Standard-Examiner,* July 28, 1939.
49. *Ogden Standard,* October 8, 1889.
50. *Deseret News* (weekly ed.), December 14, 1889.
51. Ibid., September 7, 1889.
52. Pil [pseud], "Liberalism Is Wealth," *Salt Lake Tribune,* December 5, 1889.
53. *Deseret News* (weekly ed.), December 14, 1889; *Ogden Standard,* October 8, 1889. Stephens testified in the criminal prosecution of the Novelty's arsonists.
54. *Ogden Standard,* July 11, 1889. O. A. Kennedy, who was a member of the welcoming committee, recalled the experience in "Gun Scene 'Cooked up?'" *Ogden Standard-Examiner,* July 28, 1939. The *Salt Lake Tribune's* July 18 and August 11, 1889, reports of Ogden's "new," "soon [to] be completed" Novelty Theater imply that its first five months—encompassing Kennedy's experience with the Nebraskans—were spent at a location preceding the 263 25th Street address. But Kennedy remembered the event specifically at 263 25th Street. It was not possible to resolve the discrepancy.
55. An Ordinance to Promote Morality, *Revised Ordinances of Ogden City, Utah, Embracing All Ordinances of a General Nature in Force August 1, 1894* (Ogden, UT: Authority of the City Council of Ogden City, Utah, 1894), title 10, chapter 2; *Ogden Standard,* September 13, 1889.
56. *Ogden Standard,* September 15, 1889.
57. *Deseret Evening News,* November 8, 1889. The Novelty Theater, newly erected in November 1889, endured in many capacities, serving finally as the Labor Temple at the time when it burned down in 1961.
58. *Ogden Standard,* June 30, 1892. The Novelty had also closed in June 1891 (see chapter 1, note 16) but reopened two months later. *Salt Lake Herald,* August 4, 1891.
59. *New York Times,* March 28, 1890.
60. Work Projects Administration for the State of Utah, *Utah: A Guide to the State* (New York: Hastings House, 1941), 212; O. A. Kennedy, "Col. Harvey Enrolls Boosters in Secret Monte Cristo Order," *Ogden Standard-Examiner,* May 6, 1931; Kennedy, "Special Train with Flower of South on Way to Ogden Fete," *Ogden Standard-Examiner,* May 7, 1931. Harvey's home was at 2671 Jefferson Avenue.
61. *Ogden Standard,* July 1, 1890; *Salt Lake Herald,* July 2, 1890; Kennedy, "Special Train with Flower," *Ogden Standard-Examiner,* May 7, 1931.
62. O. A. Kennedy, "King of Mardi Gras Welcomed to Ogden by Carnival Throng," *Ogden Standard-Examiner,* May 8, 1931; Kennedy, "Harvey Opens Carnival with Great Gusto; Titles Given," *Ogden Standard-Examiner,* May 9, 1931. Kennedy was on hand for many subsequent mass gatherings at

the depot, including the post–World War I troop parades and Golden Jubilee of the driving of the Golden Spike, and could speak from experience on the crowd size.

63. *Ogden Daily Commercial,* July 4, 1890. Of all the performers listed, only the Brothers Leondor appear to have been nationally known. An advertisement in the *San Francisco Call* called them "America's Greatest Gladiatorial Acrobats" on December 6, 1900, and according to the *Anaconda (MT) Standard* of December 22, 1890, they were "the lithest, strongest men on earth."
64. *Salt Lake Herald,* July 4, 6, 1890; O. A. Kennedy, "Worries Grow for Promoter of Boom Days Carnival Here," *Ogden Standard-Examiner,* May 10, 1931. Many older Ogdenites probably recalled New Orleans from its years as the port of entry for European Mormon immigrants. David Buice, "When the Saints Came Marching In: The Mormon Experience in Antebellum New Orleans, 1840–1855," *Louisiana History* 23 (1987): 225.
65. *Salt Lake Herald,* July 2, 6, 11, 1890.
66. Ibid., July 6, 23, 1890; O. A. Kennedy, "Carnival King Bares Visage to Gathering at Mask Ball," *Ogden Standard-Examiner,* May 13, 1931; Kennedy, "Carnival Ends but Fiddlers Must Be Paid; Harvey Loses," *Ogden Standard-Examiner,* May 14, 1931. Harvey seemed to suffer no permanent damage from the carnival's financial failure. In 1892—as Chamber of Commerce president—he brought home a second major trophy for Ogden from New Orleans: designation as host city for the April 1893 Trans-Mississippi Congress. *Ogden Standard,* February 27, 1892. In 1893 he moved to Chicago to publish *Coin* magazine, which advocated a free silver policy. *Ogden Standard Examiner,* April 29, 1893. He ran for president of the United States in 1932 at the age of eighty.
67. *Salt Lake Tribune,* April 12, 1890; *Ogden Daily Union,* cited in the *Salt Lake Tribune,* July 28, 1890. The *Salt Lake Herald's* Ogden section of July 11, 1890, made comparable objections: "Standing in front of some public drinking places, at nearly all times, but especially in the evening, these fellows pollute the air with their profanity and obscenity, and it has reached to a point when few ladies dare to venture in the vicinity of the places named."

CHAPTER 4, OGDEN SCRUBBED

1. *Ogden Standard,* November 1, 1909.
2. Ibid., January 2, 1906. In an editorial entitled "The Reverend Elderkin and the New Mayor," in the *Ogden Standard* on January 3, 1910, Glasmann wrote, "It was not within [my] power or any living man to suppress [gambling]...the open gambling house doors might be closed, but, if so, gambling would go on behind the closed doors."
3. Very likely the encounter between Brigham Bowman and Mayor Glasmann was embarrassing for both of them. As former editor and general manager of the *Utah Daily Union,* Ogden's Democratic newspaper, Bowman had feuded regularly in print with *Standard* owner and Republican Glasmann. In 1908 Bowman had accused Glasmann of accepting a two-hundred-dollar bribe from gamblers, which Glasmann denied. Less than a month before the Elephant House encounter, Bowman's newspaper had failed, which was on one level a triumph for Glasmann (see the *Ogden Standard,* July 13, 1910). No wonder he refused Bowman's offer of lemonade.
4. *Ogden Standard,* August 4, 1910; *Salt Lake Herald-Republican,* August 5, 1910. Glasmann's visitations were utterly tame compared to the 1892 "ultimate sin tour" of the Reverend Charles H. Parkhurst, president of New York City's Society for the Prevention of Crime. Parkhurst hired a private

detective to escort him through New York's brothels and flesh circuses and observed genuine debauchery. See Richard Zacks, *Island of Vice: Theodore Roosevelt's Doomed Quest to Clean Up Sin-Loving New York* (New York: Doubleday, 2012), 10–21.

5. *Ogden Standard,* August 12, 1910; *Salt Lake Herald-Republican,* August 12, 1910.
6. *Ogden Evening Standard,* August 23, 26, 1910; *Deseret Evening News,* August 27, 1910; *Salt Lake Herald-Republican,* August 27, 1910. David Eccles had been mayor of Ogden from 1887 to 1889. Gary Topping discusses his career as "robber baron" and "exploiter" in *Leonard J. Arrington: A Historian's Life* (Norman, OK: Arthur H. Clark Company, 2008), 154–57.
7. *Salt Lake Herald,* August 28, 1910; *Ogden Evening Standard,* September 2, 1910.
8. *Ogden Evening Standard,* August 30, 31, 1910; *Salt Lake Herald-Republican,* August 31, 1910. Elderkin had a similar falling out with Ogden's previous mayor, Alexander Brewer. *Ogden Standard,* May 17, 1909. Gambling was Elderkin's cause célèbre during his Ogden lustrum; in 1909 he publicly called upon the Utah Legislature to repeal antigambling statutes, claiming they were "repeatedly and openly" violated. *Salt Lake Telegram,* January 11, 1909.
9. James H. Timberlake, *Prohibition and the Progressive Movement, 1900–1920* (Cambridge: Harvard University Press, 1963), 166; Michael McGerr, *A Fierce Discontent: The Rise and Fall of the Progressive Movement* (New York: Free Press, 2003), 84.
10. *Ogden Standard,* May 8, 1905.
11. Ibid., January 30, February 1, 9, 1906; *Salt Lake Herald,* February 1, 1906.
12. Gordon Harrington, "The Pastorate of the Rev. Noble Strong Elderkin," chapters 10–14 in *History of Congregational United Church of Christ, Ogden.* Copy available in the Val Holley Collection, Special Collections, Stewart Library, Weber State University, Ogden.
13. *Ogden Standard,* March 30, 1892.
14. Glasmann served as mayor of Ogden from 1902 to 1905 and 1910 to 1911. He owned the Ogden *Standard* from 1894 until his death in 1916 and the *Examiner* from 1904 to 1911. The two newspapers merged in 1920. See J. Cecil Alter, *Early Utah Journalism* (Salt Lake City: Utah Historical Society, 1938), 155, 179–80.
15. *Ogden Standard,* June 24, 28, 29, July 5, 1905. The most serious criticism was that Halverson had witnessed an Ogden man's will, then later testified in court that the man had been drunk when he signed, "one of the most embarrassing occurrences for the legal profession in the history of the bar in Ogden." Halverson unsuccessfully sued the *Standard* for libel.
16. Ibid., January 24, 1906. See *Skeen v. Craig,* 31 Utah 20, 86 P. 487 (1906); *Skeen v. Chambers,* 31 Utah 36, 86 P. 492 (1906). These are both Utah Supreme Court cases.
17. *Ogden Examiner,* February 25, 1906. See chapter 3, note 35.
18. *Ogden Standard,* December 15, 1905; *Salt Lake Tribune,* December 19, 1905.
19. *Ogden Standard,* February 8, 24, 1906.
20. Ibid., March 9, 1906. Also see the *Ogden Standard,* June 22, 1906: "Judge Murphy forfeits [the gamblers'] bails [of $150 each] with a remark that the city needs the money."
21. Ibid., December 12, 1906; January 3, 1907; *Skeen v. Browning,* 32 Utah 164, 89 P. 642 (1907).
22. Larry E. Nelson, "Utah Goes Dry," *Utah Historical Quarterly* 41 (1973): 341.
23. *Salt Lake Tribune,* December 2, 2008.
24. "Temperance Advocated at Mormon Conference," *Davis County Clipper,* October 9, 1908; *Salt Lake Tribune,* December 2, 2008; Bruce T. Dyer, "A

Study of the Forces Leading to the Adoption of Prohibition in Utah in 1917" (master's thesis, Brigham Young University, 1958), 20–22.

25. *Salt Lake Telegram,* January 11, 18, 1909.
26. Dyer, "Adoption of Prohibition in Utah," 36; *Salt Lake Telegram,* January 18, 1909.
27. *Ogden Standard,* March 11, 1894; November 28, 1896; *Ogden Standard-Examiner,* February 16, 1938. Rudolph Kuchler's nephew, Ogden's Kenneth Kuchler, was associate concertmaster of the Utah Symphony Orchestra for more than half a century until his death in 2008.
28. *Deseret Evening News,* February 9, 1909; *Ogden Standard,* November 10, 1904; May 31, 1919.
29. *Deseret Evening News,* February 9, 1909.
30. Kuchler lost to former county physician Dr. Edward M. Conroy, who served 1906–7. *Ogden Weekly Standard,* November 10, 1905.
31. *Salt Lake Herald,* January 14, 1909.
32. Parley T. Wright was manager of his family business, W. T. Wright and Sons' dry goods store at 24th Street and Washington Ave. See the *Ogden Standard,* January 15, 1909.
33. Ibid., February 9, 1909; *Deseret Evening News,* February 9, 1909. Blind tiger and blind pig were terms for venues where liquor was sold illegally.
34. *Salt Lake Herald,* March 23, 1909.
35. *Ogden Standard,* March 24, 1909.
36. Ibid., March 23, 1909.
37. *Salt Lake Herald-Republican,* September 5, 18, November 3, December 23, 1909; *Deseret Evening News,* August 31, 1909. Citizens opposed to Prohibition also presented petitions, but they were outnumbered in most cities.
38. *Zamata v. Browning,* 15 Utah 400, 170 P. 1058 (1918) [Utah Supreme Court].
39. *Ogden Standard,* June 29, 1909; *Salt Lake Herald,* June 29, 1909.
40. *Ogden Standard,* March 23, 1909.
41. *Salt Lake Herald,* March 10, 1909.
42. *Deseret Evening News,* December 23, 1908.
43. Dyer, "Adoption of Prohibition in Utah," 54–55.
44. An Act Relating to the Manufacture, Sale, Exchange, Barter, and Disposition of Intoxicating Liquor (March 20, 1911), 1911 *Utah Laws* 152, chap. 106.
45. *Ogden Evening Standard,* December 22, 1910; January 5, 6, 1911.
46. Ibid., June 28, 1911.
47. *Salt Lake Herald,* March 11, 1909.
48. *Ogden Evening Standard,* May 24, 1911.
49. Ibid., June 6, 10, 1911.
50. Ibid., June 28, 1911. Contrary to the spirit of its pledge, the Ogden City Council passed major changes to the ordinance within two months, permitting all-night liquor sales by druggists and transfer of licenses and allowing saloons to operate restaurants with more than fifteen seats. Mayor Glasmann vetoed the change, but the council had the votes to override him. Responding to protests that it had violated its June pledge, the council claimed it had only promised not to change the 9:00 p.m. closing provision, which it did leave intact. Ibid., August 29, 1911.
51. Ibid., June 26, 1911.
52. Ibid., June 1, 21, 1911.
53. Ibid., June 26, 1911.
54. Ibid., June 27, 1911.
55. Dyer, "Adoption of Prohibition in Utah," 58; *Deseret Evening News,* June 27, 1911; *Ogden Evening Standard,* June 28, 1911.
56. *Ogden Evening Standard,* October 30, 1911.
57. Results of the various local-option elections appeared in the *Ogden Evening Standard* on June 25, 1913, and June 30, 1915. Most of these were

unsuccessful campaigns to transform dry cities into wet ones.

58. In 1911 the Utah legislature altered cities' municipal governments to conform with the so-called Galveston plan: "cities of the second class" (Ogden was the only one in Utah) would be governed by a board consisting of a mayor and two commissioners. Municipal Government of Incorporated Cities (March 20, 1911), 1911 *Utah Laws* 224, chap. 125. The commission form of municipal government was a Progressive Era innovation, expected to focus less on political patronage than business needs.

59. *Ogden Evening Standard,* November 8, 1911; *Ogden Examiner,* June 11, 1912.

60. *Ogden Examiner,* June 10, 1912.

61. Ibid., August 21, 1912; *Ogden Evening Standard,* August 21, 1912. According to the *Ogden Examiner* of February 20, 1913, open vice was finished in Ogden and most other western cities, and Ogden would never accept its return.

62. Jeffrey Nichols, *Prostitution, Polygamy, and Power: Salt Lake City, 1847–1918* (Urbana: University of Illinois Press, 2002), 141–67; *Ogden Evening Standard,* August 21, 1912. London gave her own version of the origins of the Stockade scheme in the *Salt Lake Herald* on July 1, 1909: "I saw there would be money in such an investment. I'm a business woman; I'm a good manager."

63. Nichols, *Prostitution, Polygamy and Power,* 158–61; *State v. Topham,* 41 Utah 39, 123 P. 888 (1912) [Utah Supreme Court].

64. *Ogden Evening Standard,* August 20, 1912.

65. *Deseret Evening News,* March 12, 1909; *Salt Lake Herald,* March 13, 1909; *Salt Lake Tribune,* March 13, 1909. On March 13, 1909, the *Ogden Evening Standard* mentioned the debate only as an aside in its editorial comment: "My, what a woman; and oh my, what men! And to think that Mr. Jimmy McCracken was gone and disclosed the whole perfidious gang to the prudish Salt Lakers." House Bill 81, which made owning a house of ill fame a felony, was enacted during that session. An Act Relating to Owning or Renting Buildings, Keeping, Residing in, or Resorting to Houses of Ill Fame (March 22, 1909), 1909 *Utah Laws* 186, chap. 88.

66. *Ogden Evening Standard,* October 12, 1911; Nichols, *Prostitution, Polygamy, and Power,* 160.

67. *Ogden Evening Standard,* October 30, 1911. In London's Stockade trial, Browning said he did not know who was running Ogden's red-light district, "but a man by the name of Ternes had charge of the office." Ibid., October 28, 1911. Ternes's career with the Ogden Police Department can be traced in the *Ogden Standard,* January 16, 1906; January 5, 1909; November 9, 1909; and the *Salt Lake Tribune,* December 22, 1908.

68. *Ogden Examiner,* December 18, 1913; *Ogden Evening Standard,* August 23, 1911. When the *Salt Lake Herald* on February 27, 1903, reported London's $12,300 purchase of the Bon-Ton restaurant (the present-day London Ice Cream Parlor building at 254 25th Street), it said she "owns most of the real estate in the vicinity of Electric Avenue as well as other valuable Twenty-Fifth Street tracts."

69. Utah Department of Commerce, Division of Corporations and Commerce, incorporation case files, series 5297, case 941, Utah State Archives, Division of Archives and Records Service, Salt Lake City.

70. Nichols, *Prostitution, Polygamy, and Power,* 149, 196.

71. *Ogden Examiner,* August 21, 1912; *Ogden Evening Standard,* August 21, 28, 1912. The raid was only the second made by the Ogden police under the search-and-seizure provisions (section 43) of the 1911 state liquor law (see note 44). *Ogden Examiner,* August 25, 1912.

72. *Ogden Standard,* November 21, 1916. Ethel Topham was in the same graduating class as Bernard DeVoto. See the *Ogden Examiner,* May 19, 1914.
73. The former London home served as a children's nursery until 1938, when it became the Paradise Club and Café. It was destroyed in a fire on May 3, 1939.
74. Nelson, "Utah Goes Dry," 342.
75. Ogden's state senators—Democrat Joseph Chez and Republican William Craig—were not necessarily Prohibitionists, but they voted for the Prohibition bill. See the *Ogden Standard,* February 12, 1915.
76. Dyer, "Adoption of Prohibition in Utah," 96; *Ogden Standard-Examiner,* December 30, 1976.
77. *Salt Lake Tribune,* March 3, 1915.
78. The state Democratic convention of 1916 was held at Ogden's Alhambra Theater on Kiesel Avenue.
79. *Ogden Standard,* February 2, 1917.
80. Prohibiting the Manufacture and Use of Intoxicating Liquors, and Regulating the Sale and Traffic Therein (February 8, 1917), 1917 *Utah Laws* 2, chap. 2; Nelson, "Utah Goes Dry," 352; *Ogden Standard*, February 9, 1917.
81. *Ogden Standard,* March 2, 1917; November 6, 7, 1918.
82. George H. Skyles, "A Study of Forces and Events Leading to the Repeal of Prohibition and the Adoption of a Liquor Control System in Utah" (master's thesis, Brigham Young University, 1962), 10; *Ogden Standard,* November 6, 1918.
83. *Ogden Examiner,* April 19, 1917.
84. *Ogden Standard,* July 26, 1917. National Prohibition, via the Eighteenth Amendment to the U.S. Constitution, was ratified on January 16, 1919, and took effect on January 17, 1920.
85. *Ogden Standard,* August 1, 1917; *Davis County Clipper,* August 3, 1917.
86. Ogden's Ray Olson, manager of the Utah League for Prohibition Repeal, acknowledged the ease of getting a drink during Prohibition in October 1933. Olson reported, "There are more saloons today in Ogden than there were in 1917....the sale and distribution of liquor in Ogden is freer today than at any time in the city's history," *Ogden Standard-Examiner,* November 3, 1933.

Chapter 5, Ogden Parched

1. The Weber Hotel was in the building that is now the vacant Windsor Hotel at 166 25th Street.
2. *Ogden Standard,* December 21, 1917.
3. Ibid., December 22, 1917.
4. Ibid., January 6, 1917.
5. The Eighteenth Amendment to the U.S. Constitution, which imposed national Prohibition, was proposed on December 18, 1917; ratified on January 16, 1919; and took effect on January 17, 1920.
6. Gus Russo, *The Outfit: The Role of Chicago's Underworld in the Shaping of Modern America* (New York: Bloomsbury, 2001), 5, 20.
7. Floyd A. Timmerman, "Bootlegger's Life Bared by Ogdenite," *Ogden Standard-Examiner,* August 30, 1925.
8. *Ogden Examiner,* May 9, 1919.
9. *Ogden Standard-Examiner,* May 26, 1927; July 20, 1928.
10. Floyd A. Timmerman, "Says Ogden Has 68 Rum Sales Shops," *Ogden Standard-Examiner,* September 3, 1925.
11. *Ogden Standard-Examiner,* January 12, 1923.
12. Ibid., February 18, 1923. Daniel Okrent in *Last Call: The Rise and Fall of Prohibition* (New York: Scribner, 2010) notes that New York's famous "21" Club on West 52nd Street employed a raid-busting system allowing a bartender, with the press of a button, to send "the entire contents of the back bar tumbling

down a shaft, past a series of bottle-breaking metal grates, and finally onto a pile of rocks in the basement. Any remaining liquid drained into a sump." (209)

13. *Ogden Standard-Examiner,* December 9, 1923.
14. Ibid., January 19, 1928; September 7, 1929.
15. Interview with Joseph Prantil, September 1, 2011.
16. "Booze Buster Saved-Car Was 'Tippled,'" *Ogden Standard-Examiner,* October 8, 1972; ibid., September 17, October 4, 8, December 26, 1922; January 5, February 2, 1923.
17. Floyd A. Timmerman, "'Joint' Men Fear Ogden Liquor King," *Ogden Standard Examiner,* September 2, 1925. Okrent, *Last Call,* 214, mentions the same bootleg formula for gin.
18. *Ogden Standard-Examiner,* January 12, 1923.
19. *Salt Lake Tribune,* December 31, 1932.
20. *Ogden Standard-Examiner,* February 10–11, 1928.
21. Timmerman, "'Joint' Men Fear," *Ogden Standard-Examiner,* September 2, 1925.
22. Floyd A. Timmerman, "Ogden Rum Makers Tip Off Rivals," *Ogden Standard-Examiner,* August 31, 1925.
23. Floyd A. Timmerman, "'Fixers' Get Ogden Rum Trade Coin," *Ogden Standard-Examiner,* September 1, 1925.
24. Okrent, *Last Call,* 134–37, 264.
25. Larry E. Nelson, "Utah Goes Dry," *Utah Historical Quarterly* 41 (1973): 345, 348; George H. Skyles, "A Study of Forces and Events Leading to the Repeal of Prohibition and the Adoption of a Liquor Control System in Utah," (master's thesis, Brigham Young University, 1962), 13–14.
26. *Ogden Standard-Examiner,* June 11, 1922.
27. Clara Decker Mohlman, "Diary," January 22, 1925, MS 325, Special Collections, Stewart Library, Weber State University, Ogden, UT. The diary covers only the first four months of 1925. My thanks to Charles Trentelman and Sarah Langsdon for notifying me about this resource.
28. *Ogden Standard-Examiner,* November 13, 1924.
29. Mohlman, "Diary," March 18, 19, 1925. A grand jury had indicted Mohlman as an Ogden city police sergeant for willfully failing to arrest a merchant who maintained gambling devices. *Ogden Standard,* March 24, 1917.
30. Bernard DeVoto, "The Bucolics of Decadence," in *The Selected Letters of Bernard DeVoto and Katherine Sterne,* ed. Mark DeVoto (Salt Lake City: University of Utah Press, 2012), appendix A, 419–23.
31. Ibid., 423, 430; *Ogden Standard-Examiner,* January 3, 5, 1921.
32. Cited in Larry E. Nelson, "Problems of Prohibition Enforcement in Utah, 1917–1933" (master's thesis, University of Utah, 1970), 121. The letter was leaked to the *Salt Lake Tribune* and published on February 5, 1925.
33. *Ogden Standard-Examiner,* October 11, 1931.
34. *Salt Lake Tribune,* April 1, July 27, 1932.
35. *Ogden Examiner,* February 1, 1918; *Ogden Standard,* April 23, 1918.
36. *Ogden Standard,* February 5, 6, 1918.
37. See chapter 4, note 61.
38. *Ogden Standard,* January 25, 1917; February 20, April 28, 1918.
39. *Ogden Standard-Examiner,* December 18, 1924.
40. The San Francisco city directory for 1916 identified Maxine Rose (a.k.a. Belle London) as proprietress of the Hotel La Rosa at 339 O'Farrell Street. She was no longer there in the 1917 directory. Both the *San Francisco Call* and *Oakland Tribune* of August 15, 1912, had called 339 O'Farrell Street a "house of ill-fame." U.S. Bureau of the Census, fourteenth census (1920), San Francisco County, p. 211, lines 7–16 show Maxine Rose, her two daughters, and seven boarders (including Thomas W. Matthews, secretary

of her Arcadia Land and Livestock Company in Ogden) at 317 Lyon Street in San Francisco.

41. *Blue and Gold* yearbook, University of California at Berkeley, 1922, p. 392. In her later life, Ethel Topham, who apparently never married, was active in the women educators' society Alpha Delta Kappa, hosting social events and speaking about her European travels. See *San Mateo Times,* October 13, 1965; December 9, 1967.
42. *Ogden Standard-Examiner,* December 24, 1924; January 8, 1925.
43. Ibid., February 1, May 20, July 7, October 14, 1924.
44. Ibid., May 9, 1924.
45. *Ogden Examiner,* March 31, April 28, August 10, September 4, 1918.
46. *Ogden Standard,* November 19, 1917.
47. *Ogden Examiner,* March 6, 1918; *Ogden Standard,* May 13, 1918; *Ogden Examiner,* July 7, 1918.
48. *Ogden Standard,* November 11, 1918.
49. Richard W. Sadler and Richard C. Roberts, *Weber County's History* (Ogden, UT: Weber County Commission, 2000), 217–20; *Ogden Standard,* January 17, 1919.
50. *Ogden Standard,* March 20, 1919; *Ogden Examiner,* March 21, 1919.
51. *Ogden Standard,* April 19, 1919; *Ogden Examiner,* April 25, 1919.
52. *Ogden Examiner,* March 21, April 19, 1919.
53. Ibid., May 14, 21, 22, 1918; *Ogden Standard,* May 21, 1918; *Salt Lake Herald-Republican-Telegram,* May 22, 1918.
54. *Ogden Standard,* April 11, 17, 1919; Anthony P. Martini, "1919: Post-War Pilots Take to the Air," chapter 10 of *Flying Machines over Zion: Aviation Come[s] to Utah, 1910–1919* (Ogden, UT: Aerospace Heritage Foundation of Utah, 1997), available online at http://www.hill.af.mil/library/factsheets/factsheet.asp?id=5973 (accessed June 9, 2011).
55. *Ogden Examiner,* May 9, 1919; *Ogden Standard,* May 9, 10, 1919.
56. *Ogden Standard,* May 9, 1919.
57. Martini, "Post-War Pilots Take to the Air."
58. *Ogden Standard-Examiner,* May 27, 1924.
59. Ibid., November 23, 1924.
60. Ibid., September 13, 1926.
61. Ibid., December 16, 1932. As the inspiration for Paramount Pictures' Majestic Mountain logo, Ben Lomond peak was a worthy choice as the hotel's name.
62. Okrent, *Last Call,* 331; *New York Times,* November 18, 1932.
63. The U.S. Senate passed *Joint Resolution Proposing an Amendment to the Constitution of the United States Relative to the Eighteenth Amendment,* JR 211, 72nd Congress, 2nd sess., *Congressional Record* 76: 4231 on February 16, 1933. The House of Representatives followed on February 20, 1933. *Congressional Record* 76: 4516. The resolution was deposited with the Secretary of State for submission to the states on February 20, 1933. *Congressional Record* 76: 4565.
64. *An Act to Provide Revenue by the Taxation of Certain Nonintoxicating Liquor, and for Other Purposes, U.S. Statutes at Large* 48 (1933): 16; Martha Swain, *Pat Harrison: The New Deal Years* (Jackson: University Press of Mississippi, 1978), 40–41; *Ogden Standard-Examiner,* March 23, 1933.
65. The *New York Times* of March 21, 1933, carried the Associated Press's chart showing the legal status of beer in each state once the Cullen-Harrison Act took effect.
66. Regulating Manufacture and Sale of Beer (August 8, 1933; 2nd special sess.), 1933 *Utah Laws* 19, chap. 10; *Ogden Standard-Examiner,* August 9, 1933. See note 81.
67. On May 18, 1932, the U.S. Senate defeated the Tydings Amendment to HR 10236, *A Bill to Provide*

Revenue, Equalize Taxation, and for Other Purposes," which would have legalized 2.75 beer, 72nd Congress, 1st sess., *Congressional Record* 75: 10519. The U.S. House of Representatives passed HR 13742, *A Bill to Provide Revenue by the Taxation of Certain Nonintoxicating Liquor, and for Other Purposes* (the Collier Bill), to legalize 3.2 beer on December 21, 1932, 72nd Congress, 2nd sess., *Congressional Record* 76: 867. The Senate failed to take up the Collier Bill before it adjourned, but with the intervention of FDR's inauguration and the swearing in of a new, alcohol-friendly Congress, the Cullen-Harrison Act passed less than one month later. See Swain, *Pat Harrison,* 40.

68. Skyles, "Repeal of Prohibition," 39–50; *Ogden Standard-Examiner,* February 18, 1933. The *Salt Lake Tribune* summarized Becker's testimony to the Utah Senate's Judiciary Committee on February 8, 1933.
69. *Ogden Standard-Examiner,* February 22, 28, 1933.
70. Manufacturing Certain Beverages for Sale Outside of State (March 21, 1933), 1933 *Utah Laws* 51, chap. 35; Skyles, "Repeal of Prohibition," 42, 46–47.
71. Herbert Asbury, *The Great Illusion: An Informal History of Prohibition* (New York: Greenwood Press, 1968), 233–34.
72. Skyles, "Repeal of Prohibition," 42, 49–50.
73. *Salt Lake Telegram,* April 7, 11, 12, 14, 1933; *Ogden Standard-Examiner,* April 10, 1933; *Salt Lake Tribune,* April 11, 1933.
74. *Ogden Standard-Examiner,* June 26, 1933; *Salt Lake Telegram,* June 26, 1933; *Salt Lake Tribune,* June 27, 1933.
75. *Salt Lake Tribune,* July 23, 1933.
76. *Ogden Standard Examiner,* June 15, October 18, 1933.
77. Skyles, "Repeal of Prohibition," 79. Utah's vote count was 101,600 for repeal candidates and 67,200 for candidates who wanted Utah to remain dry. The Utah League for Prohibition Repeal received congratulatory telegrams from Postmaster General James A. Farley, national officers of the Association against the Prohibition Amendment, and other eastern well-wishers. See *Ogden Standard-Examiner,* November 9, 1933.
78. *New York Times,* December 6, 1933; Thomas M. Coffey, *The Long Thirst: Prohibition in America 1920–1933* (New York: Norton, 1975), 315–19.
79. *Ogden Standard-Examiner,* December 6, 1933; *Salt Lake Tribune,* December 5–6, 1933; *New York Times,* December 5–6, 1933.
80. Coffey, *The Long Thirst,* 315–16.
81. Skyles, "Repeal of Prohibition," 79.
82. *Ogden Standard-Examiner,* November 9, December 31, 1933; January 3, 1934.
83. Liquor Control Act (March 25, 1935), 1935 *Utah Laws* 57, chap. 43; *Ogden Standard-Examiner,* April 3, May 31, 1935.
84. *Ogden Standard-Examiner,* June 2, October 13, 1935.
85. Ibid., November 24, December 4, 1935.
86. For example, in July 2010, undercover police staked out beer outlets in Evanston, Wyoming, and followed and arrested Utahns who purchased stronger beer and brought it into the Beehive State. See *Salt Lake Tribune,* July 3, 2010. Paul Rolly's *Salt Lake Tribune* column of April 15, 2011, noted a secret Utah drinking fraternity—the Underground Alcoholic Company—whose members pool their resources, make bulk purchases of liquor in bordering states where it is considerably cheaper, and transport it (illegally) into the state for personal consumption. See also "Utah Liquor Laws May Be Scaring Off National Restaurant Chains," *Salt Lake Tribune,* May 5, 2011; "State Lost Money after Closing Salt Lake City Liquor Store," *Salt Lake Tribune,* June 1, 2011; "Hospitality Group Sues over Utah Liquor Law," *Salt Lake Tribune,* July 1, 2011;

"Utah Liquor Laws, as Mixed Up as Some Drinks," *New York Times,* July 20, 2011; "Lack of Liquor Licenses Has Utah Applicants Paying Double," *Salt Lake Tribune,* October 6, 2011; "Clubs Cry Foul over Delayed Liquor Citation," *Salt Lake Tribune,* June 30, 2012; "Zion Curtains Are Weird," *Standard-Examiner,* March 6, 2013.

87. *Ogden Standard-Examiner,* March 18, 1966.
88. Ibid., March 29, 1966.

Chapter 6, Ogden Follies

1. *Ogden Standard-Examiner,* June 29, 1926.
2. Peery did not run in 1931.
3. For example, Peery said, "The best way to handle gambling is to legalize it and thus bring it out in the open, where it will be properly supervised and meanwhile enable the city and the state to realize badly needed new sources of revenue." *Ogden Standard-Examiner,* February 27, 1948.
4. John C. Davis, a former district attorney who disapproved of the mayor, admitted during Peery's first term that gambling money in Ogden "does find its way into the city treasury." See *Ogden Standard-Examiner,* February 1, 1935, and October 26, 1947.
5. Ibid., September 23, 1929. See Appendix A.
6. Interview with Robert Peery King, April 20, 2009.
7. The Peery estate was sold within a month of Harman Peery's death to two investment companies for $1.5 million. At that time, the estate included twenty-two buildings in downtown Ogden and was said to be the largest single real-estate sale in Ogden's history. *Ogden Standard-Examiner,* February 12, 1961; October 2, 1927. For a summary of Harman Peery's business career, see F. Ross Peterson and Robert Parson, *Ogden City: Its Governmental Legacy: A Sesquicentennial History* (Ogden, UT: Chapelle Ltd., 2001), 123.
8. Harold Peery made this clear when the council voted not to raise saloon license fees in 1909; see chapter 4, note 39.
9. Interview with Robert Peery King, Apr. 20, 2009.
10. Darrell Greenwell to Robert H. Hinckley, October 12, 1945, Robert H. Hinckley papers, MS0102, box 28, Special Collections, J. Willard Marriott Library, University of Utah, Salt Lake City. Hinckley, founder of the long-lived Hinckley Dodge auto dealership in Ogden, was wartime chairman of the U.S. Civil Aeronautics Administration. The *Salt Lake Tribune* of January 25, 1934, cited the Peery slogan.
11. *Ogden Standard-Examiner,* March 20, November 24, 25, December 4, 1935.
12. Ibid., November 28, 1935.
13. Ibid., November 24, December 6, 10, 1935; June 30, 1936.
14. Ibid., April 6, 7, 9, 1936. It was a rare instance when Peery and Glasmann agreed on anything.
15. Ibid., August 29, 1936; January 16, 1937; *Salt Lake Tribune,* January 16, 1937; Beer: Bonds of Licensees (March 6, 1937), 1937 *Utah Laws* 113, chap. 50, sec. 89.
16. *Ogden Standard-Examiner,* May 11, 25, August 3, 1937.
17. Ibid., August 31, 1937.
18. Ibid., August 29, 1937.
19. Ibid., September 1, 2, 1937.
20. Ibid., April 21, 1942. Supporting the 1:00 a.m. closing the following year, Peery argued, "Ogden is now a twenty-four hour town and people on the swing shift should be able to relax after work." See the *Ogden Standard-Examiner,* September 17, 1943. But the closing was modified once more to midnight on February 14, 1944. Ibid., February 15, 1944.
21. Ibid., May 29, 1938. Five hundred copies of the survey, entitled "A Social Service Directory," were supposedly printed and distributed by June 15,

1938. No copy was located, however. Interviewed on August 11, 2011, LeMoyne Petersen said his source was Lalovi McMurrin Hilton, Ogden police chief from February 20 to July 31, 1934, which explains the focus on conditions that year. In 1938 Hilton was superintendent of the Police Department's Bureau of Identification. Petersen was dating Hilton's daughter, Janet, at the time.

22. The houses on 25th Street were the Wyoming Rooms (238), K. C. Rooms (250), Seattle Rooms (278½), and Wilson Rooms (320½). Those on Grant Avenue were the Golden Hotel (2422½), Alexander Hotel (2446), Oak Hotel (2456), and Dixie Rooms (2468).
23. O'Neil self-published his findings in a mimeographed sheet called "The Ogdenite," vol. 1, no. 10, May 1940. Robert Chugg Ogden Collection, MS202, Special Collections, Stewart Library, Weber State University, Ogden, UT. One of several Southern Pacific employees laid off during the Depression, O'Neil lived at 2536 Lincoln Avenue. My thanks to Charles Trentelman and Sarah Langsdon for identifying and sharing this resource.
24. *State v. Tacconi,* 110 Utah 212, 171 P.2d 388 (1946). In a related case against operators of the Wyoming Rooms at 238 25th Street, former police chief Hilton testified that around 1941 it was Ogden City's practice to require prostitutes to register, be fingerprinted, and pass a health examination before they could sell sex. See *Ogden Standard-Examiner,* June 12, 1945.
25. Ibid., October 5, 1939. The clinic moved to the new (and current) municipal building on July 22, 1940. Ibid., July 21, 1940.
26. Alta Roskelley, an oral history by Marci Farr, July 14, 2008, Oral History Program, Special Collections, Stewart Library, Weber State University, Ogden, UT. *Ogden Standard-Examiner,* March 10, August 25, 1940.
27. Richard W. Sadler and Richard C. Roberts, *Weber County's History* (Ogden, UT: Weber County Commission, 2000), 254–55; *Ogden Standard-Examiner,* November 24, 1940.
28. The author's great-grandmother, Marie Bishop, used sheets to partition her living and dining rooms at 2824 Lincoln Avenue into separate sleeping quarters for newly arrived roofers. "The accommodations were spartan," recalled her daughter, "but they ate like kings." Jessie Bishop Lewis, e-mail to the author, August 4, 2011.
29. "Weekly Activity Report," Vyvyan Parmelee to Eliot Ness, September 22, 1941, record group (RG) 215, box 30, Division of Social Protection, Federal Security Agency, National Archives and Records Administration (NARA), College Park, MD. Strangely, box 30 has almost no memoranda relating to Ogden from 1942 to 1943, Harman Peery's wartime mayoral term. Most come from 1941 and 1944. Also see *Salt Lake Tribune,* August 22, 1941.
30. Paul M. Kinsie, "The Prostitution Racket Today," *Journal of Social Hygiene* 27 (1941): 327–34. The army lost seven million man-days to venereal disease in World War I. Eugene T. Weatherly, "Local Control of Prostitution in Wartime," *Journal of Social Hygiene* 28 (1942): 384.
31. Untitled memorandum, A. C. Tilley to Heber Harper, October 10, 1941, RG 215, box 30, Defense Health and Welfare Services, NARA.
32. "Weekly Activity Report," Parmelee to Ness, November 17, 1941, RG 215, box 30, Division of Social Protection, NARA.
33. *Salt Lake Tribune,* November 14, 1941. That Ogden closed brothels under federal pressure was unremarkable because 350 other cities also closed their "hitherto condoned houses." *Time,* March 29, 1943.
34. *Ogden Standard-Examiner,* November 14, 1941.

35. "Weekly Activity Report," Parmelee to Ness, November 17, 1941. Peery was convicted twice of running gambling machines at his Old Mill resort; the first conviction was nullified because of juror improprieties. *Ogden Standard-Examiner,* June 29, 1940.
36. "Community Services in the Ogden, Utah, Area: Report of Progress," March 1944, RG 215, box 30, Office of Community War Services (OCWS), Federal Security Agency, NARA.
37. "Progress Report, Region XI," Howard C. Beresford to Mark McCloskey, September 13, 1943, RG 215, box 30, Division of Recreation, Federal Security Agency, NARA.
38. Floyd A. O'Neil, "Utah's Twentieth Century History: Reprise and Nostrums," *Utah Historical Quarterly* 74 (2006): 105–6.
39. Military officers in an unmarked car described a typical Thursday night in Miami, Florida, in March 1942: "Many enlisted personnel and their girls, when not in sight of the shore patrol, were observed locked in each other's arms, petting and kissing as they moved down the streets. As they progressed farther from the middle of the town, these couples were observed disappearing into the alleyways, yards, parks, and shrubbery." Petting went on openly in "practically all the cars, even though the lights around were bright enough to make the performance easily visible from almost every direction." U.S. Army Office of the Adjutant General, RG 250, decimal file 726.1, NARA, cited in John Costello, *Virtue under Fire: How World War II Changed Our Social and Sexual Attitudes* (Boston: Little, Brown, 1986), 216.
40. Greenwell to Hinckley, March 16, 1942, Robert H. Hinckley papers.
41. Interview with Bonnie Coates, daughter of policeman Albert Brown, October 7, 2009; *Ogden Standard-Examiner,* Jan. 21, 1944.
42. *Ogden Standard-Examiner,* September 17, 1943. On one summer night, a pickpocket managed to rob almost sixty persons sleeping in the park. Ibid., August 2, 1943. The bushes and shrubs were not removed until 1954. Ibid., August 15, 1954.
43. Ibid., June 3, 1943.
44. Tom Zito, an oral history by Mary Werner, July 6, 1973, Oral History Program, Special Collections, Stewart Library, Weber State University.
45. Ogden City Commission, Minutes of the Regular Meeting of the Board of Commissioners of Ogden City, Utah, December 23, 1942, Ogden City Commission Minute Book, p. 842, Ogden City Recorder's Office; *Ogden Standard-Examiner,* December 23, 1942.
46. *Salt Lake Tribune,* December 24, 1942. Acknowledging that Mayor Abbott had closed the brothels, federal officials said prostitution in Ogden took the form of "pickups in cafes, skating rinks, dance halls, and on the street." "Summarized Report of Present Conditions in Localities in Each Region/Utah," Vyvyan Parmelee to Eliot Ness, March 10, 1942, RG 215, box 30, Division of Social Protection, NARA.
47. *Salt Lake Tribune,* December 11, 1942.
48. "Survey of Conditions in Region XI," Howard Slutes to Eliot Ness, July 3, 1943, RG 215, box 30, OCWS, NARA; *Ogden Standard-Examiner,* July 12, 13, 14, 1943; October 27, 1947. From 1935 to 1943, Darrell Greenwell headed the Utah WPA office, and the Division of Social Protection often sought his guidance even before he rejoined the *Ogden Standard-Examiner.* On August 2, 1942, Greenwell wrote Robert Hinckley, "The social workers still come to me for public relations advice. One week ago [they] had me in a huddle wondering how to

get some of the nasty situations in Ogden cleaned up." Greenwell to Hinckley, Robert H. Hinckley papers.

49. *Ogden Standard-Examiner,* July 24, 1943.
50. Ibid., July 20, 1943; *Salt Lake Tribune,* July 26, 1943.
51. *Ogden Standard-Examiner,* October 14, 15, 1943. The provost marshal said Peery's statement was inaccurate.
52. *Salt Lake Tribune,* January 27, 1934.
53. Ibid., January 25, 1934.
54. O'Neil, "The Ogdenite," October 1940.
55. Darrell Greenwell to Dean Brimhall, April 14, 1944, Dean Brimhall papers, MS0114, box 27, Special Collections, J. Willard Marriott Library, University of Utah, Salt Lake City; Darrell Greenwell to Robert Hinckley, September 6, 1944, Robert H. Hinckley papers. Beginning on April 20, 1942, the Playdium ran daily ads in the *Ogden Standard-Examiner* seeking pretty young women between eighteen and twenty-five as cashiers and floor attendants for good pay. The Eccles Building still stands at the southwest corner of 24th Street and Washington Boulevard., operating today as the Hampton Inn.
56. Peery reported the revenue in an official communication to the Ogden City Commission. *Ogden Standard-Examiner,* October 14, 1943.
57. Ibid., September 8, 9, 1943.
58. Ibid., November 10–19, 1943; Transcript of preliminary hearing, Paul Erz murder trial, Second District Court (Weber County), August 23, 1943, criminal case files, series 6954, case 4196, Utah State Archives, Division of Archives and Records Service, Salt Lake City.
59. *Ogden Standard-Examiner,* October 20, November 30, 1943.
60. During the war, 254½ 25th Street was an African American rooming house. *Ogden Standard-Examiner,* July 23, October 15, 1944; February 16, June 13, 1945. In 1939—as the Arizona Hotel—it experienced an arson attempt where William J. Leatherwood, who will be introduced in chapter 7, was a lookout. Ibid., March 18, May 18, 1939.
61. Ibid., November 30, 1943.
62. Ibid. Peery was well aware that the Weber Club, housed at the Ben Lomond Hotel, "had a ready supply of women upstairs. That's what he detested." Interview with Robert Peery King, April 20, 2009. In Peery's final term, when a citizen complained that houses of ill fame were not being closed, Peery cited a recent arrest of a prostitute and pimp at the Ben Lomond Hotel and dared a fellow commissioner to make a motion to close it. *Ogden Standard-Examiner,* December 13, 1948.
63. Karen Anderson, *Wartime Women: Sex Roles, Family Relations, and the Status of Women During World War II* (Westport, CT: Greenwood Press, 1981), 103–11. During the 1941 discussions on closing Ogden's brothels, Mayor Fred Abbott admitted that suppression "protect[s] only the soldier." He said closure scattered prostitutes, forcing them to "assume the roles of legitimate employees in business places while carrying on their profession. I am trying to take a broader viewpoint." *Ogden Standard-Examiner,* November 12, 1941.
64. "Confidential Report: Negotiations in the Utah War Area," January 10–14, 1944, RG 215, box 30, OCWS, NARA.
65. *Ogden Standard-Examiner,* January 5, 14, February 19, 1944; "Community Services in the Ogden, Utah, Area: Report of Progress," March 1944, RG 215, box 30, OCWS, NARA.
66. *Ogden Standard-Examiner,* April 7, 1944.
67. Ibid., March 14, 1944.
68. Ibid., April 13, June 30, 1944. Benson Y. Parkinson gives a detailed account of the Bramwell case and grand jury investigation in "On Trial," chapter 9

of *S. Dilworth Young: General Authority, Scouter, Poet,* available online at http://jared.pratt-family.org/parley_family_histories/helaman-pratt/histories/sdy.html (accessed June 9, 2011). Darrell Greenwell to Robert Hinckley, March 25, 28, April 1, September 6, 1944, Robert H. Hinckley papers; Darrell Greenwell to Dean Brimhall, April 14, 1944, Dean Brimhall papers. When David S. Romney was appointed to replace Bramwell as mayor, Hinckley wrote to Greenwell on April 14, 1944: "As I recall, Dave Romney was the champion slot machine player of all Ogden, even after he became a bishop. Am I right? Has he reformed? Or is the appointment a bit incongruous to say the least?" Robert H. Hinckley papers.

69. "Bill of Particulars," Second District Court (Weber County), October 2, 1945, criminal case files, series 6954, case 4251, Utah State Archives, Division of Archives and Records Service. Fifty-two of the sixty-five gambling establishments were on 25th Street. The list—showing addresses but not names—does not include the Playdium at 375 24th Street.
70. *Ogden Standard-Examiner,* November 20, 1945. Peery and Moore finally pleaded guilty under pressure from their wives, who wanted the matter ended. Interview with Robert Peery King, May 26, 2009.
71. *Ogden Standard-Examiner,* June 6, 9, 1946.
72. Ibid., May 26, 1933.
73. Ibid., August 19, 1945; *Salt Lake Tribune,* August 25, 1945. See Appendix A for Peery's philosophy on gambling ("amusement") devices in Ogden.
74. *Ogden Standard-Examiner,* November 3, 1947. Syndicated columnist Drew Pearson described the Ogden depot fight best: "The prize is the Sixth Service Command's supply depot, given to Utah for safekeeping during the war. Now California wants it back." *San Mateo Times,* October 16, 1947. The army eventually announced that Ogden would "remain the principal storage and distributing center for the Sixth Army area." *Salt Lake Tribune,* January 1, 1948.
75. *Ogden Standard-Examiner,* November 3, 1947.
76. Ibid., October 30, 1947. The *Ogden Standard Examiner* on November 5, 1941, also cited Peery's support among railroad men.
77. Ibid., January 22, 1948.
78. Ibid., July 24, 1946. The Pioneer Tavern was the predecessor of today's Kokomo Club.
79. Parole officer Lalovi McMurrin Hilton to Louis W. Thrailkill, U.S. probation officer in Boise, Idaho, December 28, 1944, Arlyn Garside papers, MS400, Special Collections, Stewart Library, Weber State University, Ogden, UT.
80. *Ogden Standard-Examiner,* February 2, March 18, 1948; April 29, May 23, 1949.
81. Ibid., September 22, 1949.
82. Ibid., February 17, 1950.
83. Interview with Robert Peery King, April 20, 2009.
84. *Ogden Standard-Examiner,* April 14, 1949.
85. Interview with Robert Peery King, May 26, 2009.

Chapter 7, Ogden Blushed

1. Although there are many stories of Rosetta's walking her ocelot on Ogden streets, her sister, Birdena, says the ocelot was "never taken out." Interview with Birdena Nance, August 20, 2009.
2. The description of the Rose Rooms is based on interviews with Robert Peery King on May 26, 2009, and Ed Simone on August 4, 2011; a tour of 205 25th St. with its then-owner, Bruce Edwards, on July 30, 2011; and Issac Goeckeritz's interviews with Maurice Richards and John Posnien for his film, *Ogden: Junction City of the West* (2007). Goeckeritz recorded lengthy conversations on DVD with many knowledgeable Ogdenites. My thanks to Charles Trentelman of the *Ogden Standard-Examiner*

for access to the Goeckeritz DVDs. The five-dollar fee was noted in the *Ogden Standard-Examiner,* September 22, November 10, 1950. An inventory of the Rose Rooms' furnishings in a 1949 temporary injunction listed contents of a front room, another room "across the hall," a waiting room, a kitchen, six bedrooms, and one bathroom. "Inventory," *State v. Prantil, et al.,* Second District Court (Weber County), July 28, 1949, civil case files, series 6659, case 24077, Utah State Archives, Division of Archives and Records Service, Salt Lake City.

3. *Ogden Standard-Examiner,* December 13, 22, 1922; April 13, 1923.
4. Ibid., March 25, July 1, 11, 1924. For Louis's first bootlegging arrest, see *Ogden Standard-Examiner,* December 24, 1923.
5. *Ogden Standard,* January 9, 1919.
6. *Ogden Standard-Examiner,* October 5, 1924; January 1, February 5, 1926; *Salt Lake Tribune,* February 5, 1926.
7. R. L. Polk's *Ogden City Directory* (Ogden, UT: R. Polk and Company, 1925–1948) shows the first floor (201 25th Street) as the Lincoln Confectionery through 1939; vacant in 1940–1941; Ben's Tavern in 1942; Kay's Tavern beginning in 1944; and El Borracho beginning in 1948. The *Salt Lake Tribune* of May 25, 1933, noted the Lincoln Cigar Store at 201 25th Street.
8. *Ogden Standard-Examiner,* November 19, 1926.
9. During the federal "lumberjack raid" of February 1928, Louis was one of many 25th Street proprietors nabbed; see chapter 5, note 20. Details of his arrests at 201 25th Street appeared in the *Ogden Standard-Examiner* on January 19, December 9, 1928; September 7, 1929; August 17, 1931; January 8, 1932; January 8, 1934; and in the *Salt Lake Tribune* on August 2, 1928; September 11, 1931. In 1930 attorney George C. Buckle, defending Louis on a persistent violator charge, convinced a jury to consider his age, fifty-five (Louis was actually fifty-three), and ignore previous convictions. *Ogden Standard-Examiner,* October 14, 1930.
10. *Ogden Standard-Examiner,* October 3, 1929; February 21, 1946. In the Troy Hotel's heyday, proprietor Martin Ramires lost his rooming license after police found liquor, empty glasses, and flasks in his possession. The application of Ramires's wife, Mary, to operate the Troy was denied because the Ogden City Commission believed she was merely a front for her husband. Ibid., January 30, February 2, March 30, 1926.
11. The Prantils were newly minted U.S. citizens when they leased 205 25th Street to the Beveridge sisters; see the *Ogden Standard-Examiner,* August 9, 1944, for Giuseppina, May 8, 1946, for Louis.
12. Family records at http://www.familysearch.org. U.S. Bureau of the Census, fourteenth census (1920), Contra Costa County, California, p. 60, lines 14–16 show John, "Dora," and "Ida" Beveridge in Port Costa township.
13. Interview with Birdena Nance, August 20, 2009; *Salt Lake Tribune,* May 17, 1932; May 4, 1935. Although the name Papiano is Italian, the wrestler was frequently described as Greek.
14. *Ogden Standard-Examiner,* October 5, 1948.
15. A bill of particulars filed in Mayor Peery's 1944–1945 conspiracy case (see chapter 6, note 69) identified Ogden gambling-machine operators, including John "Beverage" at three different addresses on 25th Street. Whether this was Ada and Birdena's father, or if he influenced the sisters' move to 25th Street, is unknown.
16. Polk's *Ogden City Directory* (1944). Leatherwood's crimes are noted in the *Ogden Standard-Examiner,* March 28, 31, May 16, 1937; March 18, 1939.

See also chapter 6, note 60. Rosetta and Birdie established a significant family beachhead on Lincoln Avenue's 2500 block from approximately 1944 to 1960. Various husbands, parents, and children moved back and forth between 2506 Lincoln (the Rose Rooms' alternate address); 2512 Lincoln, another rooming house; and 2536 Lincoln, a freestanding house. These households resembled a menagerie. Rosetta's first husband, Chester Shaw Frost, bunked at 2536 in 1953, and Birdie's former boyfriend, Grant Sprunt, resided at 2506 with his new wife and daughter in 1954. Even the prostitutes arrested at the Benevolent Hand Club in 1950 gave their address as 2536 Lincoln. See the *Salt Lake Tribune,* June 15, 1950; *Ogden Standard-Examiner,* May 21, 1953; July 6, 1954. In January 1950, an Ogden cabdriver told police that 2536 Lincoln, where Birdie was living, was "still operating from cabbies," meaning cabdrivers earned commissions when they brought fares seeking prostitutes there. "Confidential Report," January 18, 1950, Arlyn Garside papers MS 400, Special Collections, Stewart Library, Weber State University, Ogden, UT.

17. *Ogden Standard-Examiner,* January 27, August 5, 1942. Frost eventually served long sentences in the Idaho and Utah state prisons. While incarcerated in the latter, he worked in its dental laboratory and got high on its supply of narcotics. Ibid., October 18, 1955.
18. Ibid., January 21, 1945. In 1946 reports of an auto accident and a jaywalking citation, Michael Seaman's address was still 205 25th Street. Ibid., July 1, November 16, 1946.
19. Ibid., March 6, 1947.
20. Ibid., December 12, 21, 1947.
21. Ibid., July 24, 1947.
22. "Complaint," *Prantil v. Seaman, et al.,* Second District Court (Weber County), March 9, 1949, civil case files, series 6659, case 23734; *Ogden Standard-Examiner,* April 24–26, December 30, 1947. It is conceivable that Harman Peery's return as mayor on January 5, 1948, made the sisters feel a bordello might stand a chance.
23. *Ogden Standard-Examiner,* May 3, 1948; author's conversation with former Dorianaire Orvil Holley, May 25, 2009. In a public statement, the Wildlife Federation's president said, "[Our] entertainment committee hired the women to provide us with a show similar to what we have had in the past. We do not feel we have any further responsibility in the matter." *Ogden Standard-Examiner,* May 3, 1948.
24. Dean Hurst, telephone conversation with the author, August 20, 2009. City attorney George S. Barker admitted, "I got a tip as to what was going to happen [at the Wildlife jollification], so I stayed home that night." See the *Ogden Standard-Examiner,* May 4, 1948.
25. Ibid.
26. Interview with Birdena Nance, August 20, 2009. Social Security death records list William Davie's date of birth as February 10, 1908. Available online at http://www.familysearch.org
27. *Ogden Standard-Examiner,* May 7, 12, 14, July 8, 1948. Although this was William Davie's first *Standard-Examiner* appearance, his Ogden Police Department mug shot is dated April 17, 1948, so he was already known.
28. Ibid., June 9, 10, December 8, 1948; *Salt Lake Tribune,* June 10, 1948. Ducinnie may have been a variation on Duccini. Lawrence Duccini, an Ogden bootlegger, lived just one block from the Rose Rooms at 221 26th Street, but whether Rosetta acquired the name legally or merely fancied it is unknown. Official records for Rosetta and William Davie's marriage were not found. Perhaps

it occurred outside of Utah, as with her earlier marriages to Frost and Seaman—both in Idaho.

29. Anonymous source interview. Dr. Brown eventually committed suicide. *Ogden Standard-Examiner,* May 12, 1960.
30. Ibid., June 29, 30, 1948.
31. Ibid., December 24, 1948. The *Ogden Standard-Examiner* reported an earlier raid on August 2, 1948.
32. Ibid., December 13, 1948. Rosetta's conviction was mentioned belatedly in the *Ogden Standard-Examiner* on December 8, 1948. Ogden City Attorney Paul Thatcher reported "grapevine" chatter from the "underworld" that Ogden "is the junction point of two 'circuits' around which prostitutes are moved." Thatcher to Utah Attorney General Clinton D. Vernon, February 19, 1951, Garside papers.
33. *Salt Lake Tribune,* December 8, 1948.
34. *Ogden Standard-Examiner,* October 5, 1948.
35. "Complaint" and "Exhibit A," *Prantil v. Seaman, et al.,* December 21, 1948, case 23734; *Ogden Standard-Examiner,* March 11, 1949.
36. *Ogden Standard-Examiner,* June 23; July 3, 6, 1949. Chief Schooff arrested the three women, who gave their names as Candice Richards, Chickie Lamont, and Bobbie Crawford. Crawford pleaded guilty to soliciting for immoral purposes and paid a hundred-dollar fine. The Milner Hotel at 184 25th Street was the 1949 name of the present-day Marion Hotel.
37. *Ogden Standard-Examiner,* July 6, 1949.
38. Ibid., August 8, 1949.
39. "Complaint," *State v. Prantil, et al.,* July 28, 1949, case 24077. The state's case against the Rose Rooms was one of four simultaneous injunction cases; the other three targeted the Wyoming Rooms (238 25th Street); the Parkway Hotel (316 25th); and the Wilson Rooms (320½ 25th). All four were ordered closed. *Ogden Standard-Examiner,* October 5, 1949.
40. "Order," October 4, 1949; "Temporary Restraining Order," *State v. Prantil, et al.,* October 18, 1949, case 24077.
41. "Amended Answer," *State v. Prantil, et al.,* March 5, 1951, case 24077; *Ogden Standard-Examiner,* February 19, 1951.
42. *Ogden Standard-Examiner,* November 10, 1950.
43. Interview with Raymond Jones, September 10, 2011; Thatcher to Vernon, February 19, 1951 Garside papers.
44. *Ogden Standard-Examiner,* November 13, 14, 1948. Earlier in the same year, Mayor Harman Peery acknowledged rumors of payoffs to police and announced an investigation. Ibid., March 7, 8, 1948. Within a single week in February 1954, Detective Arlyn Garside received multiple offers of monthly cash payments of five hundred dollars or more to stay away from various 25th Street establishments. Garside to Police Chief Maurice Schooff, February 11, 1954, Garside papers.
45. Interview with Raymond Jones, September 10, 2011.
46. "Confidential Report of Ray Clawson and Arlyn Garside," January 19, 1949, Garside papers.
47. *Ogden Standard-Examiner,* December 13, 1952.
48. *Davis County Clipper,* November 10, 1950. I am indebted to Farmington historian Glen M. Leonard for the present-day location of the Benevolent Hand Club's site. According to article five of the Benevolent Hand Club's 1950 articles of incorporation, it was "one-half mile west of Highway 91 on Viaduct Road, near Farmington." Viaduct Road no longer exists. Utah Department of Commerce, Division of Corporations and Commerce, incorporation case files, series 7184, case 26993, Utah State Archives, Division of Archives and Records Service, Salt Lake City.
49. *Ogden Standard-Examiner,* June 20, 1950; interview

with Richard Roberts, August 4, 2011. Goeckeritz's interview with Maurice Richards.

50. Goeckeritz's interview with Richards.
51. The Key Club should not be confused with the Key Klub at 2522 Wall Avenue, an African American venue. The official name of William Davie's state-chartered Key Club was the Pan-American Political and Social Club. *Ogden Standard-Examiner,* January 14, 1951. The Key Club's predecessor at 200½ 25th Street was the Ideal Rooms, a brothel closed down in 1948. *Salt Lake Tribune,* December 8, 1948. Appendix B describes a police visit to the Key Club.
52. According to *State v. Fertig,* 120 Utah 224, 233 P.2d 347 (1951) [Utah Supreme Court], the Key Club had been operating since at least August 12, 1949. The Key Club's incorporation case file includes a wealth of correspondence in 1950–1951 reflecting Ogden and state officials' concern. See Utah Department of Commerce, Division of Corporations and Commerce, incorporation case files, series 7184, case 26677 ("Pan American Political and Social Club").
53. *Ogden Standard-Examiner,* April 29, 1950; May 16, 1951. The Key Club apparently continued to operate and sell illegal liquor after the gambling raid, Ibid., July 13, 1950.
54. Arlyn Garside, notes on dealings with Rosetta and William Davie, August 16, 1950, "Scrapbook: Arlyn M. Garside, Ogden Police Dept., 1944 to 1964," Garside papers.
55. *Salt Lake Tribune,* June 11, 15, 1950; *Ogden Standard-Examiner,* June 20, 1950. A photo published on page 2 of the *Salt Lake Telegram* on June 10, 1950, and clipped into incorporation case file 26993 shows the Davis County sheriff and county attorney inspecting half-full liquor glasses on a tray inside the Benevolent Hand Club. This photo was not published in the edition of the *Telegram* available on the Utah Digital Newspapers Web site at http://digitalnewspapers.org/
56. *Davis County Clipper,* June 16, 1950. The Benevolent Hand Club was organized on May 27, 1950. Its articles of incorporation—notarized on June 2, 1950 by attorney Maurice Richards—were almost identical to the Key Club's. It is possible that Rosetta, a proficient typist (see note 93), prepared both clubs' articles of incorporation herself.
57. *Ogden Standard-Examiner,* July 24, 1950.
58. Ibid., July 30, August 1, 1950. The initial charge against William Davie was dropped, but the city subsequently charged him with vagrancy and operating a house of prostitution. Ibid., September 19, 1950; February 11, 1951.
59. Arlyn Garside, notes on dealings with Rosetta and William Davie, August 16, 1950, Garside papers.
60. *Salt Lake Tribune,* November 5, 1950; *Davis County Clipper,* November 10, 1950. The Davies' lawyer in the Benevolent Hand Club case was Ogden's Richard Stine.
61. *Ogden Standard-Examiner,* September 13, 15, November 9, 10, 13, 14, 1950; *State v. Davie,* Second District Court (Weber County), November 9, 1950, criminal case files, series 6954, case 4934.
62. Andrew Wahlquist, e-mail to the author, September 23, 2009; "Notice of Withdrawal," October 16, 1950, case 4934. One of Rosetta's new lawyers, Warwick C. Lamoreaux, had persuaded the Utah Supreme Court to reverse Ogdenite Pete Tacconi's conviction on keeping a house of ill fame at the Golden Hotel, 2422½ Grant Avenue. See *State v. Tacconi,* 110 Utah 212, 171 P.2d 388 (1946).
63. *Ogden Standard-Examiner,* November 21, 1950.
64. *Davis County Clipper,* November 17, 1950; *Ogden Standard-Examiner,* November 14, 1950.
65. *Ogden Standard-Examiner,* November 21, 22, 23,

1950. William Davie demonstrated a pattern of violence that included threats. In addition to his threats to Sheriff Hess and Detective Garside and the attack on Sol Kaplan, Davie struck John J. Sullivan of Salt Lake with a blackjack in September 1950, but Sullivan apparently feared testifying against Davie, and the complaint was dismissed, Ibid., October 6, 1950.

66. "Order," *State v. Prantil, et al.,* February 10, 1951, case 24077.
67. *Ogden Standard-Examiner,* February 11, 19, March 27, 1951.
68. Ibid., March 29, 1951. As early as November 1950, Hendricks blamed Sheriff Wade for not notifying him of the Davies' violation of the 1949 injunction. Ibid., November 24, 28, 1950. City Attorney Paul Thatcher believed Addie Davis, the Rose Rooms' maid, was afraid to tell police what she knew about her employers because "several people who have crossed Bill Davie have been seriously beaten up by hired thugs." Thatcher to Vernon, February 19, 1951, Garside papers.
69. Club Zebra was located at 225½ 25th Street in the space occupied by the former La Siesta Hotel; the address is confusing because it was directly above the Hub Tavern at 227 25th Street and not above the Star Noodle Parlor at 225 25th. The *Ogden Standard-Examiner,* September 6, 1944, noted that a previous tenant with the address of 225½—the New West Hotel—was directly over the Hub. The Davies' involvement in La Siesta's operation is unclear; they were never charged with any crime originating there (and there were many), but La Siesta and the Rose Rooms shared personnel, including Jean Taylor and Tommy Moore. James Sandman, co-owner of the building, offered to post bond for William Davie's Key Club conviction appeal but failed to qualify. Ibid., June 5, 1951.
70. Ibid., November 26, 1950; *Salt Lake Tribune,* May 23, 1950. The Utah Supreme Court affirmed the locker system's legality in *State v. Alta Club,* 120 Utah 121, 232 P.2d 759 (1951).
71. *Ogden Standard-Examiner,* January 14, March 6, 1951. Frost succeeded White as Ogden's mayor.
72. Ibid., April 1, 16, 1951. The other raided clubs on 25th Street were the Pan Railway at 130; Latin American at 203; and Bon Ami at 262½. The Shuffleboard Club at 219 Washington Boulevard was also raided.
73. Ibid., May 16, 21, 1951.
74. William Davie was held in Weber County's jail on a certificate of probable cause during appeal of his Key Club sentence. As initially planned, the arrangement was to count as time served for his Davis County Benevolent Hand Club conviction. Weber County agreed to incarcerate Davie while the Davis County jail underwent renovations. *Ogden Standard-Examiner,* June 3, July 4, 1951.
75. Ibid., June 3, 1951. In Polk's 1951 *Ogden City Directory,* Rosetta gave her occupation as department head at the Washington Market and her address as 2281 Kiesel Avenue. She listed herself as Rose A. Seaman, even though she had annulled that marriage four years earlier.
76. *Ogden Standard-Examiner,* June 15, 1951.
77. Ibid., July 2, 4, 7, August 10, 1951. Judge Hendricks concluded the hearing by declaring Club Zebra a nuisance. During Rosetta's 1955 incarceration on federal narcotics charges, sacks of special groceries mysteriously appeared in her jail cell. Ibid., February 16, 1955. Appendices C and D contain official statements in the Hendricks-Wade feud.
78. *Ogden Standard-Examiner,* August 10, 1951.
79. Ibid., August 13, 1951. Rosetta's sentence was a fine of a thousand dollars and six months in jail,

suspended on payment of the fine. Birdie also pleaded guilty.

80. Ibid., November 2, 1951.
81. *Salt Lake Tribune,* January 31, 1952.
82. *Ogden Standard-Examiner,* February 27, 1953. Ward Armstrong recalled Rosetta bringing camera film to be developed at Armstrong Sporting Goods at 302 25th Street while wearing her prison jumpsuit. Ward Armstrong, conversation with the author, June 18, 2012.
83. *Ogden Standard-Examiner,* April 23, 1952.
84. Ibid., December 13, 1952.
85. The West Virginia penitentiary has housed women in countless high-profile cases, including Billie Holiday and Martha Stewart.
86. *Ogden Standard-Examiner,* September 23, 1954. "For the first time in my life," Mathewson wrote, "I was ashamed of my fellow citizens of Ogden."
87. Ibid., January 26, 27, 28, February 9, October 19, 1955.
88. Ibid., December 22, 1954; January 5, February 25, 1955.
89. Ibid., February 24, 1955; *State v. Nance,* Second District Court (Weber County), January 4, 1955, criminal case files, series 6954, case 5521.
90. Interview with L. G. Bingham, August 27, 2011.
91. Ibid.
92. Ibid.
93. Donna Mathewson, *Down Mexico Way* (New York: Comet Press, 1956). In her acknowledgments, Mathewson wrote, "To Rosetta I am indebted for the six Spanish words I know, and the many hours she so graciously spent being my typist."
94. *Reno Evening Gazette,* March 20, 1958; *Nevada State Journal,* March 26, 1958.
95. *Ogden Standard-Examiner,* June 24, 1959.
96. Donna Mathewson, *Bananas Have No Bones* (New York: Comet Press, 1960). In her acknowledgments, Mathewson wrote, "To my daughter Rosetta who spent many strenuous hours as my typist, my thanks."
97. Goeckeritz's interview with Maurice Richards.
98. *Idaho State Journal,* February 6, 1976.
99. Family records and Social Security death records at http://www.familysearch.org
100. Interview with Joseph E. Prantil, September 1, 2011.
101. Allen D. Roberts, nomination of the Lower 25th Street Historic District, National Register of Historic Places Inventory, September 13, 1977, available online at http://pdfhost.focus.nps.gov/docs/NRHP/Text/78003260.pdf (accessed January 13, 2012).
102. *Salt Lake Tribune,* November 7, 2005.

Chapter 8, Ogden Shrugged

1. *Ogden Standard-Examiner,* November 7, 1946.
2. Ibid., October 14, 1946; September 15, 1937.
3. Ibid., April 30, 1950.
4. White defeated Harold Welch in the general election. Incumbent Harman Peery failed to advance from the primary. *Ogden Standard-Examiner,* October 16, 1949.
5. Ibid., February 6, March 23, 1948.
6. Ibid., January 5, February 20, November 2, 12, 1950. The Arlyn Garside papers at Weber State University include unprecedented daily police reports from January 1950 suggesting that Mayor White demanded tangible evidence of police crackdowns in the first month of his administration.
7. *Ogden Standard-Examiner,* September 7, 1950.
8. Ibid., March 16, April 1, 1951.
9. Issac Goeckeritz's interview with Maurice Richards for *Ogden: Junction City of the West* (2007). As an elderly man, Richards often claimed credit for cleaning up the street, especially in "The 25th Street Your Mother Didn't Want You to Know,"

Standard-Examiner, November 29, 2001; and "Tackling 25th Street's Cleanup," ibid., December 6, 2001. In reality, much of the heavy lifting had already taken place before he was sworn in as county attorney on January 1, 1951. Richards's recollections were not always accurate. He wrote, for example, that Rosetta and William Davie "voluntarily closed up here [in Ogden] when I was elected and moved to Davis County." Actually the Davies ran houses of prostitution simultaneously in Ogden and Davis County and were arrested and put out of business months before Richards took office (see chapter 7). As the Davies' attorney, however, Richards had counseled them on their Davis County venture; on June 2, 1950, he notarized their Benevolent Hand Club's articles of incorporation and affidavit of nonprofit status. Utah Department of Commerce, Division of Corporations and Commerce, incorporation case files, series 7184, case 26993, Utah State Archives, Division of Archives and Records Service, Salt Lake City.

10. *Ogden Standard-Examiner,* August 20, 1955.
11. Ibid., February 24, 1948; April 17, 1951. There were indications that Wade's public rectitude was not what it appeared to be. On October 25, 1948, three prostitutes from La Siesta Hotel at 225½ 25th Street testified before the Weber County Commission that Wade and some friends had visited them, drunk alcohol, told "filthy stories," and made "improper advances." Questioned by the commission, Wade admitted drinking but shrugged off the other accusations, saying he had visited La Siesta in connection with a narcotics investigation and commenting, "I'd like to know how you can make improper advances to a prostitute." *Ogden Standard-Examiner,* October 25, 26, December 1, 1948; *Salt Lake Tribune,* October 27, December 3, 1948.
12. In October 1915, an Ogden correspondent reported almost two hundred African American ballots cast in Ogden's primary municipal elections. *Chicago Defender,* October 30, 1915.
13. "Community Services in the Ogden, Utah, Area: Report of Progress," March 1944, RG 215, box 30, Office of Community War Services, Federal Security Agency, NARA. Of the three restaurants willing to serve African Americans, two (at Union Station and the bus station) were considered too expensive.
14. Eric Stene, "The African-American Community of Ogden, Utah, 1910–1950" (master's thesis, Utah State University, 1994), 55–56; *Ogden Standard-Examiner,* June 16, 17, 24, 1943; March 26, 1944. The proposed venue for the Little Harlem Café is the building shown on pp. 107–8.
15. *Ogden Standard,* October 4, 1906; *Salt Lake Herald,* October 4, 1906; *Salt Lake Tribune,* February 4, 2007.
16. Stene, "African-American Community," 16–19 (Stene's sources were C. John Turner and James Gillespie); *Ogden Standard-Examiner,* February 5, 1945. Segregation of bars and clubs during World War II was widespread. Novelist Christopher Isherwood's October 16, 1942, diary entry described downtown Los Angeles nightclubs "where whites are not welcome." Christopher Isherwood, *Diaries,* ed. Katherine Bucknell, vol. 1, 1939–1960 (New York: HarperCollins Publishers, 1997), 254.
17. Joe McQueen, conversation with the author, September 21, 2011; Tom Owens, e-mail to the author, January 19, 2009. A couple of McQueen's engagements at Porters and Waiters were noted in the *Los Angeles Sentinel* on April 1 and July 15, 1954. The *Sentinel* carried a regular column of Ogden's African American news from correspondent Bessie Carr.
18. *Ogden Standard-Examiner,* February 1, April 1, 1946. An American Social Hygiene Association (ASHA) field report on Ogden dated November 8, 1945,

observed, "A [N]egro special policeman assigned to the Health Department is bringing in girls for examination and treatment that have never before been located. This man had the Tuskegee non-com VD training and was secured through the Army." "Field Report of John Hall," Legal and Protective Measures, Field Reports—Utah, box 111, folder 1, p. 114, American Social Hygiene Association, Social Welfare History Archives, University of Minnesota, Minneapolis, available online at http://purl.umn.edu/111135 (accessed December 22, 2011), hereafter cited as ASHA-UMN.

19. Conversation with Joe McQueen; *Ogden Standard-Examiner,* September 12, 1947; October 7, 1948.
20. Issac Goeckeritz's interview with Annabelle Weakley for *Ogden: Junction City of the West; Los Angeles Sentinel,* November 11, 1948. Annabelle Weakley, her husband, and Mr. and Mrs. Walter Epps vacationed together at Lava Hot Springs, Idaho, in 1953. *Los Angeles Sentinel,* June 18, 1953. Another African American venue raided by Epps was the Harlem Club at 115 25th Street. *Ogden Standard-Examiner,* December 20, 1952.
21. *Ogden Standard-Examiner,* April 14, 1954.
22. Major Farley "said that with the exception of an explosive racial situation precipitated by the closing of a colored bar by a Weber County sheriff (politics!), he was satisfied with conditions in Ogden." "Field Report of Robert S. Elliott," Legal and Protective Measures, Field Reports—Utah, May 11 and 13–16, 1954, box 111, folder 1, p. 228, ASHA-UMN.
23. *Ogden Standard-Examiner,* April 14, 1954.
24. Goeckeritz's interview with Weakley. In contrast to Sheriff Wade's apparent disdain of Annabelle Weakley, Detective Arlyn Garside of the Ogden police referred to her as "very honest," "very cooperative," "operator of a very neat, high-class place of business," and "[gives] the greatest assistance in the way of information regarding law violators." Garside to C. Ed. Lewis, September 8, 1954, Arlyn Garside papers, MS 400, box 28, Special Collections, Stewart Library, Weber State University, Ogden, UT.
25. *Ogden Standard-Examiner,* May 15, 1954.
26. Ibid., December 1, 1954. Weakley's lawyer, John Snow, had earlier defended Sheriff Wade when Judge Hendricks had cited him for contempt of court. *Salt Lake Tribune,* December 12, 1950.
27. *Ogden Standard-Examiner,* November 3, 1954. Although Weakley did not publicly endorse LeRoy Hadley's bid for sheriff, other African Americans did, including *Los Angeles Sentinel* Ogden correspondent Bessie Carr and Earline Davis; see Hadley's paid political advertisement in the *Ogden Standard-Examiner,* November 1, 1954.
28. *Ogden Standard-Examiner,* April 10, 17, 1951; January 2, 1952.
29. An ASHA field report from Ogden dated April 26–28, 1950, observed, "There is [a] question in the minds of many people as to the trustworthiness of either the police chief or sheriff. These two are at each other's throats and accuse one another's department of flagrant corruption." "Field Report of Patrick Kelley," Legal and Protective Measures, Field Reports—Utah, box 111, folder 1, p. 178, ASHA-UMN.
30. The Interstate Commerce Commission cited the "accelerating transportation revolution" as a reason to grant the first modern independent railroad merger (of the Norfolk and Western and Virginian railways). *Salt Lake Tribune,* December 27, 1959.
31. Interstate Commerce Commission figures cited in John F. Stover, *The Life and Decline of the American Railroad* (New York: Oxford University Press, 1970), 218–19.
32. *New York Times,* October 29, December 11, 1960;

Mike Schafer and Joe Welsh, *Streamliners: History of a Railroad Icon* (St. Paul: MBI Publishing, 2002), 64. The Western Pacific Railroad resisted proposed mergers until 1982, when the Union Pacific Railroad acquired it. F. Ross Peterson and Robert Parson provide a good summary of Ogden's gradual loss of its railroad economy after World War II in *Ogden City: Its Governmental Legacy: A Sesquicentennial History* (Ogden, UT: Chapelle Ltd., 2001), 196–203.

33. "Field Report of Patrick Kelley," Legal and Protective Measures, Field Reports—Utah, November 1–2, 1950, box 111, folder 1, p. 187, ASHA-UMN; *Ogden Standard-Examiner,* November 5, 1950; January 3, 5, September 12, 1951. On November 1, 1951, the center became a USO club. Ibid., February 24, 1952.
34. Allen D. Roberts, nomination of the Lower 25th Street Historic District, National Register of Historic Places Inventory, September 13, 1977, available online at http://pdfhost.focus.nps.gov/docs/NRHP/Text/78003260.pdf (accessed January 13, 2011).
35. The 1910–1911 building wave included the Lyceum Theater and Helena and Marion hotels—all still standing—*Ogden Evening Standard,* September 16, 1910; numbers 223 (now demolished), 225, and 227 25th Street; ibid., June 28, August 17, 1911; and Fred Kiesel's Van Ness Hotel (demolished in 1997) at 150 25th Street, where the Chapman House stood; ibid., October 20, 1911.
36. *Ogden Standard-Examiner,* November 25, 1940.
37. Ibid., September 16, 1935. The National Hotel, formerly the European Hotel, was built in 1891 by Boston Realty. *Ogden Standard,* December 20, 1902. The colorful Denny Smyth was its proprietor from 1894 to 1922. There is retrospective irony in the European Hotel's early publicity: "Fire escapes have been provided, although the building is known to be fireproof." Ibid., December 21, 1901.
38. *Ogden Standard-Examiner,* December 4, 24, 28, 1936; February 10, 20, 24, March 8, 11, 24, 1937. Thomas Chamberlain originally built the New Central Hotel at 218–226 25th Street as the Central Hotel in 1882 (see chapter 2). Its lot has been vacant since 1937. From 2002 to 2006, a temporary structure—the Everwood house—occupied the lot while the television series of the same name was filmed for the WB Television Network.
39. *Ogden Standard-Examiner,* September 15, 1937.
40. Ibid., September 21, 1937. The six properties on 25th Street were the National Hotel (whose surviving ground floor is present-day Brewski's); numbers 139–141, 157, 247, and 253; and 224–226, the vacant lot where the New Central Hotel had stood, which needed to be cleaned up.
41. Ibid., April 16, 1936.
42. Ibid., October 10, 1943.
43. Interview with Robert Peery King, May 26, 2009; interview with Helen Booth by Jalynn Olsen in "C. C. Keller Building, 201–205 25th St., Ogden," 1997, historic survey form, Utah State Historic Preservation Office, Salt Lake City. An Ogden resident who worked at L. R. Samuels told historian John Sillito that whenever the store received a shipment of rose-colored merchandise, he called Rosetta Davie, and she came in immediately. The informant, who did not give his name, remembered her fondly. John Sillito, e-mail to the author, July 10, 2012.
44. *Ogden Standard-Examiner,* September 17, 1950.
45. Ibid., April 4, 1950.
46. Dorrene Jeske, e-mail to the author, June 2, 2008; Dorothy Scott Harvey, letter to the author, August 3, 2008.

47. *Ogden Standard-Examiner,* November 27, 1954; April 17, 1951.

48. Subcommittee on Equal Opportunities, Committee on Education and Labor, *Juvenile Justice and Delinquency Prevention and Runaway Youth,* HR, 93rd Congress, 2nd sess., March 29–May 21, 1974, 127–135; *New Canadian,* December 5, 1978; *Long Beach (CA) Independent Press-Telegram,* August 6, 1972.

49. *Ogden Standard-Examiner,* February 3, April 1, 1960.

50. Ibid., February 4, August 12, 1960.

51. Ibid., July 3, 1957; January 10, April 6, 1958. After Helen (Mrs. Frank) Estrada was arrested for shooting Doherty, Lyle Kurisaki posted her thousand-dollar bond. *Ogden Standard-Examiner,* July 1, 1957. On the witness stand in an unrelated criminal case, Estrada was asked if she was "the same Helen Estrada" linked to Eddie Doherty in *Confidential,* a scandal magazine famous for exposés on celebrities such as Robert Mitchum, Maureen O'Hara, and Liberace. She refused to answer. *Ogden Standard-Examiner,* December 13, 1956. This *Confidential* story has not been located. The *Salt Lake Tribune* of July 1, 1957, referred to Estrada as Doherty's "girl friend." A report from Detective Arlyn Garside indicated that local men utilized Estrada as a procuress. Arlyn Garside to Maurice Schooff, April 11, 1956, Garside papers.

52. Interview with L. G. Bingham, August 27, 2011; *Ogden Standard-Examiner,* April 24, 25, May 1, 1962.

53. Ibid., June 21, 1956; July 8–9, 1958.

54. Ibid., August 31, 1958.

55. Ibid., October 16, 1946; November 20, 1967.

56. Ibid., June 1, September 28, 30, 1960. The Porters and Waiters building at 127 25th Street disappeared from Polk's *Ogden City Directory* after 1973.

57. The city issued demolition orders to Allen Roberts, then-owner of 111 and 115 25th Street, in 1975 and 1989. See *Ogden Standard-Examiner,* December 15, 1975; "Notice of Dangerous Building and Order to Demolish," ibid., November 2, 1989; attachment in Heather M. Weymouth, *The Congress House: Intensive Level Survey Research: 115 25th Street Ogden, Utah* (Ogden: Sagebrush Archaeological Consultants, 1995).

58. *Ogden Standard-Examiner,* February 14, 1961; January 15, 1962; October 4, 1967; June 6, 1969. The Labor Temple at 261 25th Street was demolished after the fire, and its lot remains vacant to the present time. The ground floor of the Weber Hotel at 268–270 25th Street still stands and houses an art gallery and gift shop. The first-floor remnant of the Montana Hotel at 162 25th is home today to a sushi restaurant, cinema art house, and tavern. The Pacific/Van Ness Hotel was finally torn down in 1997 "in spite of over a year's effort to obtain sufficient financing for the project, including significant general funds and Community Development Block Grant funds." National Parks and Public Lands Subcommittee, House Committee on Resources, testimony of Mayor Glenn Mecham, 106th Congress, 1st sess., October 5, 1999, available from the Federal News Service. An official transcript of this hearing was never printed. One of the street's worst fires occurred late in 1979 at the Reed Hotel at 204 25th Street, killing four persons and hospitalizing sixteen. *Ogden Standard-Examiner,* December 7, 1979. The three-story building was restored.

59. *Ogden Standard-Examiner,* Dec. 19, 1956; July 14, 1960.

60. Ibid., January 31, April 1, September 28, 1957; March 10, 1958; January 27, 1959; *Congressional Record* 104 (1958): 8656–657; 105 (1959): 1174–175; 106 (1960): 13771, 15252.

61. *Ogden Standard-Examiner,* August 26, 1960.

62. *Salt Lake Tribune,* August 27, 1960; *Ogden Standard-Examiner,* January 6, 1961.

63. *Ogden Standard-Examiner,* September 6, 1962; *Making Appropriations for Sundry Independent Executive Bureaus, Boards, Commissions, Corporations, Agencies, and Offices, for the Fiscal Year Ending June 30, 1963, and for Other Purposes,* Public Law 87-741, *U.S. Statutes at Large* 76 (October 3, 1962): 724.

64. Andrew Wahlquist, e-mail to the author, June 10, 2009. "I wish I had kept the script," Wahlquist wrote. "I gave the film to a professor at the University of Utah. I doubt it still exists." Wahlquist gave the photos he collected for his project—including the one on p. 14—to the Utah Historical Society.

65. For an analysis of present-day attitudes toward Ogden's historic architecture west of Washington Boulevard, see Jalynn Olsen, *Building by the Railyard: The Historic Commercial and Industrial Architecture of Ogden, Utah* (Salt Lake City: Western Regional Architecture Program, Center for Architectural Studies, Graduate School of Architecture, University of Utah, 1998).

66. *Ogden Standard-Examiner,* March 17, 1962. When he left politics, Richards said the "most satisfying chapter" in his career "was the cleaning up of vice and crime while he was county attorney" so that "Ogden's notoriety for prostitution, dope, and violent crimes declined." Ibid., November 28, 1968.

67. Ibid., November 2, 1962.

Chapter 9, Ogden Renaissance

1. *Weber Sentinel,* July 2, 2004.

2. Interview with Allen Roberts, November 30, 2011; Allen D. Roberts, "A Few Good Catalysts: 25th Street, the Scowcroft and Boyle Buildings, and Ogden's Urban Renaissance," *Utah Preservation* 8 (2004): 28.

3. *Salt Lake Tribune,* February 14, 1974; *Denver Post,* January 10, 2000; *St. Louis Post-Dispatch,* October 31, 1999. Judy Mattivi Morley thoroughly documents Crawford's accomplishments at Larimer Square in *Historic Preservation and the Imagined West: Albuquerque, Denver, and Seattle* (Lawrence: University Press of Kansas, 2006), 43–66.

4. Interview with Allen Roberts; *Ogden Standard-Examiner,* November 23, 1975.

5. *Ogden Examiner,* January 19, November 24, December 18, 1913. The 25th Street property owners said they had already been taxed for the original 1893 paving and believed the subsequent expense should be borne by the taxpayers at large. Neither Utah law nor Ogden ordinances allowed the city to take jurisdiction of the paving district if a majority of owners objected. In 1914 National Hotel proprietor Denny Smyth, informal leader of the property owners, announced that opposition had been resolved and the owners would bear the costs of paving and constructing curbs and gutters. Ibid., January 12, 1914.

6. Ibid., April 24, 1913.

7. *Ogden Evening Standard,* February 6, 1913; *Ogden Standard,* July 4, 1913. The arc lights were installed, but no further discussion of the red, white, and blue scheme was recorded.

8. *Ogden Standard-Examiner,* January 23, 28, 30, February 2, 3, 5, 1934. Although Roy Steele wanted to clean up 25th Street, he had had an illegal slot machine in his store. Ibid., November 11, 1931.

9. Interview with Allen Roberts; *Ogden Standard-Examiner,* December 15, 1975; January 17, 1976.

10. Interview with Allen Roberts.

11. James L. Porter apparently bought the Cottage Hotel at 2518 Lincoln Avenue in the final days of 1899. U.S. Bureau of the Census, twelfth census (1900), Weber County, p. 354, line 60 lists him and his family at that address. Porter leased the Cottage Hotel to new operators in July 1900, perhaps because of his newer project—the Porter Block.

Ogden Standard, December 27, 1899; July 6, 23, September 10, 1900.

12. *Chicago Tribune,* January 16, 2006; *Evansville Courier and Press,* July 2, 2006.
13. Interview with Allen Roberts.
14. After years of lower-court battles, the U.S. Supreme Court upheld the prohibition of construction of a tall tower over Grand Central Station in *Penn Central Transportation Co. v. New York City,* 438 U.S. 104 (1978).
15. *Ogden Standard-Examiner,* February 10, 1968; January 5, April 27, 1969.
16. Ibid., May 28, 1969.
17. Ibid., June 3, 1969; July 20, 1970; February 5, 8, 1972.
18. Ibid., February 13, 24, 1972.
19. Ibid., April 27, 1972.
20. Ibid., October 25, November 4, December 27, 1975.
21. *Salt Lake Tribune,* February 7, 1976; *Ogden Standard-Examiner,* January 31, February 13, 1976.
22. *Ogden Standard-Examiner,* August 15, October 10, 1976.
23. Murray Moler, "Ogden's Union Station," in Richard W. Sadler and Richard A. Roberts, *Ogden: Junction City* (Northridge, CA: Windsor Publications, 1985), 41.
24. *Ogden Standard-Examiner,* March 16, April 6, May 5, 1977.
25. Ibid., October 5, 1977.
26. Ibid., October 21, 22, 1978.
27. Ibid., June 1, 1976; Teddy Griffith, conversation with the author, January 15, 2012.
28. *Salt Lake Tribune,* April 10, 1976; *Ogden Standard-Examiner,* May 25, 1977.
29. *Ogden Standard-Examiner,* August 6, 1977.
30. Ronald Hales and Stephen Baird, *25th Street Master Plan: A Working Document* (Logan, UT: Land Design, 1977).
31. Letter from A. Stephen Dirks, August 24, 1977, in *25th Street Master Plan: A Working Document.*
32. Allen D. Roberts, nomination of the Lower 25th Street Historic District, National Register of Historic Places Inventory, September 13, 1977, available online at http://pdfhost.focus.nps.gov/docs/NRHP/Text/78003260.pdf (accessed January 13, 2012).
33. Interview with Allen Roberts; interview with Greg Montgomery, April 20, 2009.
34. Carl Porter, "Kokomo Club," *Ogden Indie* 2 (2009): 17; *Ogden Standard-Examiner,* December 7, 1979 (see chapter 8, note 58).
35. Interview with Allen Roberts; *Deseret News,* March 3, 1989.
36. Interview with Eric and Terry Zenger, January 14, 2012; interview with William Parker, May 4, 2010; interview with Heidi Harwood, January 17, 2012.
37. Interview with Margaret Hunter, January 20, 2012.
38. Interview with Mark Altice, January 17, 2012; *Deseret News,* November 15, 1997.
39. National Parks and Public Lands Subcommittee, House Committee on Resources, testimony of Mayor Glenn Mecham, 106th Congress, 1st sess., October 5, 1999, available from the Federal News Service. An official transcript of this hearing was never printed.
40. The Woodbury Corporation had purchased part of the Peery estate in downtown Ogden in 1961; see chapter 6, note 7.
41. *Ogden Standard-Examiner,* April 12, August 6, December 18, 1977.
42. Interview with Daniel Cook, January 19, 2012; interview with Jim Stavrakakis, January 17, 2012; interview with Jim Budge, January 18, 2012; *Salt Lake Tribune,* September 4, 1983.
43. *Deseret News,* March 29, 2002; *Standard-Examiner,* November 19, 27, 2002; January 15, 2008.

44. *Deseret News,* March 30, 2004; "Ben Lomond Historic Suite Hotel," *Street Magazine,* summer 2004; *Standard-Examiner,* August 25, 2005; July 17, 2008; July 16, 2009.

45. *Standard-Examiner,* August 28, 2009; Joyce Powell, conversation with the author, January 21, 2012.

46. *Weber Sentinel,* July 2, 2004. Years of immersion in old Ogden newspaper articles have not turned up a single allusion to tunnels.

47. Interview with George Pappas Jr., August 4, 2011.

48. *Ogden Standard,* September 24, November 9, 1890; December 21, 1901; December 20, 1902; March 24, 1917. The case against Denny Smyth was dismissed. *Ogden Standard,* September 13, 1917.

49. Interview with Jared Allen and tour of the planned Alleged establishment, June 23, 2012.

50. In future years, the FrontRunner will extend north to Brigham City and south to Payson. Service between Salt Lake and Provo began on December 10, 2012.

51. *Standard-Examiner,* July 4, 2005.

52. Ibid., April 28, 2009. Only three years after this criticism was leveled, the Brookings Institution reported 47 percent of the Ogden/Clearfield metropolitan area can reach a typical job within ninety minutes on public transportation, ranking eleventh in the nation. The Salt Lake metropolitan area, at 64 percent, ranked first. Adie Tomer, "Where the Jobs Are: Employer Access to Labor by Transit," available online at http://www.brookings.edu/research/papers/2012/07/11-transit-jobs-tomer (accessed July 12, 2012); *Salt Lake Tribune,* July 12, 2012.

53. *Washington Examiner,* February 23, 2011; *Washington Post,* December 16, 2011.

54. *Salt Lake Tribune,* December 18, 2011; Wasatch Front Regional Council, *Wasatch Choices 2040: A Four-County Land-Use and Transportation Vision,* available online at http://www.wfrc.org/cms/publications/wasatchchoices2040report.pdf (accessed January 19, 2012).

55. *Salt Lake Tribune,* May 26, 2011; *Standard-Examiner,* August 21, 2011.

56. *St. Louis Post-Dispatch,* October 31, 1999; *Denver Post,* December 5, 2004.

57. Jalynn Olsen, *Building by the Railyard: The Historic Commercial and Industrial Architecture of Ogden, Utah* (Salt Lake City: Western Regional Architecture Program, Center for Architectural Studies, Graduate School of Architecture, University of Utah, 1988), 3–5.

BIBLIOGRAPHY

Articles and Book Chapters

Anderson, Bernice Gibbs. "The Driving of the Golden Spike: The End of the Race." *Utah Historical Quarterly* 24 (1956): 149–56.

Arrington, Leonard J. "The Influenza Epidemic of 1918–19 in Utah." *Utah Historical Quarterly* 58 (1990): 165–82.

———. "The Railroad and the West." *Utah Historical Quarterly* 37 (1969): 4–15.

———. "The Transcontinental Railroad and Mormon Economic Policy." *Pacific Historical Review* 20 (1951): 143–57.

Bailey, Jody, and Robert S. McPherson. "'Practically Free from the Taint of the Bootlegger': A Closer Look at Prohibition in Southeastern Utah." *Utah Historical Quarterly* 57 (1989): 150–64.

"Ben Lomond Historic Suite Hotel." *Street Magazine,* summer 2004.

Best, Gerald M. "Rendezvous at Promontory: The 'Jupiter' and No. 119." *Utah Historical Quarterly* 37 (1969): 69–75.

Bolino, August C. "Mormon Philosophy and Practical Railroad Building." *Business History* Review 32 (1958): 407–22.

Buice, David. "When the Saints Came Marching In: The Mormon Experience in Antebellum New Orleans, 1840–1855." *Louisiana History* 23 (1987): 221–37.

"Camera Story of Golden Spike Fête at Utah." *Southern Pacific Bulletin* 8 (June 1919): 5.

Carmack, Noel A. "Before the Flapper: The Utah Beginnings of John Held, Jr." *Utah Historical Quarterly* 66 (1998): 292–319.

Clapp, Raymond F. "Social Treatment of Prostitutes and Promiscuous Women." *Federal Probation* 7 (1943): 23–27.

Dawson, Janice P. "Frederick Vining Fisher: Methodist Apologist for Mormonism." *Utah Historical Quarterly* 55 (1987): 359–69.

DeVoto, Bernard [Richard L. Caxton, pseud]. "The Bloody Shirt, World-War Model." *Harvard Advocate* 115 (1928): 9–20.

———. "The Bucolics of Decadence." In *The Selected Letters of Bernard DeVoto and Katherine Sterne,* edited by Mark DeVoto, appendix A, 408–57. Salt Lake City: University of Utah Press, 2012.

———. "Ogden: The Underwriters of Salvation." In *The Taming of the Frontier,* edited by Duncan Aikman, 27–60. New York: Minton, Balch, 1925.

———. "Utah." *American Mercury* 7 (1926): 317–23.

Embry, Jessie L. "Fighting the Good Fight: The Utah Home Front during World War II." *Utah Historical Quarterly* 63 (1995): 242–67.

Fleming, Thomas. "Prohibition: A Cautionary Tale." *Wall Street Journal,* January 4, 2010.

Gerlach, Larry R. "Ogden's 'Horrible Tragedy': The Lynching of George Segal." *Utah Historical Quarterly* 49 (1981): 157–72.

Glasgow, Robert W. "Something's Being Done about Downtown Denver." *Arizona Republic,* December 7, 1965: 7.

Goodman, Jack. "Jews in Zion." In *The Peoples of Utah,* edited by Helen Z. Papanikolas, 187–220. Salt Lake City: Utah State Historical Society, 1976.

Haefeli, Leo. "A Stroll through Ogden." *Tullidge's Quarterly Magazine* 1 (1881): 475–84.

Hales, Stephen W. "Rocky Mountain Carnival." *Arthur Hardy's Mardi Gras Guide* (2006): 60–65, 98.

Hitchens, Arthur Parker. "How the Army Protects Soldiers from Syphilis and Gonorrhea." *Journal of Social Hygiene* 27 (1941): 103–11.

Hollister, Ovando J. "From O. J. Hollister: Number XI." *[Denver] Rocky Mountain News,* April 15, 1869.

Johnson, Michael W. "Rendezvous at Promontory: A New Look at the Golden Spike Ceremony." *Utah Historical Quarterly* 72 (2004): 47–68.

Kennedy, O. A. "Bison Steaks and Wine Put King's Diners in Fine Mood." *Ogden Standard-Examiner,* May 11, 1931.

———. "Carnival Ends but Fiddlers Must Be Paid; Harvey Loses." *Ogden Standard-Examiner,* May 14, 1931.

———. "Carnival King Bares Visage to Gathering at Mask Ball." *Ogden Standard-Examiner,* May 13, 1931.

———. "Col. Harvey Enrolls Boosters in Secret Monte Cristo Order." *Ogden Standard-Examiner,* May 6, 1931.

———. "Depot Was Scene of Exciting Life Fifty Years Ago." *Ogden Standard-Examiner,* February 14, 1932.

———. "Gun Scene 'Cooked Up?' Scribe Still Wonders These 50 Years After." *Ogden Standard-Examiner,* July 28, 1939.

———. "Harvey Opens Carnival with Great Gusto; Titles Given." *Ogden Standard-Examiner,* May 9, 1931.

———. "Historic Spots in Ogden and Vicinity." *Ogden Standard-Examiner,* April 19, 1925.

———. "It's a Bit Difficult at 84 to Write Own Life Story." *Ogden Standard-Examiner,* September 11, 1945.

———. "King of Mardi Gras Welcomed to Ogden by Carnival Throng." *Ogden Standard-Examiner,* May 8, 1931.

———. "Ogden Makes Huge Progress in 60 Years." *Ogden Standard-Examiner,* January 3, 1932.

———. "Ogden Man Recalls How 'Invincible' Army of Kaiser Was Organized." *Ogden Standard-Examiner,* February 7, 1943.

———. "Ogden Once a Walled City." *Ogden Standard-Examiner,* June 19, 1921.

———. "Ogden River History Contains Chapters of Success and Failure." *Ogden Standard-Examiner,* August 14, 1931.

———. "Old Timer Avers Ogden Hasn't Changed So Much in Half Century." *Ogden Standard-Examiner,* July 18, 1943.

———. "Plenty Life in Ogden Boom 40 Years Ago." *Ogden Standard-Examiner,* July 14, 1929.

———. "Rumors Heard That Mormon Is Chosen as Carnival King." *Ogden Standard-Examiner,* May 12, 1931.

———. "Special Train with Flower of South on Way to Ogden Fete." *Ogden Standard-Examiner*, May 7, 1931.

———. "The Story of the Ogden Daily Commercial." *Ogden Standard-Examiner*, November 21, 1920.

———. "Stovepipe Hats, Real Estate Talk Marked Ogden of Fifty Years Ago, Newsman Recalls." *Ogden Standard-Examiner*, July 9, 1939.

———. "To the Unknown Dead in Mountain View Cemetery." *Ogden Standard-Examiner*, May 30, 1931.

———. "Wall around Ogden Early Day Enterprise." *Ogden Standard-Examiner*, August 31, 1930.

———. "Worries Grow for Promoter of Boom Days Carnival Here." *Ogden Standard-Examiner*, May 10, 1931.

Kingsdale, Jon M. "The 'Poor Man's Club': Social Functions of the Urban Working-Class Saloon." *American Quarterly* 25 (1973): 472–89.

Kinsie, Paul M. "The Prostitution Racket Today." *Journal of Social Hygiene* 27 (1941): 327–34.

Kotter, Richard E. "The Transcontinental Railroad and Ogden City Politics." *Utah Historical Quarterly* 42 (1974): 278–84.

Launius, Roger D., and Jessie L. Embry. "A Transforming Force: Military Aviation and Utah in World War II." *Utah Historical Quarterly* 63 (1995): 222–40.

[Leslie, Frank]. "Across the Continent: The Frank Leslie Excursion to the Pacific." *Frank Leslie's Illustrated Newspaper*, December 15, 1877: 242–43.

Liestman, Daniel. "Utah's Chinatowns: The Development and Decline of Extinct Ethnic Enclaves." *Utah Historical Quarterly* 64 (1996): 70–95.

Martini, Anthony P. "1919: Post-War Pilots Take to the Air." Chap. 10 of *Flying Machines over Zion: Aviation Come[s] to Utah, 1910–1919*. Ogden, UT: Aerospace Heritage Foundation of Utah, 1997. Available online at http://www.hill.af.mil/library/factsheets/factsheet.asp?id=5973 (accessed June 9, 2011).

Mayer, Joseph. "The Passing of the Red Light District." *Journal of Social Hygiene* 4 (1918): 197–209.

Moler, Murray. "Ogden's Union Station." In *Ogden: Junction City*, by Richard W. Sadler and Richard A. Roberts, 40–41. Northridge, CA: Windsor Publications, 1985.

Morgan, Dale L. "Miles Goodyear and the Founding of Ogden." Pts. 1 and 2. *Utah Historical Quarterly* 21 (1953): 195–218; 307–29.

Nelson, Larry E. "Utah Goes Dry." *Utah Historical Quarterly* 41 (1973): 340–57.

O'Neil, Floyd A. "Utah's Twentieth Century History: Reprise and Nostrums." *Utah Historical Quarterly* 74 (2006): 100–113.

O'Neil, Hugh. F. "County Split in 1868 for School Work." *Ogden Standard-Examiner*, August 23, 1936.

———. "Doctor Began Health Unit." *Ogden Standard-Examiner*, August 13, 1936.

———. "Early Elections Lacked Ballyhoo of Present-Day." *Ogden Standard-Examiner*, June 3, 1936.

———. "Early Slaying Records Found." *Ogden Standard Examiner*, August 31, 1936.

———. "List of Persons Present, Promontory, Utah, May 10, 1869." *Utah Historical Quarterly* 24 (1956): 157–64.

———. "Ogden Daily Pilot, Early Day Paper, Short Lived." *Ogden Standard-Examiner*, February 18, 1940.

———. "Start of Fire Force Traced to 1873 Blaze." *Ogden Standard-Examiner*, August 7, 1936.

Papanikolas, Helen Z. "Bootlegging in Zion: Making and Selling the 'Good Stuff.'" *Utah Historical Quarterly* 53 (1985): 268–91.

Porter, Carl. "Kokomo Club." *Ogden Indie* 2 (August 2009): 10–17.

Rappaport, Mazie F. "A Protective Service for

Promiscuous Girls." *Federal Probation* 9 (1945): 32–36.

"Red Light for Red Lights." *Time* 49, April 27, 1942, 55–56.

Roberts, Allen D. "A Few Good Catalysts: 25th Street, the Scowcroft and Boyle Buildings, and Ogden's Urban Renaissance." *Utah Preservation* 8 (2004): 26–32.

Roberts, Richard. "Rail Completion Brings Changes to Northern Utah." *Standard-Examiner*, March 29, 2001.

———. "Railroad Depots in Ogden: Microcosms of a Community." *Utah Historical Quarterly* 53 (1985): 74–99.

———. "The Utah National Guard in the Great War, 1917–18. *Utah Historical Quarterly* 58 (1990): 312–33.

Smith, John S. H. "Cigarette Prohibition in Utah 1921–23." *Utah Historical Quarterly* 41 (1973): 358–72.

Stauffer, Suzanne. "In Their Own Image: The [Ogden] Public Library Collection as a Reflection of Its Donors." *Libraries and the Cultural Record* 42 (2007): 387–408.

Timmerman, Floyd A. "Bootlegger's Life Bared by Ogdenite." *Ogden Standard-Examiner*, August 30, 1925.

———. "'Fixers' Get Ogden Rum Trade Coin." *Ogden Standard-Examiner*, September 1, 1925.

———. "'Joint' Men Fear Ogden Liquor King." *Ogden Standard-Examiner*, September 2, 1925.

———. "Ogden Rum Makers Tip Off Rivals." *Ogden Standard-Examiner*, August 31, 1925.

———. "Says Ogden Has 68 Rum Sale Shops." *Ogden Standard-Examiner*, September 3, 1925.

Tinker, Frank. "Old 25th Street Gets New Look." *Salt Lake Tribune*, September 15, 1963.

Tomer, Addie. "Where the Jobs Are: Employer Access to Labor by Transit." Available online at http://www.brookings.edu/research/papers/2012/07/11-transit-jobs-tomer (accessed July 12, 2012).

Tullidge, Edward W. "Ogden City." *Western Galaxy* 1 (1888): 429–59.

"Utah News." *Millennial Star* 33 (1871): 172–75.

Utley, Robert M. "The Dash to Promontory." *Utah Historical Quarterly* 29 (1961): 99–117.

"VD among the Amateurs." *Time* 51, March 29, 1943, 46–47.

Walker, Ronald W. "The Panic of 1893." In *Utah History Encyclopedia*. Available online at http://www.uen.org/utah_history_encyclopedia/p/PANIC_1893_Financial.html (accessed March 17, 2013).

Ward, Ruth. "Home Town Interviews." (O. A. Kennedy.) *Ogden Standard-Examiner*, October 6, 1938.

Weatherly, Eugene T. "Local Control of Prostitution in Wartime." *Journal of Social Hygiene* 28 (1942): 383–88.

White, Jean Bickmore. "The Right to Be Different: Ogden and Weber County Politics, 1850–1924." *Utah Historical Quarterly* 47 (1979): 254–72.

Wutz, Michael. "Riffing about a Century of Jazz: A Conversation with Joe McQueen at 88." *Weber: The Contemporary West* 24 (2007): 21–24.

Books

Agnew, Jeremy. *Entertainment in the Old West: Theater, Music, Circuses, Medicine Shows, Prizefighting, and Other Popular Amusements.* Jefferson, NC: McFarland & Co., 2011.

Alter, J. Cecil. *Early Utah Journalism.* Salt Lake City: Utah State Historical Society, 1938.

Anderson, Karen. *Wartime Women: Sex Roles, Family Relations, and the Status of Women during World War II.* Westport, CT: Greenwood Press, 1981.

Armitage, Shelley. *John Held, Jr., Illustrator of the Jazz Age.* Syracuse, NY: Syracuse University Press, 1987.

Arrington, Leonard J. *Brigham Young: American Moses.* New York: Alfred A. Knopf, 1985.

Asbury, Herbert. *The Great Illusion: An Informal History of Prohibition.* New York: Greenwood Press, 1968.

Athearn, Robert G. *Union Pacific Country.* Chicago: Rand McNally, 1971.

Bain, David H. *Empire Express: Building the First Transcontinental Railroad.* New York: Viking, 1999.

Bancroft, Hubert H. *History of California.* Vol. 7, 1860–1890. San Francisco: History Company, Publishers, 1890.

Bigler, David L. *Forgotten Kingdom: The Mormon Theocracy in the American West, 1847–1896.* Logan: Utah State University Press, 2005.

Bird, Allan G. *Bordellos of Blair Street: The Story of Silverton, Colorado's Notorious Red Light District.* Pearson, MI: Advertising, Publication, and Consultants, 1993.

Blue and Gold. Yearbook of the University of California at Berkeley, 1922.

Bonwick, James. *The Mormons and the Silver Mines.* London: Hodder and Stoughton, 1872.

Codman, John. *The Mormon Country: A Summer with the "Latter-day Saints."* New York: United States Publishing Co., 1874.

Coffey, Thomas M. *The Long Thirst: Prohibition in America 1920–1933.* New York: Norton, 1975.

Costello, John. *Love Sex and War: Changing Values, 1939–45.* London: William Collins Sons and Co., 1986.

———. *Virtue under Fire: How World War II Changed Our Social and Sexual Attitudes.* Boston: Little, Brown, 1985.

Crowson, Belinda. *We Don't Talk about Those Women! Lethbridge's Red Light District, 1880s to 1944.* Lethbridge, AB: Lethbridge Historical Society, 2010.

DeArment, Robert K. *Deadly Dozen: Twelve Forgotten Gunfighters of the Old West.* Norman: University of Oklahoma Press, 2003.

Denton, Sally, and Roger Morris. *The Money and the Power: The Making of Las Vegas and Its Hold on America, 1947–2000.* New York: Alfred A. Knopf, 2001.

Dwyer, Robert J. *The Gentile Comes to Utah.* Washington, DC: Catholic University of America Press, 1941.

Feitz, Leland. *Myers Avenue: A Quick History of Cripple Creek's Red Light District.* Colorado Springs: Dentan-Berkeland Company, 1967.

Francaviglia, Richard. *Over the Range: A History of the Promontory Summit Route of the Pacific Railroad.* Logan: Utah State University Press, 2008.

Haefeli, Leo, and Frank J. Cannon. *Directory of Ogden City and Weber County.* Ogden, UT: Ogden Herald Publishing Co., 1883.

Hales, Ronald, and Stephen Baird. *25th Street Master Plan: A Working Document.* Logan, UT: Land Design, 1977.

Hatch, Wilda G., and Joseph Breeze. *A Pioneer in Communications: The History of the* Ogden Standard-Examiner *and the Electronic Advancements of the Standard Corporation.* New York: Newcomen Society in North America, 1972.

Held, John Jr. *The Most of John Held, Jr.* Brattleboro, VT: Stephen Greene Press, 1972.

Higham, John. *Strangers in the Land: Patterns of American Nativism, 1860–1925.* New Brunswick, NJ: Rutgers University Press, 2002.

History of the Arkansas Valley, Colorado. Chicago: O. L. Baskin & Co., 1881.

Hobart, H. B. *Ogden City Directory for 1890: Classified Business Directory, with a Full List of Government, Territorial, County and Municipal Officers, and Guide to Public Streets and Avenues.* Salt Lake City: H. B. Hobart, 1890.

Hollister, Ovando J. *The Resources and Attractions of Utah.* Salt Lake City: Tribune Printing and Publishing Co., 1882.

Hunter, Milton R. *Beneath Ben Lomond's Peak.* Salt Lake City: Deseret News Press, 1944.

Isherwood, Christopher. *Diaries.* Edited by Katherine Bucknell. Vol. 1, 1939–1960. New York: HarperCollins Publishers, 1997.

Kenner, S[cipio] A. *Utah as It Is.* Salt Lake City: Deseret News, 1904.

Klein, Maury. *Union Pacific.* Garden City, NJ: Doubleday, 1987.

Kratville, William, and Harold E. Ranks. *Union Pacific Streamliners.* Omaha: Kratville Publications, 1974.

Lamar, Howard R. *The Far Southwest, 1846–1912: A Territorial History.* New Haven, CT: Yale University Press, 1966.

Langsdon, Sarah, and Melissa Johnson. *Legendary Locals of Ogden.* Charleston, SC: Arcadia Publishing, 2012.

Locklin, D. Philip. *Economics of Transportation.* 7th ed. Homewood, IL: R. D. Irwin, 1972.

Lyman, Edward Leo. *Political Deliverance: The Mormon Quest for Utah Statehood.* Urbana: University of Illinois Press, 1986.

Lyon, Peter. *To Hell in a Day Coach: An Exasperated Look at American Railroads.* Philadelphia: Lippincott, 1968.

McCormick, John, and John R. Sillito. *A History of Utah Radicalism: Startling, Socialistic, and Decidedly Revolutionary.* Logan: Utah State University Press, 2011.

McGerr, Michael. *A Fierce Discontent: The Rise and Fall of the Progressive Movement.* New York: Free Press, 2003.

Maguire, Don. *Gila Monsters and Red-Eyed Rattlesnakes: Don Maguire's Arizona Trading Expeditions, 1876–1879.* Edited by Gary Topping. Salt Lake City: University of Utah Press, 1997.

Marshall, William Gore. *Through America.* London: Sampson Low, Marston, Searle and Rivington, 1881.

Mathewson, Donna. *Bananas Have No Bones.* New York: Comet Press, 1960.

———. *Down Mexico Way.* New York: Comet Press, 1956.

Meyer, Agnes. *Journey through Chaos.* New York: Harcourt, Brace and Company, 1944.

[Morgan, Dale L.] *A History of Ogden.* Ogden, UT: Ogden City Commission, 1940.

Morley, Judy Mattivi. *Historic Preservation and the Imagined West: Albuquerque, Denver, and Seattle.* Lawrence: University Press of Kansas, 2006.

Nasaw, David. *Going Out: The Rise and Fall of Public Amusements.* New York: Basic Books, 1993.

Nichols, Jeffrey. *Prostitution, Polygamy, and Power: Salt Lake City, 1847–1918.* Urbana: University of Illinois Press, 2002.

Noel, Thomas J. *Denver's Larimer Street: Main Street, Skid Row, Urban Renaissance.* Denver: Historic Denver, Inc., 1981.

Okrent, Daniel. *Last Call: The Rise and Fall of Prohibition.* New York: Scribner, 2010.

Olsen, Jalynn. *Building by the Railyard: The Historic Commercial and Industrial Architecture of Ogden, Utah.* Salt Lake City: Western Regional Architecture Program, Center for Architectural Studies, Graduate School of Architecture, University of Utah, 1998.

Papanikolas, Helen Z., ed. *The Peoples of Utah.* Salt Lake City: Utah State Historical Society, 1976.

Parkhill, Forbes. *Wildest of the West.* New York: Holt, 1951.

Parkinson, Benson. *S. Dilworth Young: General Authority, Scouter, Poet.* Available online at http://jared.pratt-family.org/parley_family_histories/helaman-pratt/histories/sdy.html (accessed April 11, 2011).

Peterson, F. Ross, and Robert Parson. *Ogden City: Its Governmental Legacy: A Sesquicentennial History.* Ogden, UT: Chapelle Ltd., 2001.

Polk, R. L., comp. *Ogden City Directory.* Ogden, UT: R. Polk and Company, 1890–1974.

Powers, Madelon. *Faces along the Bar: Lore and Order in the Workingman's Saloon, 1870–1920.* Chicago: University of Chicago Press, 1998.

Remmers, Mary W. *Going down the Line: Galveston's Red Light District Remembered.* Galveston, TX: M. W. Remmers, 1997.

Roberts, Richard C. *Legacy: The History of the Utah National Guard from the Nauvoo Legion Era to Enduring Freedom*. N.p.: National Guard Association of Utah, 2003.
Roberts, Richard C., and Richard W. Sadler. *Ogden: Junction City*. Northridge, CA: Windsor Publications, 1985.
Rose, Kenneth David. *American Women and the Repeal of Prohibition*. New York: New York University Press, 1996.
———. *Myth and the Greatest Generation: A Social History of Americans in World War II*. New York: Routledge, 2008.
Rosen, Ruth. *The Lost Sisterhood: Prostitution in America, 1900–1918*. Baltimore: Johns Hopkins University Press, 1982.
Russo, Gus. *The Outfit: The Role of Chicago's Underworld in the Shaping of Modern America*. New York: Bloomsbury, 2001.
Sadler, Richard W., and Richard C. Roberts. *Weber County's History*. Ogden, UT: Weber County Commission, 2000.
Satterfield, Archie. *The Home Front: An Oral History of the War Years in America, 1941–1945*. New York: Playboy Press, 1981.
Schafer, Mike, and Joe Welsh. *Streamliners: History of a Railroad Icon*. St. Paul: MBI Publishing, 2002.
Selcer, Richard F. *Hell's Half Acre: The Life and Legend of a Red Light District*. Fort Worth: Texas Christian University Press, 1991.
———. *Legendary Watering Holes: The Saloons That Made Texas Famous*. College Station: Texas A&M University Press, 2004.
Sillito, John, and Sarah Langsdon. *Ogden*. Charleston, SC: Arcadia Publishing, 2008.
Sismondo, Christine. *America Walks into a Bar: A Spirited History of Taverns and Saloons, Speakeasies, and Grog Shops*. New York: Oxford University Press, 2011.
Sloan, Edward L. *Gazetteer of Utah and Salt Lake City Directory*. Salt Lake City: Herald Publishing Company, 1874.
———. *The Salt Lake City Directory and Business Guide for 1869*. Salt Lake City: E. L. Sloan and Company, 1869.
Snelling, Lois. *Coin Harvey, Prophet of Monte Ne*. Point Lookout, Mo.: S. and O. Press, 1973.
Stegner, Wallace. *The Uneasy Chair: A Biography of Bernard DeVoto*. New York: Doubleday, 1974.
Stone, Eileen Hallet. *Homeland in the West: Utah Jews Remember*. Salt Lake City: University of Utah Press, 2001.
Stover, John F. *The Life and Decline of the American Railroad*. New York: Oxford University Press, 1970.
Strack, Don. *Ogden Rails: A History of Railroading at the Crossroads of the West*. Cheyenne, WY: Union Pacific Historical Society, 2005.
Swain, Martha H. *Pat Harrison: The New Deal Years*. Jackson: University Press of Mississippi, 1978.
Timberlake, James H. *Prohibition and the Progressive Movement, 1900–1920*. Cambridge, MA: Harvard University Press, 1963.
Topping, Gary. *Leonard J. Arrington: A Historian's Life*. Norman, OK: Arthur H. Clark Company, 2008.
———. *Utah Historians and the Reconstruction of Western History*. Norman, OK: University of Oklahoma Press, 2003.
Tullidge, Edward W. *Tullidge's Histories*. Vol. 2, *Containing the History of All the Northern, Eastern, and Western Counties of Utah; Also the Counties of Southern Idaho, with a Biographical Appendix*. Salt Lake City: Juvenile Instructor Press, 1889.
Tuttle, Daniel. *Missionary to the Mountain West: Reminiscences of Episcopal Bishop Daniel S. Tuttle, 1866–1886*. Salt Lake City: University of Utah Press, 1987.
Warrum, Noble. *Utah Since Statehood*. Edited by Charles

W. Morse and W. Brown Ewing. Vol. 2, *Historical and Biographical.* Chicago/Salt Lake: S. J. Clarke Publishing Co., 1919.
Weymouth, Heather M. *The Congress House: Intensive Level Survey Research: 115 25th Street Ogden, Utah.* Ogden: Sagebrush Archaeological Consultants, 1995.
Whitney, Orson F. *History of Utah.* Vol. 4, *Biographical.* Salt Lake City: G. Q. Cannon & Sons, 1904.
Wilson, Neill C., and Frank J. Taylor. *Southern Pacific: The Roaring Story of a Fighting Railroad.* New York: McGraw-Hill, 1952.
Winick, Charles, and Paul M. Kinsie. *The Lively Commerce: Prostitution in the United States.* Chicago: Quadrangle Books, 1971.
Wommack, Linda R. *Our Ladies of the Tenderloin: Colorado's Legends in Lace.* Caldwell, ID: Caxton Press, 2005.
Woodhouse, Irene. *Ogden Anecdotes: Stories and Photos from Our First 50 Years.* Ogden, UT: Woodhouse Publishing, 2004.
Work Projects Administration for the State of Utah. *Utah: A Guide to the State.* New York: Hastings House, 1941.
Young, Perry. *The Mystic Krewe: Chronicles of Comus and His Kin.* New Orleans: Louisiana Heritage Press, 1969.
Zacks, Richard. *Island of Vice: Theodore Roosevelt's Doomed Quest to Clean Up Sin-Loving New York.* New York: Doubleday, 2012.

Theses and Dissertations

Barnes, Lyle J. "Ogden's Notorious 'Two-Bit Street,' 1870–1954." Master's thesis, Utah State University, 1969.
Dyer, Bruce T. "A Study of the Forces Leading to the Adoption of Prohibition in Utah in 1917." Master's thesis, Brigham Young University, 1958.
Erickson, Velt G. "The Liberal Party of Utah." Master's thesis, University of Utah, 1948.
Grow, Stewart L. "A Study of the Utah Commission, 1882–1896." PhD diss., University of Utah, 1954.
Hansen, Alma W. "A Historical Study of the Influence of the Railroad upon Ogden, Utah, 1868–1875." Master's thesis, Brigham Young University, 1953.
Hansen, Christopher. "A Mighty OAK: The Life of Olin A. Kennedy," Senior thesis, Weber State University, 1999.
Hardy, C. Brian. "Education and Mormon Enculturation: The Ogden Public Schools 1849–1896." PhD diss., University of Utah, 1995.
Johnson, David F. "The History and Economics of Utah Railroads." Master's thesis, University of Utah, 1947.
Kotter, Richard E. "An Examination of Mormon and Non-Mormon Influences in Ogden City Politics, 1847–1896." Master's thesis, Utah State University, 1967.
Nelson, Larry E. "Problems of Prohibition Enforcement in Utah, 1917–1933." Master's thesis, University of Utah, 1970.
Roybal, Linda C. "Ogden's Twenty-fifth Street: The Spaces of Which Legends Are Made." Master's thesis, Utah State University, 1997.
Skyles, George H. "A Study of Forces and Events Leading to the Repeal of Prohibition and the Adoption of a Liquor Control System in Utah." Master's thesis, Brigham Young University, 1962.
Smith, Mary M. "You Can't Say No to a Soldier: Sexual Violence in the American West during World War II." Master's thesis, University of Utah, 2008.
Sorensen, Merlin Ray. "The Ogden Tabernacle Choir, Its History and Contributions to the Cultural History of Utah." Master's thesis, Brigham Young University, 1961.
Stene, Eric. "The African-American Community of Ogden, Utah, 1910–1950." Master's thesis, Utah State University, 1994.
Thompson, Brent G. "Utah's Struggle for Prohibition,

1908–1917." Master's thesis, University of Utah, 1979.

Manuscripts and Unpublished Material

Becker Brewery collection. MS54. Special Collections, Stewart Library, Weber State University, Ogden.

Becker Brewing and Malting Company records. 1893–1954. CAINE COLL MSS31. Special Collections, Merrill-Cazier Library, Utah State University, Logan, UT.

Brimhall, Dean. Dean Brimhall papers. MS0114. Special Collections, J. Willard Marriott Library, University of Utah, Salt Lake City.

Field Reports—Utah. American Social Hygiene Association records. 1945–1954. Social Welfare History Archives, University of Minnesota, Minneapolis. Available online at http://purl.umn.edu/111135 (accessed December 22, 2011).

Garside, Arlyn. Arlyn Garside papers. MS400. Special Collections, Stewart Library, Weber State University, Ogden.

Harrington, Gordon. "The Pastorate of the Rev. Noble Strong Elderkin." Chaps. 10–14 in *History of Congregational United Church of Christ, Ogden*. Copy available in the Val Holley Collection, Special Collections, Stewart Library, Weber State University, Ogden.

Hinckley, Robert H. Robert H. Hinckley papers. MS0102. Special Collections, J. Willard Marriott Library, University of Utah, Salt Lake City.

Holley, Henry E. "Personal History." 1949. Typescript. Val Holley Collection, Special Collections, Stewart Library, Weber State University, Ogden.

Maguire, Don. "The Story of Ogden's Catholic History." 1924. MSS A4241. Work Projects Administration typescript. Utah State Historical Society, Salt Lake City.

Mohlman, Clara Decker. "Diary." 1925. MS325. Special Collections, Stewart Library, Weber State University, Ogden.

O'Neil, Hugh. F. "The Ogdenite." May 1940. Robert Chugg Ogden Collection, MS202. Special Collections, Stewart Library, Weber State University, Ogden.

———. "Utah Life in the Raw (25th Street, Ogden)." Hugh F. O'Neil Collection of Utah Documents and Reports, 1851–1955 BANC MSS P-F 311. Bancroft Library, University of California, Berkeley.

Pickett, Camille. "Maurice Schooff: Ogden's Chief of Police and His Battle against Corruption on 25th Street, 1948–1952." Val Holley Collection. Special Collections, Stewart Library, Weber State University, Ogden. (Originally a senior thesis for Brigham Young University.)

Scheer, Brenda C. "The Mormon Grid: Zion in the Desert." Paper presented at the International Center on Urban Form, Trani, Italy, 2003. Available online at http://content.lib.utah.edu/utils/getfile/collection/uspace/id/3215/filename/2052.pdf (accessed March 17, 2013).

Public Documents

Brown, Francis A. "Police Record of Ogden City." 1859–1869. MSS57. Work Projects Administration typescript. Utah State Historical Society, Salt Lake City.

Congressional Record 75 (1932).

Congressional Record 76 (1933).

Congressional Record 104 (1958).

Congressional Record 105 (1959).

Congressional Record 106 (1960).

Federal Security Agency. Defense Health and Welfare Services. 1941. Record group 215. National Archives and Records Administration (NARA), Washington, D.C.

———. Division of Recreation. 1943. Record group 215. NARA.

———. Division of Social Protection. 1941–1942. Record group 215. NARA.
———. Office of Community War Services. 1943–1944. Record group 215. NARA.
"Fire Insurance Map of Ogden, 1884." New York: Sanborn-Perris Map Co., 1884.
"Fire Insurance Map of Ogden, 1890." New York: Sanborn-Perris Map Co., 1890.
"Fire Insurance Map of Ogden, 1906." New York: Sanborn-Perris Map Co., 1906.
"Fire Insurance Map of Ogden, 1950." New York: Sanborn-Perris Map Co., 1950.
Ogden City Commission. Ogden City Commission Minute Book (1942).
———. Minutes of the Regular Meeting of the Board of Commissioners of Ogden City, Utah. October 14, 1943. Series 09731. Utah State Archives, Division of Archives and Records Service, Salt Lake City.
Ogden City Council. Minute Book A (1869); Minute Book B (1869–1871); Minute Book C (1872–1873); Minute Book H (1889–1890). Ogden City Recorder's Office, Ogden.
Ogden Police Department. "Arrest Records." 1902–1904. Series 13300. Utah State Archives, Division of Archives and Records Service, Salt Lake City.
———. "Record of Prisoners." 1904–1909. Series 13300. Utah State Archives.
Ogden, Utah. *The Ordinances of Ogden City: Revised and Passed by the City Council during the Years 1870–71.* Ogden: Ogden Publishing Co., 1871.
———. *Ordinances of Ogden City, Utah.* Salt Lake City: Salt Lake City: Deseret News Co., 1881.
———. *The Revised Ordinances of Ogden City, Utah, Embracing All Ordinances of a General Nature in Force August 1, 1894.* Ogden: Authority of the City Council of Ogden City, Utah, 1894.
Roberts, Allen D. Nomination of the Lower 25th Street Historic District, National Register of Historic Places Inventory. September 13, 1977. Available online at http://pdfhost.focus.nps.gov/docs/NRHP/Text/78003260.pdf (accessed January 13, 2012).
Second District Court, Weber County. Civil case files, 1896–. Series 6659. Utah State Archives, Division of Archives and Records Service, Salt Lake City.
Second District Court, Weber County. Criminal case files, 1896–. Series 6954. Utah State Archives.
U.S. Bureau of the Census. Ninth census (1870); twelfth census (1900); fourteenth census (1920).
U.S. Statutes at Large 16 (1869).
U.S. Statutes at Large 22 (1882).
U.S. Statutes at Large 24 (1887).
U.S. Statutes at Large 48 (1933).
U.S. Statutes at Large 76 (1962).
Utah Department of Commerce. Division of Corporations and Commerce. Incorporation case files, series 7184, series 5297. Utah State Archives, Division of Archives and Records Service, Salt Lake City.
Utah Laws 1909.
Utah Laws 1911.
Utah Laws 1917.
Utah Laws 1933.
Utah Laws 1935.
Utah Laws 1937.
Wasatch Front Regional Council. *Wasatch Choices 2040: A Four-County Land-Use and Transportation Vision.* Available online at http://www.wfrc.org/cms/publications/wasatchchoices2040report.pdf (accessed January 19, 2012).

Interviews

Olsen, Jalynn. Interview with Helen Booth. In "C. C. Keller Building, 201–205 25th Street, Ogden," 1997, historic survey form. Utah State Historic Preservation Office, Salt Lake City.

Oral History Program, Special Collections, Stewart Library Weber State University, Ogden.
Belnap, Lamar, July 26, 1973.
Hansen, Angus, July 6, 1973.
MacCarthy, Oakley, July 5, 1973.
Price, William, July 19, 1973.
Roskelley, Alta, July 14, 2008. Interview conducted by Marci Farr.
Werner, Clarence, June 29, 1973.
Zito, Tom, July 6, 1973. Interview conducted by Mary Werner.
Interviews (undated) by Issac Goeckeritz for his 2007 film, *Ogden: Junction City of the West*, which were sources for this book, available in Special Collections, Stewart Library, Weber State University, Ogden.
Frost, Norm
Gibson, Grant
McQueen, Joe
Moore, Willie
Posnien, John
Richards, Maurice
Roberts, Richard
Sadler, Richard
Weakley, Annabelle
Transcribed interviews for this book, Val Holley Collection, Special Collections, Stewart Library, Weber State University, Ogden.
Altice, Mark, January 17, 2012
Bingham, L. G., August 18, 27, 2011
Budge, Jim, January 18, 2012
Coates, Bonnie Brown, October 7–8, 2009; September 3, 2011.
Cook, Daniel W., January 19, 2012
Devine, James, July 31, 2011
Gunderson, Arlene Brown, October 7, 2009
Handy, George, September 11, 2011
Harwood, Heidi, January 17, 2012
Hunter, Margaret, January 20, 2012
Jones, Raymond, September 10, 2011
King, Robert Peery, April 20, May 26, 2009
Lamph, Max, August 28, 2011
Montgomery, Greg, April 20, 2009
Murphy, Ed, October 2, 2009
Pappas, George Jr., August 4, 2011
Prantil, Joseph E., September 1, 2011
Richards, Richard, August 4, 2011.
Roberts, Allen, Nov. 30, 2011
Roberts, Richard, August 4, 2011
Simone, Ed and Cindy, August 4, 2011
Stavrakakis, Jim, January 17, 2012
Zenger, Eric and Terry, January 14, 2012
Additional interviews
Allen, Jared, June 23, 2012
Parker, William, May 4, 2010

INDEX

Numbers in *italics* indicate images.